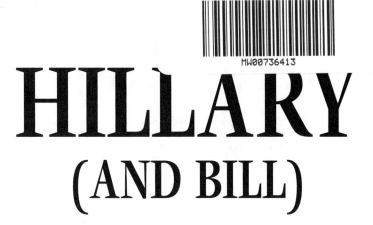

HILLARY
(AND BILL)

THE SEX VOLUME

PART ONE OF THE CLINTON TRILOGY

BY VICTOR THORN

Published by
Sisyphus Press
in conjunction with
American Free Press

Hillary (And Bill)
The Sex Volume
Part One of the Clinton Trilogy

ISBN 0-9785733-4-X

SISYPHUS PRESS

P.O. Box 10495
State College, PA
16805-0495

First Edition: January 2008: 2,000 copies

Manufactured in the United States of America

In conjunction with

AMERICAN FREE PRESS

645 Pennsylvania Avenue SE
Suite 100
Washington, D.C. 20003

www.americanfreepress.net
1-888-699-NEWS toll free

 **WING TV**

www.wingtv.net

DEDICATED TO:

Dorothy Kilgallen,
Mae Brussell,
and
Gary Caradori

Independent researchers, journalists,
and truth-tellers who were taken
well before their time

"Hillary Rodham Clinton needs to be kept very far away from the White House for the rest of her life."

—BRADFORD DELONG, deputy assistant secretary of the Treasury during the first Clinton administration

TABLE OF CONTENTS: HILLARY (AND BILL)

TABLE OF CONTENTS (CONTINUED)

PREFACE

The Rape of Juanita Broaddrick

Her name was Juanita Broaddrick. In April, 1978 Arkansas Attorney General Bill Clinton raped her. His wife – then known as Hillary Rodham – not only knew of this incident, she also took every measure possible to cover-up her husband's sexual attack (a trend that would continue for over two decades into the future).

The 35-year-old Juanita Broaddrick met Bill Clinton in 1978 while he was undertaking his first campaign for governor. After glad-handing for votes at her privately-owned nursing home, candidate Clinton told Mrs. Broaddrick that if she were ever in Little Rock, she should visit his headquarters.

As fate would have it, Juanita Broaddrick was attending a conference for the American College of Nursing Home Administrators on April 25, 1978 when she decided to contact Clinton. That's when events took a turn for the worse. As Christopher Andersen writes in *American Evita*:

> **Juanita checked into Little Rock's Camelot Hotel on April 25, 1978 with her friend Norma Kelsey. But when she called Clinton, he asked if they could meet at the hotel coffee shop instead. Then he called back and asked if they could meet in her room – the coffee shop, he explained, was crawling with reporters.[1]**

Then the nightmare began. As Clinton entered the woman's hotel room, his sexual predator tendencies immediately took over. After taking hold of Mrs. Broaddrick's wrist, he turned her in his direction and began kissing her.

> **"'No!' she stated firmly, 'Please don't do that!'"[2]**
>
> **Clinton told her, "We're both married people,"[3] whereupon she responded that she was deeply involved with another man.**

"Disregarding Juanita's objections, Bill kissed her again. This time, he bit down hard on her top lip. She tried to pull away, but he applied even more pressure with his teeth, drawing blood."[4]

According to Juanita Broaddrick, "Then he tries to kiss me again. And the second time he tries to kiss me he starts biting on my lip. He starts to bite on my top lip. I tried to pull away from him. Then he forces me down on the bed. I tried to get away from him and I told him no, but he wouldn't listen to me. I told him, please don't."[5] Within moments, Clinton's libido spun out of control. "Without letting go of her lip, he unzipped his pants, pulled up her skirt, and tore a hole in her panty hose. Then, according to Juanita, Bill Clinton forcibly, painfully, raped her."[6]

A friend, Phillip Yoakum, recounted the savagery in a letter to Broaddrick which was published by ABCNEWS.com on March 28, 1998: "I was particularly distraught when you told me of your brutal rape by Bill Clinton ... how he started trying to kiss you and ran his hands all over your body until he ripped your clothes off, and how he bit your lip until you gave into his forcing sex upon you."[7]

Pulitzer Prize-winning journalist Dorothy Rabinowitz of *The Wall Street Journal* weighed-in on February 19, 1999: "The sexual entry itself was not without some pain because of her stiffness and resistance."[8]

But her vehement objections didn't stop Bill Clinton. "Still biting down on her lip, Bill, according to Juanita, raped her. Violently."[9]

"He wouldn't listen to me. He was such a different person at that moment; he was just a vicious, awful person. It was a real panicky, panicky situation, and I was even to the point where I was getting very noisy, yelling to please stop. And that's when he would press down on my right shoulder and bite on my lip."[10]

But violating Mrs. Broaddrick wasn't enough for this sexual predator; he had to further humiliate his victim by rubbing salt into the wound.

Dorothy Rabinowitz of *The Wall Street Journal* continued her account:

> **When it was over [the rape], he looked down at her and said not to worry, he was sterile – he had mumps when he was a child.**
>
> **"I felt paralyzed and was starting to cry," Broaddrick said. Then, as Juanita Broaddrick lay battered and bruised on her hotel bed, she remembered the following about Bill Clinton – future president of the United States: "This is the part that always stays in my mind – the way he put on his sunglasses." Then he looked at me and said, "You better put some ice on that [her lip]." And then he left.[11]**

Less than half an hour after this horror story began, Bill Clinton adjusted his clothes and exited the room, leaving the woman he just sexually molested without medical help or emotional support – just like any rapist-thug on the street would do. When discovered a short while later, nursing associate Norma Rogers Kelsey described the scene to NBC News correspondent Lisa Myers: "Juanita Broaddrick was distraught, her lips were swollen at least double in size, and she told me they had intercourse against her will."[12]

Kelsey also reported that her friend was bruised and bleeding, while "NBC producers had managed to turn up four witnesses who corroborated different aspects of her allegations."[13]

Kelsey further elaborated to Paula Jones' investigators Rick and Beverly Lambert that, "The wounds were so bad that one lip was nearly torn in two."[14]

Similarly, Kelsey told Dorothy Rabinowitz that when she entered Broaddrick's room, she was "in a state of shock – lips swollen to double their size, mouth discolored from the biting, her panty hose torn in the crotch. She just stayed on the bed and kept repeating, 'I can't believe what happened.'"[15] Likewise, Kelsey reported to Fox News, "She was hysterical. Her lip was blue and bleeding and her hose were severely torn in the crotch area."[16]

Lastly, when Broaddrick returned home after the assault, her husband David recalled that "her lip was black, and mentally she was in bad shape."[17]

At this point it is important to note that lip-biting is part of the modus operandi of many rapists. In fact, *NewsMax* interviewed a Louisiana investigator specializing in sexual violence, who stated:

> **The reason rapists bite is, even with the full weight of her attacker on top of her, the woman is often able to resist the parting of her legs by locking her ankles. The rapist's arms are busy keeping her pinned down. The only weapon the rapist has left is his teeth, which he uses to bite while demanding she opens her legs. The lips are very sensitive. Biting them is so painful it distracts the victim, allowing the rapist to overcome her resistance. The victim can only hold out for so long and the blood flows into her mouth. Some women are stronger than others, and I've seen their lips half-torn from their faces before they give up."[18]**

Bill Clinton – lip biter and rapist.

When NBC's Lisa Myers interviewed Juanita Broaddrick on January 20, 1999 she specifically asked:

> **"Is there any way at all that Bill Clinton could have thought this was consensual?"**
>
> **Broaddrick was adamant, "No. Not with what I told him and with how I tried to push him away. It was not consensual."**
>
> **Myers pushed further, "You're saying that Bill Clinton sexually assaulted you, that he raped you?"**
>
> **Broaddrick was firm in her one word response. "Yes."[19]**

The damage to Broaddrick's mouth from Clinton's biting was so severe that when she finally drove back to her hometown of Van Buren, Arkansas, they had to "stop for more ice to apply to Broaddrick's swollen mouth."[20]

Before bringing Hillary Clinton into the picture, let's pause for a moment and ask ourselves: what do we have here? What has been presented thus far in the opening pages of this book?

Feminist spokesman and author Andrea Dworkin doesn't mince words when declaring, "I believe that Clinton is a rapist. I believe the woman – and if I had doubts about the woman, I trust what I perceive about him."[21]

Dworkin also categorized what he did to Paula Jones as "assault," continuing, "From there, it's a very clear line to rape ... suddenly, every time you look at this man you have to think about rape. It's harder to sleep, it's hard to work because this man is the president. That's obscenity."[22]

Or, as Candice Jackson asks in *Their Lives: The Women Targeted by the Clinton Machine*, "What does it mean that we may have permitted a rapist to run the free world for eight years?"[23] In the same vein, long-time *Washington Post* liberal columnist Richard Cohen asked, "Is it possible the president's a rapist? Am

I supposed not to care? Who is this guy?"[24]

Even one of Clinton's most intimate ex-girlfriends, Dolly Kyle Browning, confirmed his dark side. "Do I believe Billy is capable of rape? Absolutely. There is a very cruel side to Billy. He is willing to destroy anyone – man or woman – who gets in his way. That was part of his nature then, but I never saw it until later."[25] The worst part is: our former president didn't limit his sexually predatory nature to only one woman. Or, as Candice Jackson so succinctly wrote in *Their Lives*, "Juanita Broaddrick isn't the only woman ever rumored to accuse Bill Clinton of rape, but she is the only woman who has confirmed her claims publicly."[26]

Coincidentally, Sam Smith reported in *Arkansas Connections: A Timeline of the Clinton Years*, that, "Hospital nurses reported Broaddrick's incident as a rape, but the report along with photos have since disappeared."[27] When one considers how many files 'mysteriously' vanished in subsequent years in relation to various Clinton scandals (i.e. Vince Foster, Whitewater, Filegate, Travel-gate, etc), the above information is not too surprising.

Partners in Power author Roger Morris takes matters one step further when describing a female Little Rock lawyer who accused Bill Clinton of not only sexually assaulting her, but also biting and bruising her too. When her husband saw Clinton at the 1980 Democratic Convention, he confronted him and issued a very succinct warning: "If you ever approach her, I'll kill you." Here is how Morris described the then-governor's response: "Not even seeing fit to deny the incident, Bill Clinton sheepishly apologized and duly promised never to bother her again."[28]

A mountain of further evidence will be presented later in this book that illustrates Bill Clinton's sexual degeneracy, but for the moment let's turn our attention to Hillary Rodham Clinton's re-action to the above rape-related material. Now, since Hillary is widely viewed as an ardent feminist that strongly supports women's causes, one would think she'd be appalled by such a vicious, abhorrent rape.

But as always, political expediency took precedence over any

moral sense of doing what was proper, and Hillary Clinton immediately went into cover-up mode. In other words, Hillary's first
instinct was not to do the right thing, but instead to preserve her
"political viability" (to borrow a phrase from her husband).

   To reconstruct Hillary's actions, let's return to an event which
took place three weeks following the rape of Juanita Broaddrick
in Little Rock's Camelot Hotel. Christopher Andersen sets the
stage in *American Evita*:

> **There was a Clinton fund-raiser scheduled to
> be held in just a couple of weeks in Van Buren
> [Broaddrick's place of residence] at the home
> of Dr. Chris Wells. Calls were made to make
> sure an invitation had gone out to Juanita, who
> happened to be a friend of Wells. It had. In
> fact, Juanita had RSVP'd long before the inci-
> dent in the Camelot Hotel, and the host was
> certain she would be attending.[29]**

Andersen continued:

> **Hillary and Bill flew into town on a corpo-
> rate aircraft supplied by "Big Daddy" Tyson,
> and were met at the airport by a campaign
> volunteer assigned to drive them to Wells's
> home. The Clintons were unaware that their
> driver was also a close friend of Juanita's.
> The driver later told Juanita that, during the
> twenty-minute ride, Hillary and Bill talked
> about only one thing: Juanita and what to do
> about her. Hillary cautioned her husband
> not to talk to Juanita and to 'leave the whole
> thing up to me.' All Bill had to remember to
> do, she said, was to point Juanita out as soon
> as they arrived.[30]**

To reinforce this point, in an interview with the Fox News Channel's Sean Hannity, Juanita Broaddrick said, "They [the Clintons] came in, but just before they did, the driver – who had gone to the airport and picked them up – came over to me and said that – he was a local pharmacist in this area – but he told me the whole topic of conversation from the airport was you and are you going to be there."[31]

What we are now beginning to see is a Hillary Clinton far different than the one portrayed in her bio, *Living History*. In Hillary's convoluted portrayal of 'reality,' she's a long-suffering victim who is out of the loop and only finds out about her husband's indiscretions after the fact. But as you'll see in the following example – and throughout the entirety of this book – nothing could be further from the truth, for Hillary Clinton was not only fully aware of every major sexual impropriety committed by Bill Clinton (not to mention a few of her own), but she was also the catalyst in charge of covering up these atrocities.

Anyway, after obsessing over the rape of this young woman during their limousine ride, it was now time to implement their plan. Immediately following her arrival at the fundraiser, Juanita Broaddrick described what happened next. "Hillary sought me out."[32]

> **"Is Juanita Hickey here yet?" Hillary asked brightly. "Has anybody seen Juanita?"**
>
> **Bill, too skittish to come anywhere near Juanita, was of no help at all to his wife. Still, it didn't take long for Hillary to get someone to point Juanita out. Hillary made a beeline for Juanita, then cornered her and grabbed her hand forcefully enough to frighten her.**[33]

Broaddrick told Christopher Andersen, "When somebody told her where I was, she came straight for me and cornered me and grabbed my hand very forcefully."[34]

At that point, Hillary Clinton laid her cards on the table. Broaddrick recalled what Mrs. Clinton told her that night. "'I want you to know how grateful we all are for all you've done for Bill,' Hillary said, eyes glaring as if to underline another message. 'We are so grateful for all you've done for Bill, and all you'll keep doing.'

Broaddrick remembered that Hillary's grasp lingered before she let go."[35]

Juanita explained to Sean Hannity, "I almost got nauseous when she came over to me. And she took a hold of my hand and said, 'I've heard so much about you. I've been dying to meet you.' ... And I started to turn and walk away. This woman – this little soft spoken – pardon me for the phrase – dowdy woman that seemed very unassertive, took a hold of my hand and squeezed it and said, 'Do you understand everything that you do?' I could have passed out at that moment."[36]

Christopher Andersen continues, "Juanita tried to free herself from Hillary's iron grasp, but the candidate's wife did not release her grip for several seconds – enough for Hillary to feel certain that she had gotten her point across."[37]

"'She was looking me straight in the eye and I understood perfectly what she was saying,' Juanita recalled. 'I knew *exactly* what she meant – that I was to keep my mouth shut.'"[38]

After pulling away from Hillary's clutches, Juanita surmised, "In that instant, I knew that *she* knew. I never thought for a moment there was any possibility that she didn't know that her husband had raped me."[39]

In this same vein, Broaddrick further described the look in Hillary's eye and her stern demeanor. "That meant she knew what had happened almost from the beginning. But apparently it was something she was willing to overlook."[40]

"In that split second Juanita realized that Bill had confessed to Hillary, and that she was not going to let that get in the way. 'At that moment I knew what Hillary was capable of doing. And I could see in her eyes that she wasn't doing it for her husband. She wasn't even doing it for them. She was doing it for Hillary Rodham.'"[41]

The episode so traumatized Mrs. Broaddrick – only three weeks after being violently raped, bruised, and bitten – that "when Hillary moved on to the other guests, Juanita retreated to a hallway, where she became physically ill. 'I was so upset,' she said, 'all I could think of was, Oh God, I'm going to throw up.'"[42] Hillary Clinton – cover-up artist extraordinaire for her husband the rapist – the same man who five months later would stand in the same hotel where he physically assaulted Juanita Broaddrick and be declared the governor of Arkansas.

As Juanita Broaddrick watched their celebration on TV, she commented, "It was just, you know, surreal. Hillary was laughing and waving to the crowd. She was just so pleased with herself, I kept thinking: What kind of woman is this? What kind of woman?"[43]

Ironically (or sickeningly, depending on your perspective), Hillary Clinton was instrumental in establishing "the first rape crisis phone line in Arkansas."[44] Furthermore, whenever they're confronted by the rape of Juanita Broaddrick, the Clintons do what the Clintons do best – they lie.

But the fact of the matter – what actually took place behind-the-scenes after the rape – is best summarized by Christopher Andersen in *American Evita*:

> **Bill returned home in a panic. Worried that his victim might go public and derail his campaign, he decided to confide – to an extent – in the one person whose opinion he most valued. According to Bill's version of events, Juanita was a Clinton groupie who had lured him up to her room under false pretenses and seduced him. He was ashamed and sorry, and begged Hillary to forgive him.**
>
> **Hillary let fly with the customary expletives, though she was clearly more concerned**

> with the potential political fallout than with
> the mere fact that Bill had once again
> cheated on her. Just as it was becoming ap-
> parent that Hillary did not view this problem
> as insurmountable, Bill confessed there was
> more....
>
> Hillary was ashen once she was con-
> fronted with the whole story – at least Bill's
> carefully parsed version of events. But, as
> the woman who had set up Arkansas's first
> rape crisis hotline and had championed laws
> protecting victims, she almost certainly rec-
> ognized the confession of a rapist when she
> heard it.[45]

Bill Clinton: rapist; and his wife the hypocritical, amoral, politically charged cover-up artist and enabler. A match truly made
in hell.

Oddly, although most members of the feminist movement ig-
nored Juanita Broaddrick's rape, or else conveniently swept it
under the rug, Andrea Dworkin lashed out. "What Hillary is
doing is appalling. Being a feminist has to mean you don't use
your intellect and your creativity to protect a man's exploitation
of women."[46]

Dworkin was correct, because as you'll see later in this book,
Hillary Clinton has marginalized, attacked, threatened, intimidated, harassed, and/or bribed nearly every woman who has ever
spoken out publicly against her sexual predator husband. When
Juanita Broaddrick engaged in litigation against Bill Clinton the
rapist [1999], guess what happened? "In the middle of the lawsuit, Broaddrick's nursing home business found itself audited by
the IRS for the first time in its thirty years of existence."[47] Flash-
backs of Richard Nixon's dirty tricks team all over again – a concept Hillary was very well aware of.

So, to close this chapter let's cut to the chase. As Edward Klein wrote in regard to the Lewinsky affair, "The fact of the matter was, Hillary knew everything – and she knew it before anybody else. And yet, she never changed her tune. Even after the truth about Bill and Monica came out, Hillary continued to defend her husband. And while the lurid tale rocked the nation, Hillary recovered from the shock faster than everybody else."[48]

Think about it: "According to a filing in the Paula Jones case, Clinton forcibly raped her [Juanita Broaddrick]. Following the encounter, he bribed and intimidated her to remain silent about the matter."[49]

When informed that Hillary had begun another new anti-rape campaign, Juanita Broaddrick told *NewsMax*, "If Hillary can accept what Bill did to me; then she shouldn't even be involved in anything like that. You just wonder if she shouldn't start at home with this crusade."[50]

Her words are absolutely true because, as Carl Limbacher so poignantly surmises, she became her husband's "enabler, facilitator, or co-conspirator."[51] On top of that, "She had threatened to 'crucify' Gennifer Flowers, was the one who decided not to settle with Paula Jones, and then later signed off on a despicable attempt to trash Kathleen Willey after she accused Bill of sexual assault."[52]

Yet for some reason the mainstream media have never portrayed Hillary Clinton in this light. Why? Because the corporate-controlled press has also, to a large extent, been a Bill Clinton enabler and Hillary Clinton facilitator. Stated differently, they've been running a huge protection racket to maintain Hillary's political viability.

Try to absorb what Limbacher is saying. "If reporters accepted the clear implications of all the evidence pointing to Hillary Clinton's involvement in trashing her husband's accusers, then she could no longer be depicted as a long-suffering victim,"[53] or a figurehead for the women's movement.

Presto! If Hillary is ever seen by the public as part of an attack force which focuses its fury on the women who have been sexually abused – and even raped – by her husband, then he is instantly written off as "a de facto accomplice of the worst order."[54]

But instead of saving the women who were abused and destroyed by her husband, she sold her soul to attain even higher political office. Every step she made revolved around self-preservation and advancement – damn the sins (her own or her husbands). "Mrs. Clinton has sold out her sex as part of a Faustian bargain with a predatory rapist on the chance that she might one day become president of the United States."[55] Bill Clinton is a perverted monster and sexual deviant, and when it comes to Juanita Broaddrick, Hillary "was an accomplice at some level to rape."[56]

What has been written thus far isn't the tangled web of some vast right-wing conspiracy, nor is it a by-product of the rambling tinfoil hat-wearing crowd. It is, sadly, the bitter, publicly documented truth about a degenerate couple so intent on political advancement that their very souls are blacker than charcoal.

Juanita Broaddrick was raped by Bill Clinton, and as Lisa Myers of NBC News told her after an historic interview (which was subsequently delayed by the network until after the president's impeachment hearings were over), "The good news is, you're credible. The bad news is, you're very, very credible."[57]

Juanita Broaddrick – along with many other women – has been telling the truth for decades about Bill Clinton's sexual abuses and Hillary's reign of terror to protect him.

Regrettably, despite all the previously related evidence, there still may be those who don't believe that Bill Clinton is a rapist. To combat even the most hard-core skeptics with their heads in the sand, ponder the following example. While attending a 1999 nursing home conference in Little Rock, Clinton confessed his guilt to Ms. Broaddrick. "In person, Bill Clinton called her [Broaddrick] out of the meeting. One friend confirms seeing the pair talking. Immediately, Broaddrick says, Clinton 'began this profuse apology,' saying to her, 'Juanita, I'm so sorry for what I did. I'm not the man that I used to be. Can you ever forgive me?

What can I do to make this up to you?'"[58]

But Bill Clinton *isn't* a changed man, as witnessed by the lies and abuses of Gennifer Flowers, Kathleen Willey, Paula Jones, Monica Lewinsky, and so many others. In fact, he didn't change one little bit. He's still as exploitative as ever, and his wife continues to run roughshod over those who threaten her political ambitions.

To close, the words of Monica Lewinsky's attorney, William H. Ginsburg, best summarize this situation. "If the president of the United States did this – with this young woman [Monica Lewinsky] – I think he's a misogynist."[59]

A misogynist is a woman-hater, and as we all know by now, Bill Clinton *did* do *this* with a woman who was young enough to be his daughter – right there in the Oval Office on many occasions (and please realize Hillary knew all about it way before it ever became a public feeding frenzy on the nightly news). But Bill Clinton did something far worse than receive oral sex from Monica Lewinsky, engage in childish phone sex with her, or watch as she masturbated with a cigar. Bill Clinton raped Juanita Broaddrick, and this makes him a woman-hater of the very worst kind.

Bill Clinton is a sick, sick man who ultimately became president when, in reality, he should have been serving time in a state penitentiary; and his wife – the daughter of the devil himself – is even more dangerous because she has unendingly served as the brains behind a vast secret team which was used to further defile the women her husband had already degraded via his sexual degeneracy.

INTRODUCTION

The Clinton Lie Machine

The book you are reading is not filled with distractions that are used to divert your attention from the more serious aspects of the Clinton's lives, specifically their crimes. A perfect example of this technique was when Hillary Clinton – appearing with her husband in 1992 on *60 Minutes* to minimize repercussions from the Gennifer Flowers scandal – deliberately took a jab at a certain country western singer. "I'm not some little woman just standing by her man, like Tammy Wynette."[60] The media conveniently spent as much effort creating a fake feeding frenzy over this comment as they did revealing that Bill Clinton had been having a prolonged affair with Ms. Flowers (which, in all honesty, was *another* distraction in and of itself). The same distraction-style strategy occurred when Hillary took another swipe at traditional values by quipping, "I suppose I could have stayed home and baked cookies and had teas."[61] Likewise, I'm not going to waste your time or mine (as so many other authors have) by dwelling on Bill Clinton's infamous haircut aboard *Air Force One* where his "mammoth plane idled on the runway at Los Angeles International Airport, closing down two of the airport's four runways, delaying thirty-seven flights, and costing commercial carriers $76,479 while a ludicrous Hollywood coiffeur by the name of Christophe trimmed Clinton's frizz for fifty-six minutes at a cost of $200."[62]

Similarly, my research will not concern itself with policy issues such as social security, the budget, deficits, health care, or homosexuals in the military (the first big public relations snafu-distraction of the Clinton presidency). Also, to the disappointment of those who specialize in divide-and-conquer techniques, we won't be delving into partisan politics, the illusory left/right paradigm,

or the vicious bashing Democrats and Republicans continually inflict upon each other.

No, what follows will highlight something far more monumen-
tal – the crimes of Bill and Hillary Clinton. Sure, dozens of books
have been written about this couple (if you check the bibliography, you'll find that I've used nearly every one of them as source
material); but regrettably, most of the authors fall short in their
efforts for one primary reason: they fail to state in any unequiv-
ocal way that Bill and Hillary Clinton are two of the most criminal
political figures to ever exist in this country, and that they should
either be facing life imprisonment or capital punishment.

Of course there have been a few excellent books written about
them, but none that comprehensively tie it all together in the
manner this trilogy does. In fact, what you are holding in your
hands is the one book which could single-handedly prevent
Hillary Clinton from entering the White House. The information
regarding her is that damaging, and if the mainstream media actually reported it, Hillary could not survive.

You may wonder, what specifically are we referring to? Well,
in these pages you'll learn how:

> • **Bill Clinton was selected – from a very
> early age – to become president of the United
> States, and therefore an entire mythology was
> created concerning his "biological father" (all
> of which is a ruse) while he was being raised
> among figures known as "The Dixie Mafia."**
>
> • **Bill and Hillary Clinton had a pre-
> arranged marriage to facilitate their rise to
> political power, and both were recruited into
> the CIA during their college years to serve as
> operatives for the Agency (an association
> which still exists to this day).**
>
> • **Hillary Clinton has had been directly in-
> volved in nearly every major scandal of the**

> last thirty years, including Watergate, White-
> water, Iran-Contra, Inslaw and PROMIS, the
> BCCI banking debacle, the disastrous S&L
> bailouts, drug trafficking in Mena while her
> husband was governor of Arkansas, Travel-
> gate, Filegate, Waco, the murders of Vince
> Foster and Ron Brown, OKC, and the shoot-
> down of Flight 800.

But when confronted with the overwhelming amount of evidence chronicling their involvement in these crimes, the Clintons do two things: they lie, and they lie some more. We will prove this in these pages. What follows is a brief collection of strongly held beliefs (from a wide variety of sources) that focuses first on Hillary Clinton's honesty (or lack thereof), and that of her husband Bill.

• *New York Times* columnist William Safire branded Hillary a "congenital liar."[63]

• Liz Moynihan, wife of departed (and much respected) New York Senator Patrick Moynihan, on Hillary: "She's duplicitous. She would say or do anything that would forward her ambitions. She can look you straight in the eye and lie ... lying isn't a sufficient word; it's distortion – distorting the truth to fit the case."[64] Mrs. Moynihan also revealed to friends that "she found Hillary to be one of the strangest people she had ever met."[65]

• Dick Morris in *Rewriting History*: "Hillary's memoir is one continuous cover-up ... the cover-up is more disturbing than the scandals themselves."[66]

• When Hillary announced that she was running for an open New York senate seat in 2000, she patronized the baseball crowd by stating, "I've always been a Yankees fan."[67] When NBC News morning host Katie Couric pointed out that "Hillary had always claimed to be a Cubs fan in the past,"[68] Mrs. Clinton explained that she used to watch the Yankees on one of the super-stations as a child. The only problem is; no "super-stations" beamed the

Yankees into the suburbs of Chicago on a regular basis during the 1950's. In fact, there wasn't even the concept of "super-stations" in the black-and-white '50s. It was a total fabrication on Hillary's part to garner more votes.

• Lying about the September 11, 2001 terrorist attacks is the lowest of lows, but with Hillary, no depths are low enough to plummet. Get a load of this whopper. "She invented a story about 9/11 on the *Today* show, implying to Katie Couric that her daughter, Chelsea, had narrowly missed being on the grounds of the Twin Towers at the time of the attacks."[69] Hillary continued, "Chelsea had gone on what she thought would be a great job. She was going to go around the towers. She went to get a cup of coffee and that's when the planes hit. She did hear it. She did."[70] But Chelsea let the cat out of the bag and refuted her mother's version of events during an interview with *Talk* magazine by saying that "she was alone at a friend's Union Square apartment in Manhattan that morning when her host phoned to tell her what had happened."[71] In other words, she was "at a friend's apartment on the other side of town and watched the horrific events of the day unfold on television. She did not mention a jog around the towers or getting coffee when the planes hit."[72] Why do you think Hillary fabricated such a tall tale?

• How about the *Late Show with David Letterman* episode where, to prove how much of a New Yorker she was during her initial senatorial campaign, Hillary took a supposedly impromptu "quiz" about the Empire State. "Letterman quizzed her on the state flower, the state bird, the state tree, the state motto, and more."[73] Amazingly, Hillary got every single question correct! The only problem was, Hillary "had been given the questions in advance."[74] Worse, "Hillary agreed to do the interview only if she knew the questions in advance."[75] So, "Hillary would pretend to search her memory as Letterman asked each question, seeming to stall for time, and then blurt out the answer at the last moment."[76] "To make things even easier, comedy writers provided Hillary with a couple of snappy one-liners."[77] In the end, the entire charade was a ruse ... "It was all acting. It was all a fake."[78]

• Then, of course, Hillary can't even tell the truth about the origins of her own name. As Hillary's version of the story goes, when her mother was pregnant, she read a few articles about the mountain climber Sir Edmund Hillary who became world famous for scaling Mount Everest. "So, when I was born, she called me Hillary, and she always told me it's because of Sir Edmund."[79] But here is where a few "facts" get in the way. Hillary was born in 1947, and "Sir Edmund didn't climb Everest until May 29, 1953 – five and a half years *after* Hillary was born."[80] Thus, when Hillary came into the world and was given her name, "The great adventurer was still an obscure beekeeper living in New Zealand."[81]

• But why stop at lying about her name? Why not continue it with her book, *It Takes a Village*. "Hillary had claimed to have written the book herself, only to have it later revealed that Simon & Schuster had paid a $120,000 advance to Georgetown journalism professor Barbara Feinman."[82] Not wishing to share the limelight or admit that the book was ghostwritten, the name Barbara Feinman didn't even "make the acknowledgements page of *It Takes a Village*"[83] or merit a simple thank you. When the ghostwriter made it known publicly that she wasn't pleased with this arrangement, "Hillary wanted Simon & Schuster to withhold one-quarter of her down payment."[84] "Eventually, Hillary came through with the final payment – but only after Feinman reportedly threatened to sue."[85]

• This tale becomes even more interesting because sources say that Hillary became incensed with Feinman when – in another one of her heightened bouts of paranoia – she felt the author had leaked information to Bob Woodward for his book *The Choice*, where he chronicled how Hillary had "conversations with the ghost of Eleanor Roosevelt."[86] Yes, fringe spiritualist Jean Houston "used hypnosis to guide Hillary into a séance/conversation with Eleanor Roosevelt"[87] to "solicit her advice on a range of subjects."[88] Maybe Eleanor's ghost should have taught Mrs. Clin-

ton how to lie a little bit more convincingly, because Hillary
seems to get caught in every tangled web she weaves.

• There are many other instances of her deception and phoniness, like the time she attempted to soften her image as a radical
feminist before the Arkansas voters by telling them "she tried to
sign up with the Marines but was rejected."[89] Or, "Because Hillary
had the image of being a cold, arrogant, power-hungry attorney,"[90] she told reporters that she and Bill were thinking about
adopting a baby! Hell, Hillary can't even speak in a convincing
fashion during interviews, as could be seen from her famous Gennifer Flowers appearance on *60 Minutes* in 1992 where she "spoke
with an audible southern drawl."[91] "This woman from a Chicago
suburb who was educated at Wellesley and Yale had, until recently, spoken in the neutral tones of the Midwest."[92] So, by all
appearances, Hillary had transformed herself into a gun-toting
wannabe adoptive-mother Marine who spoke like a character on
Hee Haw. Is there anything at all real about this woman?

• Despite these examples, it didn't stop Hillary from trying to
convince New Yorkers that she was 'one of them' during her state
senatorial carpetbagger campaign in 2000. Dick Morris recalls, "I
saw Hillary frequently from 1980 until 1990. But never, not once,
did she evince the slightest, remotest interest in New York, city
or state.

"She never asked what it was like to live there ... she showed
no curiosity about the city's schools, crime, taxes, drug problems,
politics or anything else."[93] "She was not born in New York. She
had never lived there. She did not attend school there, and none
of her ancestors hailed from there. She had, in fact, never spent
more than a few days there before deciding that she wanted to
use one of New York's two senate seats as a springboard to the
presidency."[94] Her opponent in 2000, Rick Lazio, put it even
more succinctly, "Hillary Clinton has never lived a day of her life
in New York outside the Plaza Hotel."[95]

• What Hillary has done, though, is live off *you* and your tax
dollars. Peggy Noonan hit the nail on the head by stating that,

"for almost all her adult life – [Hillary has] lived in taxpayer-funded government housing. She has not had to make out a check for the mortgage or scramble to pay the rent; she has not had to pay the electric bill or shop for food or put gas in the car. The cars, most of her adult life, have been government sedans, driven by aides, state troopers, and later the Secret Service."[96] To screw the system even more, while Clinton was governor their "nanny was officially listed as a security guard"[97] while "a state legislator had to threaten to launch an investigation before she stopped using state troopers to do her errands."[98]

Bill Clinton's deceit is equally as pronounced.

• Robert J. Samuelson, *Washington Post*, June 9, 1993: "Clinton lies. I could put it more delicately, but that would miss the point. Sometimes the lies are blatant untruths. Sometimes they are artful distortions, technically true but misleading. But the effect is the same ... his distortions are brazen, unrelenting and unusually specific."[99]

• David Horowitz of *Front Page Magazine*: "Bill Clinton is more readily understood as a borderline sociopath."[100]

• Andrew Sullivan, *New Republic*: "In Bill Clinton we had for eight years a truly irrational person in the White House, someone who, I think, lived on the edge of serious mental illness. He was and is a psychologically sick man."[101] Sullivan continued, "Clinton was not psychologically healthy enough to have been president of the United States."[102]

• Howard Kurtz, *Washington Post*: "Clinton had an almost congenital inability to tell the unvarnished truth."[103]

• John R. Starr, former editor of the *Arkansas-Democrat Gazette*, labeled Bill Clinton "that lying son of a bitch,"[104] in addition to saying that "he was an arrogant, no-good son of a bitch ... a dirty rotten scoundrel."[105]

• Tony Snow, syndicated columnist, Fox News television host, and current White House spokesman: "When people elect a president, they not only want a person who promotes good policies, but also someone on whom they can depend. They like to think they're electing a Lincolnesque figure – and not a Caligula of the Ozarks."[106]

• Jimmy Breslin, long-time New York City columnist: "Bill Clinton is nothing more than a cheap waitress chaser."[107]

• Patrick Matrisciana, author of *The Clinton Chronicles*: "If you know Clinton long enough, you came to realize lying wasn't second nature to him; it was first."[108] "Everyone thought Bill was a strange character. If you could ever get someone who was close to him to level with you, they would always say the same thing: the man is strange; he's 'different' from the rest of us."[109]

• Michael Kelly, *New York Times Magazine*: "The president's essential character flaw isn't dishonesty so much as a-honesty."[110]

• *New York Times* editorial, December 16, 1998: "We say that from the platform of our record of consistently criticizing Mr. Clinton's ugly little lies, his abject failure to lead by example and to speak truthfully to the American people ... he is, in sum, a man you cannot trust whether you have his handshake, his signature, or his word on the Bible."[111]

• Jesse Jackson, *National Review*, October 30, 2003: "There is nothing that this man won't do. He is immune to shame. Move past all the nice posturing and get really down in there on him, you find absolutely nothing ... nothing but appetite."[112]

• Hunter S. Thompson, *South Bend Tribune*, September 6, 1998: "Bill Clinton would have played the Jew's harp stark naked on *60 Minutes* if he thought it would get him elected. He is the Willy Loman of Generation X, a traveling salesman who has the loyalty of a lizard with his tail broken off and the midnight taste of a man who'd double date with the Reverend Jimmy Swaggart."[113]

• Charlton Heston, NRA annual meeting, June 1998: "Mr. Clinton, sir, Americans don't trust you with our health care systems. Americans don't trust you with gays in the military. Americans don't trust you with our 21-year-old daughters, and we sure, Lord, don't trust you with our guns!"[114]

• Bert Dickey III, long-time Democratic strategist, campaigner, and fundraiser: "I think he's a habitual liar. He's done it all his life, and it's just the way, business as usual. I don't think he's got a conscience."[115]

• Meredith Oakley, Arkansas columnist and author of *On the Make: The Rise of Bill Clinton*: "His word is dirt."[116]

• Air Force Major General Harold N. Campbell called Clinton a "dope-smoking, skirt-chasing, draft-dodging, womanizing Commander-in-Chief."[117]

• Former U.S. Senator Bob Kerrey (D-Neb), *Esquire* magazine, January 1996: "Clinton is an unusually good liar. Unusually good. Do you realize that?"[118]

• One of Hillary's close friends characterized him as such: "I don't like saying this, but he lied to her. He's a very good liar."[119]

• James Ellroy, author: "Bill Clinton is a lying, thieving, perjuring, perjury-suborning, justice-obstructing, woman-harassing, misogynist sack of shit."[120] He also added, "Bill Clinton, who, like most serial sexual harassers, is a candy ass who's physically afraid of other men."[121]

• Christopher Hitchens, *Vanity Fair* columnist and author, "Bill Clinton has all the traits of a psychopath."[122]

• Senator Joseph Lieberman (D-Conn): "His behavior is not just inappropriate, it is immoral. And it is harmful."[123]

• Michael Isikoff, *Uncovering Clinton*: "Clinton was far more psychologically disturbed than the public ever imagined ... Clinton's scale required routine, repetitive, and reflexive lies to conceal itself."[124]

• David Broder, *Washington Post*, "This is a guy who reconstructs his own history to suit his needs."[125]

• R. Emmett Tyrrell, author of *Boy Clinton*: "A peculiarity about Clinton's lies that sets him apart from the other presidential prevaricators is that his lies are often so obvious as to cast temporary doubt on his intelligence or his contact with reality."[126] "Clinton is a constant liar who has, on occasion, devised lies that are truly extraordinary. He tells huge lies when a little white lie would be sufficient and perhaps even pardonable ... There is no reality beyond himself. He lies like a man totally unencumbered by conceptions of right and wrong. He lies like a sociopath."[127]

• James Woods, actor, *Washington Post*, January 1999: "He's a certified liar, a card-carrying liar, and lying is the cancer at the base of the spine of every crime ever committed."[128]

• Kevin H. Watson, author of *The Clinton Record*: "William Jefferson Clinton is truly a man like no other, for I cannot find any competitor in the number of lies and deceptions he has perpetrated upon the American public."[129]

• Jill Abramson, *Wall Street Journal*, "Nobody collects friends like Bill Clinton – and nobody puts them to better use."[130]

• Gennifer Flowers, former mistress: "Bill Clinton turns out to be a man I would compare to a Mafia don."[131]

• Clinton's courtroom perjuries were so extensive that "his law license was suspended for five years"[132] for lying during his Paula Jones sexual harassment civil suit. Federal District Judge Susan Webber Wright stated, "The record demonstrates by clear and convincing evidence that the president responded by giving false, misleading and evasive answers that were designed to obstruct the judicial process."[133]

• During "the Lewinsky affair, he lied under oath in two separate sessions, urged Monica to lie under oath, coached a potential witness in his employ in an attempt to get her to repeat falsehoods, asserted bogus executive privileges, and lied to everyone in the White House and the nation."[134]

• David Schippers, December 10, 1998 to the House Judiciary Committee: "The President has lied under oath in a civil deposition, lied under oath in a criminal grand jury. He lied to the people, he lied to his Cabinet, he lied to his top aides, and now he's lied under oath to the Congress of the United States. *There's no one left to lie to.*"[135]

• Because "he had lied about his relationship under oath"[136] with Monica Lewinsky, "Clinton had been the second president to be impeached, the first to be hauled before a grand jury, the first to have to give a blood sample for a DNA match, and the first to be held in contempt for lying to a federal judge."[137]

- "Clinton was charged by Arkansas bar authorities with making false statements of material facts in a federal legal proceeding and engaging in conduct that was dishonest, deceitful, and prejudicial to the administration of justice ... In his plea bargain Bill Clinton acknowledged knowingly violating the judge's orders to testify truthfully and accepted a five-year suspension of his license to practice law."[138]

- George Stephanopoulos, after watching Clinton's 'I never had sexual relations with that woman' speech on TV: "Now, full of self-righteous fury, he was lying with true conviction. All that mattered was his survival. Everyone else had to fall in line: his staff, his cabinet, the country, even his wife."[139]

- Ross Perot once wisecracked that he "wouldn't consider giving Clinton a job anywhere above middle management."[140]

- This guy will even lie about his own race, rationalizing why he chose to have his post-presidential office in Harlem. "I love it. I feel at home here. This *is* home."[141] "That's why I went to Harlem. Because I think I am the first black president."[142]

- That's not the only time the race card was deceptively played. During numerous political campaigns Clinton attributed his racial tolerance to seeing a number of black churches being burned during his youth. There was only one problem. "It was revealed that there had not been any churches burned in Arkansas during that time span."[143]

- Lieutenant Colonel Robert Patterson, one of only five trusted aides responsible for carrying the nuclear "football" in case a nuclear launch was ever necessary, relates how Clinton even lied on the golf course. "I decided to document, just for fun, the president's scoring transgressions. Using the cardboard lid from a boxed lunch the White House valets had prepared for the outing, we secretly kept President Clinton's score. Hole after hole, we noted his actual score. At the end of the course, we were able to sneak his scorecard from his golf cart and compare it with the scores we had kept. Sure enough, when the press interviewed him following his round, he claimed he shot a 79. Actually, it was a 92."[144]

• Paul Greenberg provided an excellent overview of Clinton's emptiness in the *Arkansas Democratic Gazette*. "It is not the duplicitousness in his politics that concerns so much as the polished ease, the almost habitual, casual, articulate way he bobs and weaves. There is something almost inhuman in his smoother responses that sends a shiver up the spine. It is not the compromises that have made that trouble so much as the unavoidable suspicion that he has no great principles to compromise."[145]

• Lastly, one of the most glaring examples of Clinton's deceit occurred in 1990 while he was running for his fifth term as Arkansas governor. Because many in the state were convinced that Clinton was simply using this last potential election victory as a springboard for the presidency, he was asked point-blank by reporter Craig Cannon, "Will you guarantee us that if reelected, there is absolutely, positively no way that you'll run for any other political office and that you'll serve out your term in full?" Clinton replied, "You bet! I'm gonna serve four years ... I made that decision when I decided to run ... that's the job I'll do for the next four years."[146] But "scarcely nine months into his fifth gubernatorial term, Clinton officially broke his promise not to seek another office, a promise he had made in full knowledge that it would never be kept. But, as Clinton had advised intimates, he had to tell the lie or he might not have been reelected, and he needed that reelection to enhance his viability as a presidential candidate."[147]

The Clintons are even described jointly as a form of tag-team deceivers.

• In *Boy Clinton*, author R. Emmett Tyrrell describes the couple as being, "cheats, users, liars, and as greedy as their worst vision of a Republican. Both are without dignity."[148]

• Deceased author Barbara Olson on the Clintons' untruthfulness: "It had become second nature to both. The abuse of power. The destruction of people who are in their way, the lying, even when the truth might be entirely acceptable – these are the Clinton's *modus operandi*."[149]

• Peggy Noonan, *The Case Against Hillary*: "The Clintons are unusually brazen. They lie in plain sight, with boldness, with utmost confidence in their ability to carry it off ... they seem to feel they *deserve* to carry it off. Bill Clinton lies, as William Safire has noted, 'when he doesn't have to.' Hillary is, as Safire has observed, 'a congenital liar'."[150]

• Maureen Dowd, *New York Times*, August 4, 1999: "Everyone is fed up with the creepy dynamics of this warped marriage. We have lost all hope of getting any shred of authenticity from either Bill or Hillary. They have chosen tactics over truth with such consistency that it's impossible to accept anything they say."[151]

• Bob Herbert, liberal writer, *New York Times*, February 26, 2001: "The Clintons are a terminally unethical and vulgar couple, and they've betrayed everyone who has ever believed in them."[152]

• Hamilton Jordan, White House Chief of Staff under Jimmy Carter, on the Clintons as grifters (*Wall Street Journal*, February 20, 2001): "Grifters was a term used in the Great Depression to describe fast-talking con artists who roamed the countryside, profiting at the expense of the poor and the uneducated, always one step ahead of the law, moving on before they were held accountable for their schemes and half-truths."[153]

• Senator Strom Thurmond: "In a receiving line at the Capitol, the president and first lady greeted Strom Thurmond with smiles and handshakes. As they later described the scene to a friend, they heard Thurmond say, 'You're two turds.' 'Pardon?' said the president. 'You're two turds,' the senator repeated."[154]

• Movie mogul David Geffen, March, 2007: "I don't think anybody believes that in the last six years, all of a sudden Bill Clinton has become a different person. Everybody in politics lies, but they do it with such ease, it's troubling."[155]

In all honesty, we could conceivably fill an entire book with such quotes, but at this point you get the picture. The Clintons are habitual, pathological, incessant, grotesque, unrepentant liars; and if this truth were ever laid out before them, they'd continue to do one thing: lie. Or, as Kevin H. Watson has outlined in *The Clinton Record*, Bill and Hillary use a Four-Step Lying Program:

- Complete denial
- Plausible denial
- Partial admission of guilt
- Make the crime seem less criminal

In case you're wondering, we're spending so much time on this subject for one very specific reason: as you read this book you'll be confronted with a wide array of material that is very damning to the Clintons. As this information registers in your mind, remember this very important point – the Clintons lie ... pathologically, habitually, and unendingly.

Plus, when directly confronted with evidence of their crimes, it's their word (or version of events), versus thousands of others who have seen through their veil of deception. In the bibliography at the end of this book, you'll find 120 + different books cited, plus dozens of articles and documentaries. In all, the individuals who have produced these works include: religious figures, political analysts, professors, radio show hosts, award-winning journalists, lecturers, researchers, military officers and veterans from all branches of the armed services, investigative reporters, pilots, best-selling authors, publishers, law enforcement officers, former intelligence agents, whistleblowers, media consultants, financial analysts, editors, television reporters, elected and appointed government officials, Pulitzer Prize winners, political commentators, attorneys and legal analysts, syndicated columnists, psychologists, biographers, political activists, speechwriters, FBI agents, documentary filmmakers, Emmy award winners, consultants, international financiers, IRS agents, relatives, state troopers, an FAA investigator, private detectives, plus ex-girlfriends and victims.

It's their word as a collective whole versus that of known liars Bill and Hillary Clinton. In addition, every word written in this book can be verified from multiple sources, and as you'll see, they are painstakingly footnoted for reference.

Bill and Hillary Clinton are criminals, and they are also liars of the worst sort. If murdered researcher Danny Casolaro were alive today, this is the book he would be writing; for if Hillary Clinton is selected to be our next president, it will be the final nail in this country's coffin. The era of Bush-Clinton-Bush-Clinton must end immediately, or this once great nation is destined to crumble like other empires before it.

The Clinton Lie Machine – and especially Hillary Clinton – must be stopped now before she inflicts any further damage on the United States of America.

This 1993 file photo shows U.S. President-elect Bill Clinton with his mother, Virginia Kelley, in Little Rock, Arkansas, minutes before Clinton delivered a farewell speech to the people of Arkansas before leaving for Washington to be inaugurated as president. Virginia Kelley, 70, died January 6, 1994, in Hot Springs, Arkansas. (J.DAVID AKE/AFP/Getty Images)

CHAPTER ONE

Who Was Bill Clinton's Real Father?

In regard to modern American politics, the biggest myth taught by our public school system is that anybody can grow up to become president. But if we were brutally honest about this situation, we'd have to admit that to attain the Oval Office, one needs wealth, power, and connections. Inexplicably, Bill Clinton appeared to be the exception to this rule, because if we're to believe his carefully crafted family history, Bubba's youth was "one spent in barefoot poverty."[156] But as R. Emmett Tyrrell tells us, Clinton constantly misrepresents his childhood and "lies with the ease and grace of a great athlete at the pinnacle of his powers."[157] Political author Jack Cashill reiterates this point with great clarity:

> In *First in His Class*, the *Washington Post's* David Maraniss reports on a life that was almost luxurious given the time and place. The Clintons had turned the living room of the family's comfortable middle class home into a veritable "shrine" to young Billy's many accomplishments.
>
> The refrigerator was stocked to his tastes. His bedroom, and he never had to share one, was the largest in the house. He had his own bathroom, perhaps the only teen in the state so blessed. Meanwhile, in the carport sat the black four-door finned Buick that young Bill drove to Hot Springs High School. For special occasions, like a trip to the whites-only country club, there was also the family's cream yellow Henry J coupe. By nineteen, Clinton

was driving a white Buick convertible with red interior. The notion he was "poor" or came from "the wrong side of the tracks" is laughable.[158]

Not too shabby for 1950s America in one of the nation's poorest states. So, the "legend" that Bill Clinton was simply an impoverished lad from Hope, Arkansas is nothing more than a fable, for as we'll soon see, he wasn't even raised in Hope; but instead the mob-run mecca of Hot Springs.

But prior to delving into that topic we need to explore one of the great mysteries of 20th century politics: who was Bill Clinton's real father? Of course we all know the popular rendition of events about how Clinton's 'biological' father – Bill Blythe – died:

> **On May 17, 1946 Blythe was speeding down Route 60 when he blew a tire, causing his midnight blue Buick to roll over. Pulling himself from the wreckage, he collapsed in a drainage ditch – and drowned. William Blythe III [Bill Clinton] was born three months later.[159]**

Although the date of Bill Blythe's death in Sikeston, Missouri is certain, many of the other details told by the Clintons aren't. Let's look at the timetable. Bill Blythe met Bill Clinton's mother in 1943, and they were subsequently married "on September 3, 1943 in Texarkana, Arkansas"[160] shortly before he was shipped overseas during World War II. Now, Bill Clinton was born on August 19, 1946 – "a healthy full-term infant."[161] This point is crucial, for if we deduct nine months from his birth date, we have a conception date of mid-November, 1945.

If we're to believe Bill's mother in her autobiography, "Bill came home in November 1945."[162] Similar to her son, Virginia Clinton Kelley was also a liar, for "Army records pinpoint December 7 as

Blythe's date of discharge."[163] This date is confirmed by Pulitzer Prize-winner David Maraniss, who found that Blythe was "honorably discharged at Camp Shelby, Mississippi on December 7 [1945]."[164] Then, after making a few quick visits along the way, "It is unlikely, given travel times in those days; they [Blythe and Virginia Cassidy] could have seen each other until December 10."[165]

Again, as Meredith Oakley describes in *On the Make*, Clinton's mother gets her 'facts' wrong. "I was five months pregnant with Bill when his father was killed in an automobile accident, Virginia recalled later, although in fact her son arrived full-term three months later."[166] By doing some simple mathematics, we arrive at a conception date of November 1945, but "nine months before, August 19, 1945, Tech 3 Bill Blythe was still in Italy."[167]

David Maraniss continues this saga. "For years afterward, there were whispers in Hope about who little Billy's father was, rumors spawned by Virginia's flirtatious nature as a young nurse and by the inevitable temptation of people to count backwards nine months from the birth date to see who was where doing what."[168] Just like her son, though, whenever the facts didn't add up, Virginia Clinton Kelley created her own. To combat rumors that Bill Blythe was not her son's actual father, "Her answer was that Billy was born a month early ... because she had taken a fall and the doctor was concerned about her condition."[169]

So, just like that (at least in the Clinton's twisted world of deceit), everything was supposedly explained away. But Gail Sheehy very convincingly disputes this rendition of a premature birth with firsthand testimony. "I found the one person still living who had been present at the birth of the future president: the delivery room nurse, Wilma Booker."[170] Sheehy continues, "I asked Nurse Booker if Bill Clinton's birth could have been premature. 'No, not at that weight,' she replied unequivocally. 'I remember he was a nice-size baby, between eight and nine pounds.'"[171] Yet again, the Clinton myth does not even remotely coincide with the facts. Something is very fishy here.

The story gets even stranger, though, for after the couple reunited in late 1945, they moved to Chicago. But "by May 1946, Virginia was back in Hope."[172] Thus, the couple had only been to-gether a few months when they separated – Virginia pregnant and living with her parents in Hope, Arkansas.

So, the question remains: who was Bill Clinton's real father? Over the years, there has been wild speculation about this topic, with some saying that Arkansas Governor Winthrop Rockefeller sired Clinton, while others have tagged it on John F. Kennedy. But since verifiable data is lacking, it would be presumptuous of us to "identify" Bill Clinton's true father, especially since these records are certainly not attainable (or not even in existence any longer).

However, it is important to weigh every possibility since Bill Clinton "is almost certainly America's first bastard to be elected president."[173] The most predominant thought on this subject is one echoed by Peggy Noonan in *Hell to Pay*: "Local hearsay held that Bill was the bastard son of a car salesman, not Virginia's hus-band, Bill Blythe of Texas."[174] Joyce Milton suggested the same possibility in *The First Partner*: "Gossips in Hot Springs whispered that Bill Clinton, born seven and a half months after Blythe's re-turn from overseas, was actually the son of a car salesman Vir-ginia had been dating in his absence."[175]

As you will see, this car salesman could either be Virginia's second husband, Roger Clinton; or, even more dramatically, a Hot Springs high roller who later became known as "Uncle Raymond" Clinton. Some writers have taken this scenario one step further, such as R. Emmett Tyrrell: "An alternate explanation that has cir-culated through Hot Springs for years is that Virginia had never even met Blythe and had a baby out of wedlock by some still un-known father."[176] One of London's most respected publications, the *Independent*, reduced this matter down to its least common denominator by calling Clinton *nullius filius* ("nobody's son").[177] Further, even Slick Willie himself had questions. "Doubts con-cerning Bill Clinton's paternity persisted, even in the mind of Bill Clinton. To one of his closest confidants in Arkansas he confessed that he had grown up 'wondering who my father really was.'"[178] Whatever the case, it seems extremely unlikely that William Blythe – a known wanderer, roustabout, adulterer and proven bigamist – was Bill Clinton's father. Further weight is added to this argument when we find that Bill Clinton "is the first president who has not made these [his medical] records public."[179] One has to ask: what could Bill Clinton's medical records hold that he doesn't want the public to see? Could it be a blood type that doesn't match that of his supposed paternal parent?

The ramifications become even more bizarre because, "On February 1, 1993, President Clinton fired his White House doctor, who claimed he was let go for refusing to give Clinton allergy shots without first seeing the president's medical records. The records remained closed to public scrutiny."[180]

Dr. Burton Lee, the physician in question, weighed in on his dismissal:

> **"I was not happy about how the serum came to us, delivered to the White House gate, no covering letter, no idea what was in the bottle or why it was mailed," said Dr. Lee, who called the president's Little Rock physician, Dr. Susan Santa Cruz, to request his full medical records. Dr. Santa Cruz said she'd have to get Hillary's permission to release the records. Two hours later, Dr. Lee was fired.[181]**

Clinton has also "turned down requests from the *New York Times* for an interview with his health correspondent Dr. Lawrence Altman,"[182] while there are also enigmatic references to something called the "Betsey Files." To unlock this mystery, one must delve deep into the Clinton literature where they'll find that after longtime aide Betsey Wright was pushed by the wayside, "ten storage boxes containing the paper trail on various sensitive questions about the Clintons' past"[183] were turned over to Webster

Hubbell. Contained in these files "was material on Bill Clinton's medical history."[184]

The big question, of course, is: why won't Bill Clinton divulge the contents of his medical records? Could it all lead back to the identity of his *true* biological father? The solution to this problem would be quite readily determined if we could simply interview Mr. William Blythe. But as was stated earlier, he died in an auto accident three months prior to Bill Clinton's birth.

As you will see, even this incident isn't cut-and-dried, and is instead shrouded in controversy. For starters, as is par for the course, "Accounts of the accident given by Virginia and her son have varied through the years."[185] Thus, it seems the Clintons have patterned their stories according to what type of spin they want to put on the event.

One detail is fairly certain – Blythe was flying at a high rate of speed along Route 60 through Missouri. Here is how David Maraniss describes those last fateful minutes:

> **It seemed that everyone was out on the road that night, moving too slowly for Blythe's taste. He passed Elmer Greenlee, who was on his way home after closing his roller rink. He passed Roscoe Gist, who was driving home with his wife after a night at the movies. He passed both men so fast that they took note of the big, dark Buick as it went by.[186]**

Somewhat later, Blythe's automobile careened off the road. We can't be any more specific about the details because many of the accounts vary. In her autobiography, Virginia Clinton Kelly stated that the Buick was found "lying upside down in a cornfield."[187] On another occasion, she alluded to him drowning, because "it was after a big flood, and all the ditches on each side of the highway were overflowed."[188] Bill Clinton himself has reported, "He was

thrown out of the car and landed, unconscious, in a ditch filled
with water. He actually drowned."[189] David Maraniss wrote that
Blythe was found "near the service ditch of a farm road intersect-
ing the highway,"[190] while Meredith Oakley's version has him "cat-
apulting through the windshield some twenty-five feet into a
trench running alongside an alfalfa field."[191] Charles Allen and
Jonathan Portis wrote that Blythe was supposed to have "drowned
in only a few inches of water,"[192] whereas Christopher Andersen
has the man "pulling himself from the wreckage [and] collapsing
in a drainage ditch."[193] As you can tell, there is quite a bit of dis-
parity between these various accounts.

Here's where the story begins to resemble a *Twilight Zone*
episode. Although Blythe's car was discovered, "the doors to the
Buick were closed. The radio was still playing. The headlights
shone into a nearby field. The car was empty."[194]

Virginia Clinton Kelly partially confirmed Pulitzer Prize-winner David Maraniss' account by writing, "Elmer [Greenlee] and
his dad pulled over and Elmer got his flashlight. They went down
the bank to the car and saw that the driver's door was open – but
there was no sign of the driver."[195] If you've noticed, Kelly's story
is contradicting other versions, for she has stated that the car was
found in a cornfield, while others said it was a drainage ditch of
some sort. Which is it?

She continues, "They flashed the light on the ground immediately around the car, but there was still no driver to be found. By
this time, other people with other flashlights were beginning to arrive at the scene. The Greenlees organized the group into a large
circle around the car, and they all walked slowly, flashing farther
out into the field. No driver."[196]

Mrs. Clinton Kelley concludes, "It occurred to them that the
driver must be pinned underneath the car, so they all lent a hand
and started rocking it, and soon they had the car righted. It was
amazing, Elmer said – as though the driver had vanished. Elmer
was curious, so the next day he went down to the funeral home
and asked if they had ever found anybody out at the wreck the

night before. Yes, said the mortician ... it was the darnedest thing, he only had one small bruise on the back of his head, which certainly wasn't enough to kill him."[197]

Maraniss gave a similar rendition, "The only bruise on his body was a bump on the back of his head,"[198] while Oakley described it as such: "The only sign of trauma was a small scratch on his forehead."[199]

Now, let's pause for a moment and rationally analyze this situation. Blythe was motoring at an exceptionally high rate of speed (as if being chased). He careens off the road and his Buick ends up overturned. One would conclude, as did Meredith Oakley, that his head would more than likely crash through the windshield (due to forward momentum). Therefore, if we use other automobile accidents as a gauge, wouldn't Blythe's face be lacerated with numerous gashes – a bloody mess, to put it mildly – from the impact? Yet all other accounts have the *only* bruise being on the *back* of his head (as if he were struck with some sort of object). Plus, no actual body was found for an inordinately long period of time ... as if it had simply disappeared. How is that possible?

Could it be that William Blythe was the first in a long line of "Clinton Body Count" victims? Before dismissing this possibility, remember that there's a strong likelihood that Blythe wasn't even Clinton's actual father. So, to create a legend of the poor, victimized widow – while at the same time concealing the true identity of Clinton's father – Blythe was simply murdered (a blow to the back of the head) while an automobile accident (with no body) was staged alongside a remote Missouri highway. Then, sometime later, Blythe's body was given to a shyster mortician who did work for the Dixie Mafia.

As you'll discover later, this exact same scenario was duplicated numerous times in the future with Dr. Fahmy Malak in Little Rock filling the role of state medical examiner on-the-take. Another example of the physician-assisted cover-up of a murder occurred when a bullet hole was found in the back of Commerce Secretary Ron Brown's head after his plane crashed in Croatia. In addition, when we consider the obvious murder of Vince Foster (with a moved body) and the deaths of two "boys on the tracks" near Mena, Arkansas, the probability that Blythe was murdered increases dramatically.

In the end, was William Blythe simply a fall guy – a phantom father who was conveniently taken out of the picture before he could speak (similar to Lee Harvey Oswald)? Verifiable proof will probably never be found, but it certainly fits the *modus operandi* of Bill Clinton and the Dixie Mafia.

Speaking of which, the next piece of the puzzle in understanding Bill Clinton is the town of Hot Springs, Arkansas and its notorious Dixie Mafia. To begin, although Clinton often refers to his birthplace of Hope, he was raised, by and large, in Hot Springs, described by columnist Joe Klein as "a notorious Bible Belt Gomorrah."[200] Michael Isikoff characterized Arkansas politics (which always gravitated toward Hot Springs) as a mingling of "bizarre characters, Southern folklore, [and] the strange mix of rumor, fact and tabloid fantasy."[201]

As political author Roger Morris writes, this was "Meyer Lansky's and Carlos Marcello's town, the Springs generated so much illegal gambling income that the take rivaled some Las Vegas casinos even into the 1960s, and the Clintons were no mere innocent bystanders but an integral part of this remarkable scene."[202]

In case you haven't figured it out, Hot Springs was a mob town, "a fount of vice and official venality, gambling and prostitution, protection rackets and other graft that constituted a backroom criminal economy."[203] "Al Capone and his archenemy Bugs Moran"[204] holed-up there. [Capone died in 1947.] Later on, "a Justice Department investigation in the early 1960s concluded that the picture-postcard Hot Springs had the largest illegal gambling operation in the United States."[205]

Researcher Pat Matrisciana describes its smarminess. "Hot Springs is a place apart. It's like the corner of every barnyard where all the manure is piled. You know where it is, and if you get in it, it's by choice. It was a town where many people operated beyond the law. There was open gambling, open prostitution, horse racing, and quite a few saloons and clip joints."[206]

Why do you think Bill Clinton spent so much energy talking about Hope and avoiding Hot Springs? It's because this is where his criminal roots and criminal character were formed. "Clinton came up in that atmosphere of smoke and mirrors, where the fix was in. The rules that applied to other people didn't apply; he never played by the rules. The city was a con."[207] "Among the regular purchases were politicians themselves, legendary for bribery, graft, and vote fraud. Prostitutes and madams publicly paid the authorities a monthly pleasure tax."[208] Now are you beginning to see where Clinton learned his tricks of the trade? He fit right in with the criminal element.

"In the 1930s, Hot Springs represented the western border of organized crime in the U.S. With the local syndicate headed by Owney Madden, a New York killer who had taken over the mob's resort in Arkansas ... Madden got the assignment from his boss, Meyer Lansky."[209] Another overseer was Morris Kleinman, who insured that "the Hot Springs set up was so luxurious and safe that it became known as a place for gangsters on the lam to hole up until the heat blew over."[210]

Another prominent figure was its mayor. "For twenty years Hot Springs had been run single-handedly by its mayor, a dapper, ruthless political boss named Leo P. McLaughlin, who had rigged the town so that its prime industry was gambling. Gambling was flat-out illegal in Arkansas ... but every week McLaughlin's people paid off a number of state officials up to and including the governor."[211] Years later, drug trafficking in Mena, Arkansas would replace illegal gambling, with the same payoffs going through Governor Bill Clinton and his wife Hillary. Or, as Roger Morris writes, "Organized crime adapted and maintained its presence, making Arkansas a pivotal province of its drug empire as it had once made the old spa an open city for its vacationing warlords."[212]

But Hot Springs wasn't all vice and illegality; respectable criminals such as the powerful Stephens & Company family (with direct ties to the Rockefellers) set up shop there, along with the mighty Rose Law Firm (later to employ Hillary Rodham Clinton). Interestingly, Arkansas had always been a state of interest to the prominent Rockefeller clan (especially John D.). At one time it was "the sixth largest producer of crude oil in America,"[213] while Winthrop Rockefeller "was voted Arkansas man of the year in 1956, [and] his famous name allowed him to gain the office of governor in 1967. It was then that a young Arkansas Democrat, Rhodes Scholar, and DeMolay member [Freemason] named Bill Clinton may have gained the attention of Rockefeller."[214] The significance of these individuals in relationship to the crimes of Bill and Hillary Clinton will become very evident later in this book.

Bill Clinton's own mob-moll mother described Hot Springs in these glowing, romantic terms: "It [was] a place where gangsters were cool, rules were made to be bent, and money and power – however you got them – were the total measure of a man."[215] It sounds like she not only accepted this situation, but embraced it whole-heartedly. In fact, Virginia Clinton Kelly had "on-call intimate relationships with organized crime figures,"[216] as did her father. In her own words, Virginia described how her father and Roger Clinton (her second husband) operated a bootlegging operation. "Roger started a little business venture with my father ... as a service to the doctors and lawyers and other 'right people' who wanted a toddy and were willing to avoid driving all that distance. My father maintained a supply of selected beverages at the grocery store – under the apples ... Roger was the supplier and Daddy handled sales."[217]

Being that the above bootlegging racket took place in Arkansas – a dirt poor state – near the end of the Depression; and considering that Mrs. Clinton's father was perpetually broke, she wonders (a bit disingenuously), "I don't know how my father got the money to open the grocery store, but there was a rich man in town who used to lend him money when times were tough ... Daddy never had to sign a thing to borrow money because the man knew he was good for it."[218]

Does this sound like the way legitimate bankers operate, or the Mob? Well, the man who "supplied the Cassidy grocery store [Bill Clinton's grandfather] with bootleg whiskey"[219] was Roger Clinton – his stepfather – and the person who Roger took orders from was one of the most influential figures in the future president's life – Uncle Raymond Clinton (one of the potential candidates named as being his true biological father).

Raymond Clinton owned a Buick dealership that "became a gathering place for powerful, politically savvy men in Hot Springs."[220] But such a description doesn't do justice to this man's real line of work. "Raymond Clinton was widely known to make his fortune and gain his influence from much more than 'out-front' business or investments. He ran some slot machines that he had scattered throughout town, said former FBI agent and Garland County Sheriff Clay White. There was also convincing evidence of the prominent car dealer's links to organized crimes and to the still formidable Ku Klux Klan."[221]

Writer Sam Smith takes this scenario even further. "The uncle's Buick agency and other businesses and real estate were widely thought to be facades for illegal gambling, drug money laundering and other ventures. He was a minion of the organized crime overlord who controlled the American Middle South for decades, New Orleans boss Carlos Marcello."[222]

Roger Morris confirms this statement. "Uncle Raymond could not have run his backroom slot machines or numbers rackets without subservience and kickbacks to Carlos Marcello in New Orleans."[223]

So, we must see Uncle Raymond as a "political wheel-horse"[224]"whom his mother called a Big Wheel."[225] How "big" was this bagman for Carlos Marcello? Well, the CIA's notorious dare-devil pilot Barry Seal (who would go on to become the biggest drug trafficker in this country's history) "is now established to have been working for the same Marcello crime family that took its skim from Uncle Raymond's slots."[226]

We're not talking about nickel and dime hoodlums here. Uncle

Raymond – Bill Clinton's mentor – was a major league mobster. "He was definitely politically connected, a nephew would say. If you wanted to get something done, Uncle Raymond was in a position to do it."[227] So much that, "By the 1960s Raymond Clinton had powerful friends beyond Hot Springs as well. He was a generous patron of Arkansas' senior U.S. Senator, John McClellan ... while also an avid backer of then-staunch segregationist Governor George Wallace of Alabama, personally driving Wallace whenever he visited Arkansas."[228] To put it mildly, this guy was a player.

So, in Bill Clinton's own words: "When I launched an apparently impossible campaign for Congress, Raymond and Gabe Crawford co-signed a $10,000 note to get me started"[229] (i.e. Mob money). Mr. Crawford – who it should be noted "presided over a backroom bookie operation that was one of Hot Springs' most lucrative criminal enterprises"[230] – also "offered the candidate unlimited use of his private plane, and Uncle Raymond not only provided several houses around the district to serve as campaign headquarters, but will secure a $10,000 loan to Bill from First National Bank of Hot Springs."[231]

Is the picture beginning to become clearer? Bill Clinton wasn't a poor, unknown child from Hope that just happened to stumble into politics. He was an integral part of the Dixie Mafia. Here is how Ambrose Evans-Pritchard described this outfit: "Less famous than the Cosa Nostra, the Dixie Mafia was, and still is, far more dangerous."[232]

"Clinton's Uncle Raymond, a politically connected car dealer in Hot Springs, and Lee Williams, an aide to Senator Fulbright, used their influence to get Clinton a berth in the ROTC program at the University of Arkansas"[233] – a move that would allow Clinton to dodge the draft and avoid the Vietnam War.

R. Emmett Tyrrell elaborated: "Young Clinton's connections quickly extended beyond the orbit of Uncle Raymond's Buick dealership. During the Rhodes Scholarship interviews Clinton attracted the favor of two senior partners at the Rose Law Firm [also deeply entangled with the Dixie Mafia], Gaston Williamson and

William Nash, both of whom had been Rhodes Scholars themselves."[234] Clinton even bragged in his autobiography how he visited the Capitol building in Washington DC and "had lunch with
J. William Fulbright, chairman of the Foreign Relations Committee, and John McClellan, chairman of the Appropriations Committee."[235]

Yes, just your ordinary little hayseed orphan from backwater
Arkansas. At least that's what the Clintons want you to believe. In
reality, Clinton was a fledgling DeMolay (Freemason initiate) who
"in 1988, DeMolay International inducted into its Hall of Fame."[236]
He was also, during his teenage years, known as "Billy Vote Clinton"[237] because of his penchant for trying to become president of
every organization in school; and there were even murmurs of
vote fraud, as "several students believed the high school's political
system was rigged ... on behalf of favored students like Bill Clinton."[238] The mob's been notorious for such actions in the past;
why not utilize them for their favorite son?

Before dismissing this notion, frame the scenario in this context. In 1963, when Bill Clinton was dining with Congressmen
Fulbright and McClellan in the Senate dining room, he was also
placed in another privileged position. "On July 24, 1963, almost
four months to the day before his assassination, John F. Kennedy
shook his [Clinton's] hand in the White House Rose Garden."[239]

But that's not all. As David Moraniss writes in the prologue to
First in His Class, following his speech, "Kennedy shook hands
with a few Legion officials at his side and turned as though he
might head back to the Oval Office, but he did not. As the president walked toward them, the boys surged forward. Clinton was
the first to shake his hand ... the Boys Nation photographer was
nearby, snapping away. Kennedy suddenly retreated, smiling,
and headed back to the White House."[240]

Imagine, of all the teenagers in America, Bill Clinton was not
only selected to be there that day, but he was the *first* (and quite
possibly the only) student that President John Kennedy chose to
shake hands with. Plus, the photo of these two became world fa-

mous – a very integral part of what would later become the Clinton legend.

Finally, as stated earlier, there are those who have speculated that JFK could have been Bill Clinton's actual father. I won't take that leap of faith, but the coincidences and similarities between them are eerie:

- Both families were bootleggers (Joe Kennedy and Uncle Raymond/Roger Clinton)
- Both were extremely charismatic
- Both were serial adulterers
- Both families had integral organized crime connections
- Both men used illegal drugs
- both were what was known as "youthful presidents"
- Both were handsome
- both had disastrous public relations debacles (Bay of Pigs & Waco)
- Both were romantically involved with Mob molls (Judith Exner and Gennifer Flowers)
- Both were romantically involved with Hollywood celebrities (Marilyn Monroe and Barbara Streisand)

So, who was Bill Clinton's real father? Bill Clinton's father was the Mob – whether of the backroom bootlegging variety or the backroom illegal business deal variety – for Bill Clinton *is* the Mob. He was born into a Mob-oriented family, lived in a Mob-run town, and carried on the Mob's ways as governor, and later president. Bill Clinton is corruption, sleazy deals, kickbacks, drug trafficking, and murder. And, to make matters even more dire and dangerous, he married a woman – Hillary Rodham – whose Mob-like ways make him look like a choir boy at Sunday mass.

It took a while for Hillary to become the polished public figure she is now.

CHAPTER TWO

Sister Frigidaire: Future Mob Queen

By all appearances, Hillary Clinton grew up in a seemingly typical 1950s *Father Knows Best* household. Here is how the *American Conservative Union* describes their situation:

> **The Rodhams were conventional middle-class suburbanites who lived northwest of Chicago. They were comfortable, but neither rich nor socially prominent. Hillary's father, Hugh Rodham, started a small custom-drapery business after World War II, and eventually he was successful enough to afford a house in Park Ridge, a community composed largely of the more affluent blue-collar workers and the less affluent white-collar workers.**[241]

But does the story end there, or are there more similarities to the lives of Bill Clinton and Hillary Rodham than meet the eye? "Hugh Rodham was born in Scranton, Pa.,"[242] and it seems that he was able to afford many of the luxuries in life. "He drove a Cadillac … and maintained a summer home at Lake Winola in the Poconos."[243] In addition, according to Hillary herself, "My father paid cash for our two-story brick house on the corner lot of Elm and Wisner Streets"[244] – very rare for 1950s middle-class America.

How was Hugh Rodham able to attain such lofty successes, and have what – at the time – was quite a bit of disposable income? Roger Morris writes that after moving to Chicago, it wasn't done "merely by long hours at the sewing machine or hanging curtains in his one, or two-man drapery business, but by lucrative, much coveted contracts with hotels and especially airlines – the sort of contracts in the 1950s and 60s believed by law enforcement officials, reporters, and others to be controlled and dispensed by organized crime."[245]

Some researchers over the years who have suggested a link between Hugh Rodham and the Gambino or Gotti crime families, but at the present time such claims have not adequately been substantiated. In addition, "There is no evidence Hugh Rodham Sr. was Mob-connected either in Chicago or his hometown of Scranton, also infamous for syndicate rule. But as with so much else in the Clintons' history, the sheer coincidence is striking."[246]

So, we see a convergence between the upbringings of Bill and Hillary Clinton, "for much of its life, until the 1960s, it [Hot Springs] was a thriving center for illegal gambling – much like Scranton."[247]

We must ask, then: how connected to politics and organized crime was the Rodham family? One answer is found in *State of a Union* where author Jerry Oppenheimer writes, "The political Rodhams were backroom politicians, fixers, purveyors of patronage, operators"[248] and "the seed of the Rodham politico strain first blossomed with George Rodham."[249] Over time, Hillary's great-uncle George went on to become "the only *elected* politician in the family. And he was the only big-time politician the family had until Hillary came along."[250] Eventually, "Rodham caught the eye of Lackawanna County Republican ward leader and political boss Bernie Harding, and soon became his protégé."[251]

Veteran *Scranton Times* reporter Joseph X. Flannery assessed the situation in these terms. "If Bernie was George's mentor, you can believe George was a major power figure in Scranton."[252] Ultimately, "like Bernie Harding, George Rodham had become a political boss."[253]

What are we to deduce from this news? If Hot Springs, Las Vegas, Atlantic City, or the smoky backrooms of Chicago are any indicator, then anybody who becomes a political boss in a Mob-run town is almost certainly in on the fix. George Rodham certainly was. "While Rodham attended council meetings once or twice a week, he conducted most of his political business in secrecy, in the backyard of his modest North Scranton house, a location where no one could overhear what favors were being dealt and what deals were being made."[254]

There are also stories about Hillary's aunt Anna May Rodham who ran a less-than-reputable establishment called Rodham's Hotel, described as "a fleabag hotel and beer-gin joint ... in the heart of Scranton's infamous red-light district."[255] Oppenheimer tells us that while "there's no evidence on record that Hillary's great-aunt by marriage was a madam, it's probable that Rodham's Hotel offered a haven for ladies of the evening and their clientele."[256]

On top of that, in 1999 a Jewish newspaper called the *Forward* did some digging and discovered that "Hillary's grandmother's second husband, whom she married in 1933, was a Jewish businessman from Chicago by the name of Max Rosenberg."[257] For whatever reason, "for years Hillary had kept the Rosenbergs' existence a closely guarded secret."[258]

Although Hillary's lips were sealed on this matter, Max Rosenberg was somewhat of a Chicago player and insider. Soon, "with Rosenberg's counsel, Hugh Rodham [Hillary's father] decided to become the first Rodham to run for public office since George Rodham, the Scranton city councilman. As Rosenberg told Hugh over and over again, money is important but politics is power."[259]

Sensing that a fortune could be made off Detroit's "post-war car hungry America,"[260] Hillary's brother Tony recalled that "Dad was in the process of buying parking lots, and he was being shut out by some big parking lot companies at the time. He had some land he wanted to buy, and they wouldn't let him turn it into a parking lot, so he wanted to get elected as an alderman and change the zoning laws so he could have a parking lot."[261]

Realizing that he had to become acquainted with the 'right' kind of people, "Rodham would claim to friends years later that he had already forged a friendship with a powerful politician, a shrewd Irishman by the name of Richard J. Daley, who would become known as the last of the big-city bosses."[262]

According to Tony Rodham, "His father had learned about the 'I scratch your back you scratch my back' school of politics from his Uncle George in Scranton."[263] Curiously, Hillary has gone to great lengths to conceal this "kind of backroom wheeling and dealing that was the hallmark of politicians such as her great-uncle George Rodham, or Chicago's 'Boss' Daley, or even her own father, who hoped political office could help line his pockets with parking lot profits."[264]

Oppenheimer concludes his excellent study of Hillary's secret political past with the observance of a close family friend. "The reason why Hugh decided to get into politics in the first place, and the political alliances he forged in Chicago, embarrassed Hillary. She didn't want to be connected to any of it. She wasn't proud of why her father had thrown his hat into the ring. Probably more importantly, she felt it wouldn't help Bill or herself politically if the people of Arkansas and the country knew about it. It's part of Hillary's weirdness."[265] Ironically, in regard to corruption and self-enablement, Hillary outshined her father in spades (and that's putting it mildly).

So, instead of hearing the truth about Mrs. Clinton's sordid political past, what do we get? Tired old anecdotes about what a strict disciplinarian her father was, how her mother proclaimed that "there's no room in this house for cowards,"[266] or how "her spirit was unbreakable."[267] Then, naturally, we learn how Hillary was "the girl voted most likely to succeed by her senior class,"[268] and how she "won so many awards that it was embarrassing."[269]

Likewise, Hillary laments in her autobiography about her humble roots. "All the girls [at Wellesley] seemed not only richer but more worldly than I."[270] Amusingly, Hillary sang the same old song for the next thirty years, riding all the way into the White House on her class-warfare strategy. Christopher Andersen also has Hillary whining to her parents, "I'm not smart enough to be here"[271] shortly after arriving at college.

Nor is Hillary troubled by articles which refer to her as being homely or unbecoming, as long as they cover-up her deeper, darker family secrets. "She was totally unconcerned abut how she appeared to people,"[272] said one classmate, while her mother stated matter-of-factly, "When she was fifteen or sixteen and other kids were starting to use makeup and fix their hair, she wasn't interested."[273] Others described the teen in similar, less than glowing terms. "She had an average figure and thick legs; she wore purple glasses and unfashionable sack dresses. Hillary wasn't considered a great catch, a friend admits. Guys didn't think she was attractive."[274]

At that time, even intimacy wasn't Hillary's forte. "Like the makeup and clothes, sexuality was one of the rites of suburban passage for which she had neither the time nor enthusiasm."[275] Her iciness was so apparent "that she was compared by her classmates to a sexually frigid nun, and nicknamed Sister Frigidaire."[276] R. Emmett Tyrrell sums it all up in this very succinct passage, "She is not easy company. In fact, she is a very difficult human being."[277]

Are you beginning to understand the dichotomy we're faced with, and what is being played out before us? The Clintons don't mind in the least – in fact, they go to great lengths promoting – when authors and biographers spend their time on pablum such as Hillary's makeup or Bill's down-home stories from Arkansas. But ponder this point: Hillary's autobiography is 532 pages long, while her husband's is 957 pages. That's a total of 1,489 pages, but not once in those pages do we learn about their family history of being political fixers, their involvement in prostitution and illegal gambling, their relationship with corrupt political bosses on the take and Mob figures, or how each has a long association with organized crime.

Not a word in 1,489 pages! Nor does either utter a peep about how Hillary became a mob queen at the Rose Law Firm, as the governor's wife in Arkansas, as first lady, and potentially as president of the United States. Do you think that these exclusions were merely accidents or oversights, or do you think they were by design?

Shown here, a very young and still pimply-faced Bill Clinton.

CHAPTER THREE

Operation CHAOS: Campus Co-Eds

"THE SPEECH"

I t is my contention that during their college careers, Bill and Hillary Clinton were recruited into the CIA under a program called Operation Chaos where they performed surveillance, informed upon, and tried to contain the anti-Vietnam War protest movement. I believe their status as CIA operatives remains in effect to this day.

As outlined previously, we will continue to show that Bill Clinton was one of the "chosen ones" from an early age, and was thus placed on a path which eventually led to the White House. Hillary Rodham, on the other hand, wasn't so fortunate and had to actually *prove* herself before any doors were opened.

Her first big test – actually, the culmination of her entire life up until that point – rested upon something which has come to be known as "the speech." The time was May, 1969 and Hillary "was chosen to deliver a commencement address at Wellesley College"[278] to coincide with her graduation. But hers was no ordinary presentation, for "Wellesley had never had a student speaker."[279] In Hillary's own words, she "thought it [graduation] would be uneventful"[280] until an insider named "Eleanor 'Eldie' Acheson decided our class needed its own speaker at graduation."[281] But Acheson was not a typical student; she was "the granddaughter of President Truman's Secretary of State Dean Acheson."[282]

Hillary continues the lead-up to this momentous event. "Wellesley had never had a student speaker, and President Ruth Adams was opposed to opening that door now. She was uncomfortable with the student milieu of the 1960s. I had weekly meetings with her in my capacity as president of college government, and her usual question to me was a variant on Freud's: 'what do you girls want?' "[283]

Indeed, the ultimate question appears to be: why would a decades-old-tradition suddenly be broken by placing Hillary at the podium, especially since her "chief lieutenant at Wellesley College was Eleanor Acheson"[284] who functioned as a lightning rod to get the wheels turning? "The conservative *Boston Herald* wrote that Hillary and her Wellesley College allies resembled the Bolshevik women's auxiliary in their fur caps and high boots."[285]

Creating even more suspense were some of the dignitaries in attendance at this commencement, including "Paul Nitze, the diplomat, and Eldie's distinguished grandfather Dean Acheson ... [who] actually later asked Hillary for a copy of her speech."[286] "Other prominent people from business, the financial world and government were in attendance, drawing more press coverage than usual."[287] In addition, another invited speaker that day was "Senator Edward Brooke, the Republican senator from Massachusetts."[288]

So, the stage was set, and after Senator Brooke delivered what would be considered a typical commencement day speech, Hillary stepped to the podium and "began insulting the featured speaker ... the first black senator since Reconstruction."[289] Hillary's bombshells sent tremors through the Wellesley administration, for "they had checked the script beforehand, but Hillary quickly dispensed with it."[290]

"Hillary's rhetoric shocked many as being rude. 'She really trashed Senator Brooke,' recalls a Wellesley professor."[291] Brooke, singled out as a "Hollow Man – was stunned, hurt – and convinced that this was no extemporaneous speech. 'As far as I could tell, she was not responding to anything I was saying,' he later observed. 'She came that day with an agenda, pure and simple.'"[292]

What could this agenda be? Well, let's look at it this way. To become known in the political arena, you need a pivotal event to grab the public's attention, and then as a result create a 'legend" around that incident. Therefore, Hillary's potential handlers knew that she needed to do something radical which would merit notice and/or controversy. Plus, with a host of Washington insiders in attendance (including, I think it's safe to say, members of the Agency itself), this event was Hillary's testing ground. To become a part of the secret cabal, one has to prove that they're capable of handling the heat, especially when recruitment into the CIA is involved. That day, would Hillary step up to the plate and hit a home run, or would she whimper and straggle away like a dog with its tail between its legs?

"Hillary followed with an unrehearsed response, chewing out the United States senator, as one account described it, for being out of touch."[293] [For the record, no one, including Senator Brooke and school officials, believed that Hillary's comments were unrehearsed, but were instead part of a carefully orchestrated plan that was delivered meticulously for maximum impact.]

Another one of Hillary's backers at the time was Alan Schechter (who would later become a renowned globalist and Fulbright scholar) who organized a "last-minute campaign within the class"[294] to get Hillary in the limelight. "To audible gasps from the crowd she scolded Brooke for his fey performance. Schechter recalled that Ms. Rodham, "gave it to him, no ifs, ands, or buts about it."[295] Even Eleanor Acheson herself commented, "Some people, largely mothers, thought it was just rude."[296]

Then, to serve as her crescendo, Hillary uttered these words that could have been taken straight out of Aldous Huxley's *Brave New World*: "We are not interested in social construction, it's human construction [we are interested in]."[297]

At that moment, Hillary passed the test and the CIA knew they had their woman. Some in the crowd were noticeably disturbed by this speech, and "only minutes into the address she seemed clearly to be losing some of the audience."[298] In fact, "a sizable number of people in the audience – including short, sullen Hugh Rodham, a dyed-in-the-wool Republican who admitted that at that moment he wanted to 'lie on the ground and crawl away.'"[299]

But the remaining attendees were different; they gave Hillary a "thunderous seven-minute standing ovation"[300] (which, if you think about it, almost nears infinity in regard to standing ovations). Or, as Christopher Andersen reported, "Predictably, when it was over, Hillary's mesmerized classmates leaped up to their feet and cheered."[301]

Additionally, Hillary was profiled in an article entitled *The Class of '69* where "excerpts of her address were published by *Life* in a collection of student commencement speeches, accompanied by her first national photograph, showing a round-faced austere young woman with long straight hair, peering out through thick rimless glasses."[302]

The effect of this performance was so riveting that "Marge Wanderer, the mother of student Nancy Wanderer, told *Frontline*, 'I will never forget it because Nancy said to me at the end of graduation, take a good look at her. She will probably be president of the United States someday.'"[303]

To increase her visibility, "Hillary subsequently appeared on Irv Kupcinet's nationally televised talk show, [and] by the time she entered Yale Law School in 1969, Hillary was a celebrity in the radical counterculture, thanks to the boost from Big Media."[304]

Hillary was on the map, and there was no turning back now.

YALE: RADICALS VS THE ESTABLISHMENT

Despite what a number of partisan authors have written (those with a Democrat-Republican axe to grind), the first elementary notion we need to remember in regard to Bill and Hillary Clinton is that they are not – nor have they ever been – "radicals." Let us repeat, for this point is essential to understanding the Clintons: they have never been radicals, subversives, reactionaries, anti-government rebels, or revolutionaries. Instead, they both realized from an early age (due to their many establishment connections) that they needed to *embrace* the System rather than tear it down. Sure, Bill and Hillary *looked* like hippie left-wing activists (him with his long curly hair and bushy beard, she with her granny glasses and sandals); but these 'costumes' were nothing more than either a by-product of the times; or, more accurately, a CIA *affect* used to infiltrate certain fringe and outsider groups.

Regrettably, too many researchers have painted Bill and Hillary as commie radicals or extremists, but both have spent their entire lives cozying up to establishment politicians and business leaders, or those engaged in criminal enterprises (the two seemingly opposite sides of the coin oftentimes working hand-in-hand with each other). In simplest terms, the Clintons have not only embraced the System, they have become a part of it. Similar to how I described Bill Clinton's father as being the Mob, they have now come to epitomize a system which is corrupt, bloated, and rotten to its core.

This point can be proven through their actions, for "Hillary had started at Yale with a certain notoriety ... [and] having had her picture in *Life* magazine hadn't hurt her reputation any either. She had already met some of the big names in Washington."[305]

With this sentiment in mind: "By the end of her first year at Yale, Hillary was already known around campus as a major voice in the student antiwar movement."[306] The most glaring problem, though, was that her voice was not authentic (as we'll see later in this chapter). Film reviewer Michael Medved was certainly aware of the young student's popularity at the time, as he said quite fittingly to London's *Sunday Times* in 1992: "Hillary Rodham was a star. Everyone knew about her speech at Wellesley and talked in reverential tones about the extraordinary wisdom and eloquence that her address had displayed."[307]

Yes, Hillary's well-planned "performance art" speech was quite a coup, and at Yale she had other ideas in mind while play-

ing *faux* antiwar activist. Specifically, "At Yale, Hillary's rolodex
of lifetime political contacts grew fat."[308] Who are some of the individuals that she became intricately involved with? How about
"future Labor Secretary Robert Reich; future U.S. Trade Representative Mickey Kantor; future deputy Secretary of State Strobe Talbott; and future Justice Department nominee Lani Guinier."[309]
Also, as noted earlier, Hillary met Eldie Acheson (who later "became John Kerry's liaison with the gay community"[310]), Tara
O'Toole (nominated for Assistant Secretary of Energy), and
Roberta Achtenberg (Assistant Secretary for Fair Housing).

   Hillary also became acquainted with, and later worked for, a
mythic establishment family – the Edelmans. "Peter, a former
aide to Robert F. Kennedy, first contacted Hillary after reading
about her Wellesley commencement speech in *Life* magazine."[311]
His wife – civil rights lawyer Marian Wright Edelman – "used her
growing clout to establish the Washington Research Project."[312] As
these doors were opened, Hillary was "invited to speak to the
[League of Women Voters] the following spring [1970]."[313] Furthermore, "In the summer of 1970, Edelman assigned Hillary to
work with a Senate subcommittee chaired by Senator Walter
Mondale of Minnesota."[314] On top of that, she also added the
names of Burke Marshall ("considered an attorney general-in-
waiting for a future Democratic administration"[315]), and legal
scholar Professor Kenneth Keniston.

   Hillary also tells an interesting story about how she was involved in a 1968 *Rockefeller* campaign.

> **[Congressman Charles] Goodell asked me
> and a few other interns to go with him to the
> Republican Convention in Miami to work on
> behalf of Governor Rockefeller's last-ditch ef-
> fort to wrest his party's nomination away
> from Richard Nixon. I jumped at the chance
> and headed for Florida."[316]**

But wasn't Hillary, at least according to conventional wisdom, supposed to be a radical feminist Democrat during her college years? It seems she didn't completely lose her Goldwater girl roots, and instead put political expediency above and beyond any deeply entrenched political ideology. Also, as you'll see, it certainly isn't the only affiliation the Clintons have had with the mighty Rockefeller family, who *epitomize* the establishment.

Continuing this story, at the Fontainebleu Hotel in Miami Beach, Hillary and four other women "staffed the Rockefeller for President suite, taking phone calls and delivering messages to and from Rockefeller's political emissaries and delegates."[317]

Are you beginning to see a picture emerging? Hillary wasn't out for any high-minded cause, nor was she an honest to goodness subversive. As R. Emmett Tyrrell and Mark Davis write in *Madame Hillary*, "There are those who fight to overthrow the system; then there are those who walk through the system, undermining it, subverting it from within. Hillary's always been one to walk through."[318] Douglas Eakeley, a Rhodes Scholar and former roommate of Bill Clinton, expands upon this scenario even further. "By the time Bill Clinton arrived on campus one year behind Hillary, [he] was a relatively unknown quantity compared to Hillary Rodham upon entry to Yale Law School."[319] Indeed, "Hillary's secret was that she never appeared to be a radical – even when espousing radical causes. She worked *within* the system, sensing where power lay, and how to play to it."[320]

But the single most important contact that Hillary Rodham made during those years – and one who would ultimately become the Clinton's primary handler, fixer, and mentor – was longtime Bilderberg member Vernon Jordan.

Here is how Hillary describes their first meeting at a nationwide symposium on youth and community development which was being held at Colorado State University in Fort Collins:

I was sitting on a bench talking with Peter Edelman when our conversation was inter-

rupted by a tall, elegantly dressed man.

"Well, Peter, aren't you going to introduce me to this earnest young lady?" he asked. That was my first encounter with Vernon Jordan, then the Director of the Voter Education Project of the Southern Regional Council in Atlanta.[321]

Prior to moving on, do any of the above-named contacts (and those listed are but a few contained in Hillary and Bill's voluminous rolodexes) sound like anarchists, hard-core rebels, or violent reactionaries? Of course not; these figures were (or were to become) the System ... just like Hillary. So don't be fooled by the hyper-charged rhetoric; Hillary always had her eye on the prize, and she would use any means necessary to obtain it.

Speaking of which, one of the most controversial individuals that Hillary became entangled with was Saul Alinsky, a radical organizer and author of *Rules for Radicals*, described as "the left-wingers operating manual for revolution."[322] On the surface, some may object that I'm contradicting myself, for how could Hillary aspire to become part of the establishment while at the same time catering to radicals? But as I said earlier, don't be swayed by smoke and mirrors. Instead, ask yourself: with whom did Hillary eventually align herself – an establishment luminary like Vernon Jordan, or Saul Alinsky, who staged a "fart-in"[323] during a Chicago protest? And believe me, the opportunity was there if Hillary had so desired. "Alinsky offered her [Hillary] a job after she graduated, [but] she turned him down."[324]

Granted, "Hillary was involved in inviting Alinsky to speak at Wellesley,"[325] while her "undergraduate thesis was an admiring paper on radical organizer Saul Alinsky."[326] [By the way, "Hillary's thesis is under lock and key on the campus of Wellesley (because her husband's) administration unilaterally cut off public access to the senior theses of all presidents and first ladies in 1993."[327] How convenient, don't you think, and so typical of Hillary's Big

Brother tactics which we'll discuss later.]

Still, despite this youthful infatuation with Alinsky, Hillary never forged a long-term bond with him because of their fundamental differences in how power should be obtained. In regard to the System, "Alinsky had a rule for pure attack: pick the target, freeze it, personalize it, and polarize it."[328]

Alinsky also advocated the dictum: "Make the enemy live up to their own rule book. You can kill them with this, for they can no more live up to their own rules than the Christian Church can live up to Christianity."[329]

The System *is* corrupt, but has Hillary Clinton *ever* tried to significantly change it? No; she's instead become an intimate part of this very corruption. And rather than attacking the status quo, she's embraced it; a thought which would have mortified Alinsky.

In the same breath, Hillary (along with "Dick Morris, an Alinsky protégé and New York street organizer turned political consultant"[330]) did learn some valuable lessons from this man. The following is how Tyrrell and Davis describe Hillary's First Rule of Politics: "In the struggle for power, tactics take precedence over principles. As *Rules for Radicals* puts it, 'Ethical standards must be elastic to stretch with the times.'"[331]

Alinsky also advocated (with eerie relevance to Hillary's political career): "Power is the very essence, the dynamo of life ... It is a world not of angels, but of angles, where men speak of moral principles but act on power principles; a world where we are always moral and our enemies are always immoral; a world where reconciliation means that when one side gets the power and the other side gets reconciled to it, then we have reconciliation."[332] [Note: This reminds us of Hillary's "vast right-wing conspiracy" when reading these words and her feigned moral outrage when Bill got caught committing adultery against her yet again.]

Alinsky further declared, "Power is not static; it cannot be frozen and preserved like food; it must grow or die,"[333] which ultimately leads to what may constitute the very essence of Hillary Rodham's being:

> **Hillary's Third Rule: The continuous struggle to win brings meaning to one's life.** Again, the *locus classicus* is found in *Rules for Radicals*: "Knowing that the mountain has no top, that it is a perpetual quest from plateau to plateau, the question arises, 'why the struggle, the conflict, the heartbreak, the danger, the sacrifice? Why the constant climb?'"[334]

Is there any passage which could better describe not only the Sisyphean struggle that Hillary has undertaken over the past three-plus decades, but also her insatiable, cancer-like hunger for power which has laid not only countless careers (and lives) of others by the wayside like twisted wreckage, but also decimated her own life and that of her family? Imagine the various scandals and humiliations Hillary has endured over the decades, beginning right from the start in Arkansas (a state which she despised). Why did she do it, and why does she continue? An answer is forthcoming later in this book. But for now, please remember that even though Hillary didn't accept Saul Alinsky's against-the-grain philosophy, she did put much of it to political use during her career.

The final "radical" element in this section that must be addressed was Hillary's association with the Black Panthers, and especially a man named Robert Treuhaft, who "dedicated his entire legal career to advancing the agenda of the Soviet Communist Party and the KGB."[335] But prior to delving into this subject, it should be noted that by the time Hillary "spent the summer of 1971 as an intern in Treuhaft's law office in Berkeley,"[336] she had already been recruited into the CIA. Thus, did she travel to northern California because she so dutifully believed in the Panther/ Communist cause, or was it to perform surveillance on these individuals? The answer will become apparent later in this chapter.

Ask yourself: would Hillary Rodham stake her entire political future on entities as tainted, taboo, and marginalized as the Black Panthers and someone labeled by the House Un-American Affairs Committee as "among the thirty-nine most dangerously subversive lawyers in the country,"[337] especially when the 60s were already kaput? [John Lennon officially put the R.I.P. stamp on the 1960s when he sang 'The dream is over' in 1970.] Flower power was dead and gone. Why would Hillary throw her entire career away over a failed pipedream? Considering how strategic, practical, and cunning she is, the thought is inconceivable; and those who say otherwise are either severely myopic, or they're deliberately leading you down a dead-end road.

A more accurate description of events is that Hillary, after infiltrating and containing the anti-war movement at Yale for the CIA, was "repositioned" (so to speak) to do the same to one of the last fringe revolutionary groups still existing in America. Remember: the 1970 Kent State Massacre officially ended student mobilization in America. Now all that remained were splintered factions like the Panthers or Weather Underground.

Would Hillary stake her neck and future political aspirations on a group that was doomed to failure? Not a chance. She wanted to side with the victors! Granted, "By the winter of 1970, Hillary had been named associate editor of the *Review*. Most of that issue was devoted to the Black Panther trial."[338] In this publication, "rifle-toting pigs, representing the police, [are] thinking: Niggers, niggers, niggers."[339]

If Hillary's true motivation was to overthrow the System, the establishment would have washed their hands of her in a millisecond. Conversely, if she was put in place in an "official capacity" to observe and report back to her CIA handlers, then the matter takes on an entirely different complexion. On the other hand, both "Treuhaft and his wife, Jessica Mitford, were avowed communists, and Treuhaft for years served as the attorney for the Communist Party, USA."[340] Coincidentally, "Hillary's involvement with the firm [Treuhaft, Walker, and Burnstein] wasn't made public until *San Francisco Chronicle* columnist Herb Caen mentioned it in a column shortly after Clinton was elected president in 1992."[341] Consider: do these actions sound like they would originate from an avidly career-minded opportunist like Hillary Rodham, or simply a CIA cover job that had been revealed many years after the fact?

Tellingly, when Hillary and Jessica Mitford crossed paths again in 1980 while Bill Clinton was governor of Arkansas, the subject was seemingly a "liberal" *cause celebre* – the death penalty. But after corresponding with Hillary, then flying to Little Rock, "the visit ended on a sour note"[342] when Mitford described Bill Clinton as being "too preoccupied with his own ambitions to care about prison reform."[343] Yes, when push came to shove, the Clintons always sided with the establishment and placed their own advancement above and before any other supposed 'cause' or fringe affiliation.

So, by the early 1970s, Hillary Rodham had clearly set her path in life, and it most certainly was not allied in any way, shape, or form with faltering revolutionary groups like the Black Panthers or obscure communist lawyers in Berkeley. No, Hillary Rodham was then, and continues to be today, the dynamic force in her relationship with Bill Clinton; and if selling out the peace movement or Black Panthers for the CIA was part of the Faustian deal that had been made to get ahead (or being a Watergate snoop a year or two later), then Hillary was more than willing to sign her name on the dotted line. Tragically, although Hillary's star was most certainly on the rise during those turbulent times in the late 60s and early 70s, she also became enslaved (maybe more so than any other political figure in history) to the very Beast to which she had sold her soul.

GEORGETOWN-OXFORD CONNECTIONS

I f you're not yet convinced that the subjects of this book have been embraced by the globalist establishment (and vice versa), let's turn our attention to former president Bill Clinton, who is a "Rhodes Scholar, a CFR member, a Trilateral Commission member, a Bilderberg participant, and most of his appointees are at least one of the above."[344] On top of that, Clinton was inducted into the DeMolay Hall of Fame (i.e. Freemasonry), plus he attended three of the most renowned internationalist universities in the world: Georgetown, Oxford, and Yale. [As a side note, Yale University is also the home of Skull & Bones (the Bush family's notorious secret society), and it has long been a hotbed for CIA recruitment over the years. Yale history professor Gaddis Smith even went so far as to say, "Yale has influenced the Central Intelligence Agency more than any other university, giving the CIA the atmosphere of a class reunion."[345]] As we know, Bill and Hillary both attended Yale University; and other than George Bush Sr. [former CIA Director], it's hard to picture any other current day politician who is more of an insider than Bill Clinton.

In addition, while vast numbers of students on college campuses around the country were rebelling against "the System" during the 1960s, here is how Bill Clinton and his fellow establishment classmates at Georgetown were described at that time in relationship to the rebellion surrounding them.

> **Most of the campus was "absolutely unconscious" of the moment [said] Walter Bastian, a classmate. "Going into business was judged a good thing, serving in government was deemed useful" was how still another classmate and Clinton friend explained their mentality. "All of the institutions whose reputations were stained during that era were all seen at Georgetown as honorable places in which to spend one's life."[346]**

Yet becoming a part of this system was Bill and Hillary's highest aspiration. Real "radicals" don't you think? Even the courses they took thrust them into what was then – and still is today – the corrupted, mainstream government. "The curriculum in which Bill Clinton enrolled in the fall of 1964 was prescribed training for prospective diplomats or others in international relations."[347]

So, what do we have with Bill Clinton? Georgetown is an infamous Jesuit-run university; while his next stop was Oxford, home of the Rhodes scholarship made famous by Cecil Rhodes and his globalist-oriented Round Table. Yale, of course, is one of the CIA's primary recruitment centers. The CFR (Council on Foreign Relations) is an American offshoot or branch of England's Royal Institute of International Affairs (RIIA) which "was to guide public opinion toward acceptance of one-world government or globalism."[348]

Likewise, the Trilateral Commission was co-founded by notorious internationalists David Rockefeller and Zbigniew Brzezinski; and as you'll see, Bill Clinton even attended a Bilderberg meeting in 1991 – coincidentally, the year before he was "selected" to be president.

Further data will be provided on all of the above subjects later in this trilogy, but for now ask yourself: how troubled are you by this information? Circa 1991, Bill Clinton was a relatively unknown governor from the second poorest state in the union. But after years of being groomed in the finest globalist institutions known to man, he attended a highly-guarded Bilderberg meeting in Baden-Baden, Germany, and in 1992 – the next year – he became president of the United States. On top of that, he's supposedly just some little orphaned kid with a promiscuous mother from Hope, Arkansas. Are there just a few too many coincidences for all of these events to perfectly fall into place, or can you accept this situation as being normal? We all know the way the world works, and supposedly poor kids from Nowhere, Arkansas, with dead bigamist fathers don't grow up to be president.

So how did Bill Clinton?

Here's a clue: "the only one of his tutors mentioned in Clinton's acceptance speech at the Democratic Convention [July, 1992]"[349] was Carroll Quigley, legendary Georgetown professor and author of the seminal pro-political conspiracy book, *Tragedy and Hope*, which elaborates on the creation of "a world system of financial control in private hands able to dominate the political system of each country and the economy of the world as a whole."[350]

At this point we have to ask ourselves two more questions: is this the type of political system we want for the United States, and who is this mysterious man named Carroll Quigley? Entire books have been written about him, so I'm not going to spend a lot of time covering his career or philosophies. I will say, first of all, that Quigley was a penultimate insider and "in 1962 the Center for Strategic and International Studies was established on the Georgetown campus, where it maintained close ties with the School of Foreign Service. CSIS included a number of people on its staff who had high-level CIA connections. Quigley moved in these circles until his death in 1977."[351]

In a nutshell, Quigley's views on world politics were as such: "Democrats and Republicans, while maintaining a democratic illusion for popular consumption, were fundamentally subservient to powerful special interests. Political parties are 'simply organizations to be used,' and big business has been 'the dominant element in both parties since 1900' ... 'the argument that the two parties should represent opposed ideals and policies ... is a foolish idea. Instead, the two parties should be almost identical so that the American people can throw the rascals out at any election without leading to any profound or extensive shifts in policy.'"[352] Does this scenario sound reminiscent of the Bush-Clinton-Bush-Clinton cycle that we've been experiencing for the past quarter-century?

With this overview in mind, it should be known that Quigley – the insider elitist internationalist – had become known as a "mentor" to young Bill, and "it was Quigley who first encouraged

Clinton to do graduate work in England, and later he provided Clinton with one of several letters of recommendation required by the Rhodes scholarship review committee."[353]

Quigley's profound influence (or could it be called preferential treatment?) was so pronounced that "out of 230 students in his freshman course, Quigley had given two A's."[354] If you do the mathematics, that's less than a one-percent rate for A's in his class; and guess who received one of them – Bill Clinton, not particularly known as the most diligent student.

Again, I'd say that's not too shabby for a poor kid from swamp-water Arkansas who – presumably – was born on the wrong side of the tracks.

But world famous professor Carroll Quigley wasn't the only one rolling out the red carpet for Bill Clinton. He had also "been encouraged by Senator Fulbright to begin the process of seeking a Rhodes scholarship."[355] During the selection process for this coveted studentship, "among his Rhodes interviewers were senior partners of the famous Rose Law Firm in the Arkansas capital."[356] [Yes, the same Rose Law Firm for whom Hillary Clinton would later work while her husband was governor.] In the end, it seemed as if the outcome was already a foregone conclusion. "Clinton won his Rhodes Scholarship among thirty-two in the nation."[357]

The odds that Bill Clinton appeared to be overcoming seem infinitesimal … but strangely, the ball continued to keep bouncing his way, especially when during this process "he interned on Capitol Hill with Arkansas senator and chairman of the Senate Foreign Relations Committee J. William Fulbright."[358] [To understand what a high-roller Fulbright was, check out his credentials: "Rhodes Scholar, law instructor, president of the University of Arkansas at thirty-four, and prominent in Congress by forty."[359]]

At first glance, it almost seems as if everybody everywhere was trying to do everything humanly possible to get Bill Clinton ahead. Why? What did this *one* single kid from the anonymous outreaches of Arkansas have that *everybody* was trying to push to the top of the mountain to grab the golden ring? This trend was so pronounced that it truly extended to the top echelon of control, for "another power behind Clinton was Winthrop Rockefeller, two-time Republican governor of Arkansas, who reportedly functioned as a father figure."[360] [More on Mr. Rockefeller's influence a little later.]

The next person to enter Clinton's orbit was the brother of a famous man whose hand he had shaken only a few years earlier – John F. Kennedy.

"Eager to meet Robert Kennedy, having met Kennedy's martyred brother, Clinton as class president invited the senator and former attorney general to make a speech at Georgetown, and proudly escorted Kennedy around the university."[361] Teenage Bill Clinton didn't have just *one* brush of greatness with a Kennedy family member. No, he shared the limelight with both Bobby and JFK!

Truly amazing, don't you think, especially when this is how Bill Clinton described himself during those times when he was hobnobbing with senators, governors, and even the president's brother: "I was nobody from nowhere. My family had no money, no political influence, nothing."[362] Please recall what so many individuals stressed in the introduction to this book – the Clintons lie ... and lie and lie.

The only significant blight on this seemingly amazing run of fortune was Bill's stay at Oxford University in England. As John Austin notes in the introduction to his book, "In addition to all the other lies he has gotten away with for over twenty years, Bill Clinton has always claimed to be a Rhodes Scholar.

The truth is he never completed the course and, instead, went to Russia and made anti-American statements and speeches."[363] Others, such as Dr. Paul Fick, confirm this fact: "He received a scholarship at Oxford but did not complete the Rhodes scholarship program."[364]

"THE MEETING," LESBIANISM &
A PREARRANGED MARRIAGE

There is a specific reason why Bill Clinton didn't finish his course work at Oxford: he had, by that time, already been recruited into the CIA and had been reassigned to do other "tasks." But prior to delving into this crucial aspect of Bill (and Hillary's) lives, I'd first like to skip ahead to their years together at Yale University, and especially how they met in what many are convinced was the first step of a very carefully crafted, prearranged marriage designed to take this predestined couple all the way to Washington, D.C. and the White House.

To begin our story, we must recall that after Hillary delivered her infamous Wellesley speech and appeared in *Life* magazine and in other media, she was on her way to becoming a star.

> **A second year student, Hillary was already well established at Yale, a formidable presence, when Bill arrived in fall 1970. She had arrived on campus the year before, already a celebrity of sorts. Everyone knew about the speech she had given at her Wellesley commencement, in which she confronted Senator Edward Brooke, the graduation speaker, and that Hillary's remarks had received wide media attention. Hillary's star status was assured, at least in certain rarified circles. People at Yale knew who she was. In a class full of celebrities – and everyone at Yale Law School considered him or herself a celebrity to some degree – she stood out.**[365]

As you will see throughout the course of this book, it has *always* been Hillary who was the mover and shaker – not Bill.

Law school acquaintance Carolyn Ellis recalls, "The story of what she had done at Wellesley preceded her. We were awed by her courage. She arrived with many of us thinking of her as a leader already."[366]

David Brock takes it even further. "Among these politically committed Ivy Leaguers, Hillary was the authentic item, but Bill was a pretender from the Arkansas backwoods."[367] His less-than-positive opinion of Bill continued. "He was regarded by his classmates not as a future president but as a glad-handing hillbilly in floodwater pants. 'There were forty or fifty guys at Yale who seemed better presidential material than Bill Clinton,' according to classmate Richard Grande."[368]

So, let's cut to the chase and put this matter into perspective. For whatever reason, quite a number of people set their aim on a boy from Arkansas named Bill Clinton, and subsequently opened a plethora of doors which would lead to his meteoric success. The only problem was Bill wasn't what was considered a nose-to-the-grindstone kind of guy. Sure, he was ambitious and hungry; but also lazy. He liked to chase pretty girls; tool around in one of Uncle Raymond's fancy (and free) Buicks; tell down-home watermelon stories; and hang out with his chums in Little Rock. Nor was Clinton a serious student; and it's not hard to imagine him selecting an evening of Big Macs at McDonalds over a night at the library learning about the history of Afghanistan.

Still, Bill was the "chosen one," and to get him into an appropriate position to rise through the ranks, the powers-that-be needed a yin to his yang ... someone with an iron will and a brash ruthlessness that would even make even the Devil himself quake in his shoes.

Enter Hillary Rodham.

Where Bill was a slacker, Hillary was an attacker ... the perfect political couple. Now, the only remaining necessity was joining their two paths together. Enter Robert Reich, a fellow Clinton classmate at Oxford who also "had known Rodham since her undergrad days when she had traveled from Wellesley up to Dartmouth to attend a meeting Reich had organized of student leaders."[369] Again, the convenience factor of a Rhodes Scholar and globalist-in-training (Robert Reich, who was also born in the same hometown as Hillary's father, Scranton Pa.) – who would later become the Clintons' Secretary of Labor – serving as the conduit seems a little too pat and prearranged, as if some very powerful forces had set things in motion well before "the meeting" ever occurred.

Speaking of "the meeting," let's first examine Bill and Hillary's oft-told 'official' version where the couple are at opposite ends of the Yale library.

> **Looking up, she [Hillary] espied the usually boisterous Clinton staring at her while appearing to be in conversation with another student. He hastily looked away and she went back to her book. This routine was repeated several times until finally she got up and walked the considerable length of the library to where he sat.**
>
> **"Look, if you're going to keep staring at me and I'm going to keep staring back," she reportedly said, "I think we ought to know each other's name. I'm Hillary Rodham."**
>
> **"I was dumbstruck," Bill would later claim. "I couldn't think of my name."[370]**

Another similar version has Hillary declaring, "Look, you have been staring at me for weeks, and I've been staring back. So at least we ought to know each other's name."[371]

Cute, wouldn't you agree; but is it factual? Remember, the Clintons have lied about their family histories, their births, their relatives, and even the origin of their own name (i.e. Sir Edmund Hillary). As you'll see, these people are such pathological liars that they couldn't even tell the truth about how they met!

First of all, Hillary has readily admitted on numerous occasions to having horrible eyesight. Was she able to ascertain all of this detail from that distance when she probably couldn't see past the first set of shelves? Secondly, as Meredith Oakley surmises about Hillary's supposed "first move": "It was a typically bold move on her part, if not a typically honest one, because Hillary already knew his name."[372]

Third, Bill and Hillary had been staring at each other for *weeks*, yet according to David Maraniss, "They were introduced to each other in the cafeteria during the first week of law school by Bob Reich."[373] Also, instead of there being such instant fireworks that it caused Bill to forget his own name, Reich tells us a different story. "I said, 'Bill, this is Hillary; Hillary, this is Bill,' but obviously it didn't take."[374]

Early Clinton supporter Paul Fray relays a conversation he once had with Hillary.

> **I asked her one day, "Where were you when you met Bill?"**
>
> **She said, "I was standing there in the registration line."**
>
> **I said, "Well, how did the conversation start?"**
>
> **She said, "Oh, you know – he just sort of asked me where I was from and I told him I was from Illinois – and the next thing I know, his leg was rubbing up against mine!"**
>
> **Not the best tale for a fundraiser, perhaps – or for a convention, or for *Current Biography*. Still, it does have a definite ring of reality to it.**[375]

So now we have them meeting in: (a) the library, (b) a cafeteria, and (c) a registration line. If I'm not mistaken, their meeting is starting to resemble the multiple versions of how Bill Clinton's "biological father" was purportedly killed in an automobile accident. It's hard to keep all their stories straight.

There is another aspect of this tale which seems disingenuous at best, as Jerry Oppenheimer writes. "There are other reasons to take the established story with a grain of salt. Despite the repeated punch line – 'I couldn't remember my name!' – There was little about Hillary's physical appearance at the time that would render a young man speechless. By all reports, she cut a distinctly unprepossessing figure at Yale, with her Coke-bottle glasses, drab brown hair, and somewhat solid shape. She was rarely seen in anything but shapeless clothing, and eschewed makeup of any kind."[376]

A nationally known film reviewer who attended Yale at the time doesn't buy their cock n' bull story in the least: "[Michael] Medved for one is sure the cute-meet tale is bogus. 'I think the thing about him seeing her in the library is garbage,' he said. 'Not a chance. I'm sure if God has videotapes somewhere, and you could replay it, you'd see.' The leg-rubbing story sounded a lot realer, he thought."[377]

Let's be honest. Bill Clinton was a player; a self-perceived Arkansas stud who liked his women to be sizzlers and beauty queens. Does anyone really believe that Hillary Rodham would make him forget his name? Sometime later I'm going to show what Bill Clinton's real opinion of women is, but for now let's just say that he was the kind of guy who wanted a trophy by his side and a model on his arm. Is it plausible that the vintage 1970 Hillary Rodham would be his idea of a dream girl?

Before weighing in, consider the following accounts; but be forewarned, this information is of a delicate nature. I am presenting it not to be cruel, but to show how Bill Clinton and Hillary Rodham's eventual marriage wasn't one of physical attraction or intimacy, but a prearranged political union that was conceived, arranged, and consummated to further an agenda which far-extended beyond either of their personal lives.

To lay an initial foundation for this topic, we need to do a bit of psychoanalysis of Ms. Hillary Rodham. "According to friends ... Hillary saw herself as an ugly duckling. In particular, she hated her body. A small boned woman from the waist up, she was squat and lumpy from the waist down, with wide hips and thick calves and ankles."[378]

This negative self-perception was not enhanced by any of Hillary's fashion choices either. "As a young woman at Yale Law School and later in Arkansas, Hillary felt so hopelessly unattractive that she did not bother to shave her legs and underarms, and deliberately dressed badly so that she would not have to compete with more attractive women in a contest she could not possibly win."[379] As trooper L.D. Brown observed years later, "Hillary possessed a deep-seated insecurity unlike any other I have ever seen. She felt awkward and inadequate around the more poised and beautiful people she was forced to interact with ... she was especially jealous of attractive women."[380]

It gets worse. Here is how a former Clinton paramour, Dolly Kyle Browning, described a character based directly on Hillary Clinton (Mallory Cheatham) in her novel, *Purposes of the Heart*: "The dowdy-looking woman stepped up beside him [Bill Clinton's character] and Kelly realized that she was of their generation, not middle-aged as her first glance had indicated. Kelly wondered why Cameron would have such a person in the plane with him in public. She was wearing a misshapen brown dress that must have been intended to hide her lumpy body. The garment was long, but stopped too soon to hide her fat ankles and thick calves, which to Kelly's amazement were covered with black hair. Thick brown sandals did nothing to conceal her wide feet and the hair on her toes ... the eyes ... bulged out of focus behind coke-bottle thick lenses in dark, heavy frames, competing with the dark, thick eyebrow which crossed from one side of her forehead to the other ... she noticed that the woman emitted a definite odor of perspiration and greasy hair. Kelly's heart went out to the poor creature."[381]

Browning continued. "Hillary smelled. I had never smelled an odor like that. I was so shocked. I just didn't believe this could really be Hillary. I thought it was one big cosmic joke. This couldn't be the woman I'd heard Bill was serious about. I honestly thought this was an actress he had hired to play Hillary, and that suddenly he'd burst out laughing. After a few minutes, it dawned on me that this was no joke."[382]

Do you genuinely think that Bill Clinton – a man in his mid-twenties with unabashed political ambitions – would seriously want a woman like that by his side? Aren't political wives supposed to be a benefit to the candidate in question, not a hindrance? Plus, Mary Lee Fray, a long-time family friend, described their shock when first seeing Hillary. "My husband was looking for a beauty queen. That's what Bill had always dated."[383] Mary Lee then contacted her mother, saying, "Mother, she's very plain, to the point you could call her homely."[384]

Her husband Paul took an even harder line. "Paul was put out. He was also stunned – This was Bill's true love? The woman he had told Paul he had intended to marry? That hair, those glasses, that outfit. 'I thought, my God, Bill Clinton, you son of a bitch – you could have any damn woman on the face of the earth, and you brought one that looks like the south end of a mule going north.'"[385]

At the risk of beating this dead horse further (no pun intended), here are a few other various descriptions of Hillary in those days:

> • "The good-looking blond in the clingy white summer dress was not prepared for the sight of Hillary – matted hair, thick glasses, body odor (even in the oppressive Arkansas heat, Hillary abstained from wearing deodorant)."[386]

> • "She had a weight problem, and she wouldn't diet. She wore these big khaki skirts and striped blouses and that wasn't changing. She didn't have a body for a dress."[387]

> • "She had a bad complexion on her face."[388]

> • "She was not somebody who was considered date bait, because of her weight and her presentation she was

not a glamorous figure by any stretch of the imagination."[389]

Lastly, Hillary's dilemma grew even worse later in life. As Edward Klein writes:

> **After giving birth to Chelsea on February 27, 1980, Hillary's silhouette changed dramatically. Though she never released her medical records, a physician who had observed her at close quarters told the author of this book that he suspected Hillary had contracted an obstetrical infection which was serious enough to damage the lymphatic vessels, carrying excess fluid from her legs back into central circulation. He said that she was left with a condition called chronic lymphedema, an incurable (though not fatal) disorder that causes gross swelling in the legs and feet, which Hillary covered up with wide-legged pants."[390]**

Bill Clinton knew how important an "appealing package" was to any candidate, and after he first started campaigning in the 1970s, he actually had groupies. "You had these women, especially older married women, getting in their cars and following him from rally to rally, just to hear him. They were listening to the same speech over and over again."[391]

What the hell was he doing with Hillary, a woman whose physical appearance brought nothing but grief to him, especially from his family? To understand this point, one needs to realize that Bill Clinton wasn't just *any* kid to his mother. Arkansas journalist John Brummett illustrates this point nicely. "It really was extraordinary. The way she talked about him. Everybody loves their kids, but with her, it was like she'd given birth to the messiah."[392] [Again, quite a peculiar scenario, especially when the dead father, Bill Blythe, was a booze-hound, roustabout, bigamist and philanderer. Are we to believe that it was *his* seed that created this supposed messiah?]

Anyway, Virginia worshiped her son; but Hillary was another matter entirely. "Bill's mother, Virginia Kelly – a flashy woman who liked a good time – took an instant dislike to her son's plain-Jane girlfriend."[393] Mary Fray summarized the reaction in a few words, "Virginia loathed Hillary then."[394] The Clinton household nearly became a battleground, for "Virginia and sixteen-year-old Roger [Bill's stepbrother] were disapproving and distant to the point of rudeness."[395] Bill's mother, whose opinion he highly valued, even called her "scraggly"[396] at one point.

Jerry Oppenheimer elaborated further: "[Virginia's] antipathy toward Hillary went far deeper. Both Virginia and Roger, Bill's teenage brother, were visibly shocked when she came through the door. It seems odd to think that such relatively minor traits – wearing no makeup, letting your hair hang loose in no particular style, dressing sloppily – could provoke such a response in the early 70s, but the South was (and is) a different country from the urban North. As one woman put it later, succinctly, Hillary came down – and the entire state of Arkansas went uhhh."[397]

In all fairness, Hillary's opinion of Bill's family was equally as insipid. "The tension and contempt for the mother was there from the first time she set foot in that house. She didn't particularly care for Arkansas, and she sure as hell didn't care for her future mother-in-law and nasty little brother-in-law."[398]

If that's not enough, this tangled web gets even stickier, for in addition to Hillary's appearance, there were also the rumors (which still linger today) of her lesbianism. Before dismissing this notion, consider that Hillary's first college – Wellesley – was notorious as being a haven for lesbianism.

There was a strong tradition of lesbianism at Wellesley; though it had not always been

> **called by that name. In the late nineteenth and early twentieth centuries, Wellesley girls who had lesbian relationships called them "smashes," "mashes," "crushes," and "spoons."**
>
> **In those early days of the college, Wellesley women who loved other Wellesley women did not consider themselves strange, since the relationships they formed were the norm rather than the exception. So many of the college's female professors lived together in lesbian relationships that a union between two women came to be known as a "Wellesley marriage" or "Boston marriage."[399]**

There are also rumors floating around that Hillary is linked to a "lesbian group known as the Sisterhood,"[400] while one of Hillary's Wellesley classmates stated, "the notion of a woman being a lesbian was fascinating to Hillary. But she was much more interested in lesbianism as a political statement than a sexual practice. A lesbian was suddenly not the eccentric old maid of Victorian literature, but a dynamic young woman who had thrown off the shackles of male dominance. Hillary talked about it a lot, read lesbian literature, and embraced it as a revolutionary concept."[401]

There was another reason why such speculation arose. "In large part, the rumors were founded on Hillary's tough, aggressive manner, her military barracks vocabulary, and her defiant refusal to do anything about her unkempt appearance. To Arkansans, she *walked* like a lesbian, *talked* like a lesbian, and *looked* like a lesbian. Ergo, she *was* a lesbian."[402] But there was more to the picture than mere speculation. "She ran around with dykes everywhere she went. She would go on the road. Spend weeks. And she would be out with known lesbians. That's how she got the label that she was a lesbian; from all of the stuff she did."[403]

Yes, such behavior and lifestyle choices might be accepted at

Wellesley, but in the middle America of Bill Clinton's Arkansas, "traditional homemakers couldn't relate to Hillary, and rumors that she was a lesbian began to circulate almost immediately."[404] Here is yet another explanation for the prolific rumor mills. "Because she had stringy brown hair, dressed like a social worker, scorned makeup, wore Ben Franklin glasses, and laced her speech with four-letter words, gossips spread the word that she was a lesbian. Christopher Andersen quotes an Arkansas woman as saying, 'Some of the women she was close to were tough-as-nails types. They wore unflattering, boxy business suits, let their hair go gray, and swore like sailors.'"[405]

Obviously such derogatory talk did not help the up and coming candidate.

> **[Paul] Fray confronted Hillary and told her that the lesbian rumors were hurting Bill's chances with the conservative voters in Arkansas. "This rumor has to be faced," Fray said firmly. "It's nobody's god damn business," Hillary shot back. Fray stood his ground. He urged her to deny the rumors publicly, thereby putting them to rest. "F*** this s**t," Hillary replied.[406]**

Even more hilarious was Hillary's backlash at her detractors, especially the *men* of Arkansas: "Instead of taking this kind of talk seriously, the First Lady of Arkansas dismissed it with such remarks as, 'When I look at what's available in the man department, I'm surprised more women aren't gay.'"[407]

Finally, what follows is a story that extends right up to the time when Hillary was First Lady.

> **Most of the members of her Wellesley class attended a twenty-fifth reunion that was held in 1994 at the White House. One of these**

women was Nancy Wanderer. Nancy married in her junior year, but after decades of marriage, she began a sexual relationship with another woman. For a short time, she played musical beds with her husband and girlfriend under the same roof. But she finally divorced, went back to school and became a law professor, and moved into a full-time lesbian relationship with her lover.

At the class's 25th reunion dinner, Hillary made a point of sitting next to Nancy Wanderer. The two old friends chatted for an hour or so – not about their mutually tumultuous marriages, but about menopause and other middle-age health concerns.

At one point, Hillary leaned toward Nancy and asked if she could touch her closely cropped hair. After Nancy recovered from her surprise, she gave Hillary permission to go ahead. Hillary reached out and ran the palm of her hand over Nancy's butch cut.

"Maybe," said Hillary, "I'll get a haircut like this and really shock everyone."[408]

If allusions to lesbianism weren't enough, there's strong evidence to suggest that the Clintons had little, if any, sex life at all with each other. Author Edward Klein notes that, "From her days in Wellesley onward, Hillary was often mistaken as asexual."[409] Roger Morris concurs about Hillary's frigidity and how others perceived it during her college years. "She dated little in her first year, and some thought her lonely despite her outward, sometimes flaunted indifference to sex."[410] [Please remember Hillary's nickname during high school – Sister Frigidaire.]

Her husband Bill, of course, would never even remotely be described as being tepid about sex, for even after "falling in love" with Hillary, "he continued to see other women, even after they moved into an apartment just off campus."[411] Needless to say, this trend continued unabated for the next thirty-plus years.

But some may wonder: what about Bill and Hillary specifically? "Their romance (if it could be called that) was not based on mutual physical attraction. Bill frequently found sexual release elsewhere. And Hillary, who had never placed much store in sex, did not seem to mind."[412] As one investigator said quite aptly, "From day one they had an agreement. It was a swinging relationship."[413] As for their daughter Chelsea; simply another political prop. "Hillary told her closest friends that they had Chelsea just so they could be a cute couple. It was all just for show."[414]

What's even more peculiar is that, possibly, Hillary may have been a virgin before Bill deflowered her. "One man who saw her socially before Clinton insisted that she had been with no one often – or in an intimate relationship, as she was with Clinton from the beginning. 'She certainly wasn't his first, but he may well have been hers,' he said, and that's as significant as anything else in what followed."[415]

Hillary Rodham a virgin? If this is the case, in lieu of their staged "meeting" at Yale University, Gail Sheehy quips, "They have been looking at each other with mixed feelings of fascination and apprehension ever since."[416]

In the end, what are we to make of this "arrangement"? Was Bill and Hillary's an honest to goodness marriage based on love, respect, and mutual attraction; or was it merely a calculated business deal with the ultimate prize being the White House – not only for one of them, but for *both* of them?

Let's examine what we've covered this far. Bill Clinton cheated on Hillary for at least three decades; she certainly wasn't his "type" of girl physically; his family, friends, and even the entire home state of Arkansas hated her; Hillary was quite possibly a lesbian or bisexual; and evidence that they had an energetic love life is lacking (or nonexistent).

To begin our analysis, let's first ask: who had the political muscle and backing in this relationship? Answer: Bill Clinton, as can be seen from the array of high rollers and power-brokers who bent over backwards to push him forward. On the other hand, who exhibited the moxy, cunning, organizational skills, and brains to bring this plan to fruition? Answer: Hillary Rodham.

So, each needed the other, but when push came to shove, Hillary needed Bill more (at least initially) because he had the designs of power already imprinted upon him. Or, as Edward Klein so duly noted, "As a woman coming of age in 1971 – still the infancy of the feminist movement – Hillary knew she could not achieve power on her own. She needed Bill Clinton to take her to the mountaintop."[417]

Thus, when Bill and Hillary signed on as rogue operatives of the CIA, another deal was cut ... one that would give her a shot at the ultimate prize. Hillary had to sell her soul, but in return, here is what awaited her: "He's going to be president of the United States"[418] she told Bernard Nussbaum in the early 1970s when Clinton was still a nobody and had never even run for public office yet. When Nussbaum objected, Hillary railed, "You don't know what you're talking about! I know this guy. You don't. He is going to be president. You think it's silly. Well, someday you'll eat your words."[419]

Was Hillary's performance simply bravado/blind faith, or did she already know something that no one else did? Novelist Charles McCarry thinks it's possible that more was going on than met the eye. "His Hillary figure is a Marxist operative, assigned to the candidate back in college. ... Hillary was the dragon lady, the controller, the political dominatrix, the one with a master plan."[420]

If such a scenario wasn't the case, why would Hillary have made the decisions she made over the years? In her own right, she could have been a nationally known attorney, congresswoman, or even on the Supreme Court. But what did she do? Go to Arkansas! "My parents didn't even know where Arkansas was ... they thought I'd end up in Washington, D.C. doing some-

thing with my life,"[421] she said in 1976.   Hillary continued,
"*Arkansas?*   God, before I met Bill I wasn't even sure where it
was."[422]   Another one of her associates agreed.   "It made absolutely no sense for Hillary to go there. Arkansas felt to all of us,
except Bill, like the end of the earth!"[423]

Think about it. "By most measures, Arkansas ranked forty-
ninth among the fifty states, which is why the state's unofficial
motto is: Thank God for Mississippi."[424] When learning of her decision to relocate to Arkansas with Bill (and obviously take on a
public role subordinate to his), her friends and associates were
mortified. Robert Levin recounts an amusing story told by Sarah
Ehrman.

> **When we arrived in Fayetteville it was the
> day of the Texas-Arkansas football game and
> the entire town was full of screaming college
> kids yelling: "Sooie Sooie, pig, pig, pig!" [The
> University of Arkansas Razorbacks are also
> known as "The Hogs."] It was just an aston-
> ishing sight. I said to Hillary, "For God's
> sake, Hillary, are you crazy? You're not going
> to stay in this town. *Why* are you doing
> this?" "I love him," she said.[425]**

But was it simply *love*, especially when, as Roger Morris de-
clares, "Her real cause was Hillary."[426] Indeed, from an early age
Hillary had aspirations far beyond the suburbs of Chicago. "In
her high school yearbook, Hillary wrote as her life's goal, 'Marry
a senator and settle down in Georgetown.'"[427] [I think she did one
better than that!] Further corroboration comes from Hillary's first
mentor, the Reverend Donald Jones. "From an early age, she
dreamed of living in the White House."[428]

To achieve this end, "Hillary hitched her star to the charismatic
Bill Clinton. She followed him back to Arkansas because, as she
told several friends, she believed that he was going to be president

one day. According to Reverend Don Jones, Hillary and Bill started plotting his run for the White House as early as 1982 – almost ten years before he actually declared his candidacy."[429]

This goal was their real love. Hillary knew what she wanted, and even more importantly, she knew how to get it. "She was so ambitious ... already knew the value of networking, of starting a Rolodex even back then. She cultivated relationships with teachers and administrators even more than with students"[430] (just like Bill was also doing).

Their plan was already so forged in Hillary's mind (and undoubtedly those of the handlers who existed above her) that a very interesting insight can be derived from the following passage by former roommate Sara Ehrman in 1974. "Ehrman told friends that she had come home one August evening to find Hillary packing her bags. When Ehrman asked where she was going, Hillary said, 'I'm going to Arkansas to marry Bill Clinton.' Ehrman asked if Bill knew this. 'Not yet' came the reply!"[431]

Hillary must have been pretty certain, and by all accounts, Bill was too. "There was little doubt in his mind at eighteen that he *would* be elected to public office someday and that he would work toward the presidency. Several of his Georgetown colleagues say that Clinton made no secret of his presidential ambitions."[432] Another acquaintance put it even more clearly. "He was someone who was on the way to somewhere else and in a hurry to get there."[433] But Edward Klein sums it up best of all. "Since the age of seven, Bill's goal has been to become president of the United States."[434]

But Bill Clinton (and especially his handlers) knew he couldn't attain the White House on his own; he needed an animus or doppelganger that could serve as his flipside and fulfill those functions for which he wasn't properly equipped. In other words, both Bill and Hillary needed each other, which brings us back to "the meeting" and how Bill and Hillary – supposedly strangers – eyed one another from afar.

"The only trouble was; Hillary's story was blatantly untrue.

In fact, Bill first became aware of Hillary through her work as coeditor of a far-left journal called *The Yale Review of Law and Social Action*."[435] Also, "Bill had seen Hillary around the campus, and though she was hardly his physical type, he was interested in meeting her."[436]

So why did he want to meet her? It obviously wasn't for sex, and over the years, Bill's status as a sexual predator has caused them an inordinate number of problems, as can be derived from this scene a few years after their meeting at Yale. "In the summer of 1975, she [Hillary] visited friends back East, and explored her options outside Arkansas. She told her friends that she was considering leaving Bill because of his womanizing. 'I know he's ready to go after anything that walks by,' she confessed. *'I know what he's doing.'*"[437]

Even back in the mid-70s Hillary was fully aware of her husband's adultery (despite how she publicly lies about this matter). More important, though, is the fact that his betrayal of their wedding vows wasn't what actually bothered her. "Hillary did not really care what Bill did with other women, as long as it did not hurt the Clintons' career. The truth was; Hillary considered leaving Bill because she was worried that she had backed a loser."[438]

Do you get it? Hillary didn't care if Bill was a rapist adulterous chauvinist pig ... she just didn't want a loser candidate that couldn't win an election! It was one thing to fool around on the side; but if Bill couldn't get her to the mountaintop, that's another story. It was political ambition – not love – that fueled her drive, as can be seen from this very poignant letter Hillary wrote to Bill in 1974:

> **Dear Bill,**
> **I still do not know why you do the things you do to hurt me. You left me in tears and not knowing what our relationship was all about.**
> **I know all about the little girls around**

there. If that's what it is, you will outgrow this. They will not be with you when you need them. They are not the ones who can help you achieve your goals. If this is about your feelings for Marla, this too shall pass. Let me remind you, it always does.

What you're feeling now isn't real. Don't trust it. Listen to your head, not your heart.

Remember what we talked about. Remember the goals we've set for ourselves. You keep trying to stray away from the plan we've put together.[439]

What "plan" was Hillary talking about? Or, as Jerry Oppenheimer asks in regard to their relationship, "How much was organized plan? Could two people forge a true commitment from an intellectual blueprint?"[440] Yes, "this letter ... seemed to be talking about something utterly outside her experience. A plan that needed to be adhered to? Some sort of strange pact? Goals. Achievement. What did any of this have to do with love? Just what kind of relationship was this?"[441] Further, "She wasn't using feminine wiles, she was literally trying to argue him back into the relationship, point by point – as if she were the lawyer and he was the jury. And what a relationship! A studied plan; a course of action you could 'stray from.' Just what was this, anyway?"[442]

Place this scenario into the context of how Bill explained his relationship to a former lover. "She gets me started, kicks my butt, and makes me do the things I've got to do."[443] The *Manchurian Candidate-Stepford Wives* ramifications are eerie, with Hillary playing both roles – subservient controlled wife and manipulative handler. But in the end, she could never leave him. Why? Because "Hillary accepted Bill's womanizing as the price of political power."[444] How bizarre!

OPERATION CHAOS

I n a book entitled *CIA: Secrets of the Company*, an interesting passage appears in regard to one of the subjects of this book. "It will probably be some years before the real nature of the relationship between Bill Clinton and the CIA emerges."[445]

Luckily, not all that many years have had to pass thanks to some invaluable research compiled by a number of hard working journalists. In fact, it can now be said, without hesitation, that Bill Clinton and Hillary Rodham were recruited into the CIA during their early college years, and have had a direct relationship with the Agency ever since. For now, though, we are simply going to examine how the Clintons became involved with this clandestine organization, and also some of their early assignments.

To begin, although Bill Clinton has often trumpeted his status as an "outsider," he was the exact opposite from an early age. One of the first instances where he rubbed shoulders with the elite of his time was in the late 1960s. "After graduating from Georgetown, he [Clinton] was invited to a conference on Martha's Vineyard for young anti-Vietnam activists attended by Larry Rockefeller and fellow Rhodes Scholar Strobe Talbott."[446]

On the surface, such information seems to feed into the conventional wisdom that Clinton was a radical, left-wing activist. But again, pop mythology does not always constitute reality. "While a student at Georgetown, according to his housemate Tom Campbell, Clinton had not actively participated in anti-war efforts."[447] Being that Georgetown is a direct suburb of our nation's capital, many opportunities presented themselves for Clinton to be a protester, such as "New York City in April 1967, the march on the Pentagon the following autumn, and the Chicago 1968 demonstrations."[448]

But the young undergraduate remained surprisingly passive and uninvolved. "This was in part due to Clinton's job with Senator Fulbright, but it also reflected the Georgetown student's general disinterest in the war."[449]

But then all of a sudden, "John Gardner of the Urban Coalition (later the founder of Common Cause) organized a weekend retreat in Martha's Vineyard for about forty young leaders, to explore ways that [they] could continue the important work started in the campaigns. Among those attending the retreat were ... Larry Rockefeller, Strobe Talbott ... and Bill Clinton."[450]

Again, his status wasn't too shabby for a poor little boy from Arkansas. Also, please note the presence – yet again – of a Rockefeller in Clinton's midst, along with Strobridge "Strobe" Talbott, "the son of a wealthy Ohio investment banker and prominent Republican."[451] Talbott went on to become *Time* magazine's editor-at-large, deputy secretary of state under the Clintons, and is described as a "world federalist" aspiring to create "a political body that would make, interpret, and enforce international law."

As a result of this conference at a swanky locale made famous by the Kennedy family, "A group of predominantly upper-class young activists created the Vietnam Moratorium Committee. This group helped organized college students in scores of American cities and abroad to protest the war in October and November 1969."[452]

One must ask, though: why was Bill Clinton even invited to this event? According to Cliff Jackson, who knew Clinton at Oxford, "No one was more surprised than he that Clinton later became involved in organizing antiwar demonstrations in London because 'that is *not* the Bill Clinton I knew.' Clinton, he said, was perceived as a 'hypocrite, a fake, and a phony because he wouldn't stand up for his convictions,' and he 'caught all kinds of flak from what we perceived as the extremist element.'"[453] Ultimately, Jackson attributes Clinton's involvement in this 'cause' to other motives, as can be seen from this quote in Meredith Oakley's *On the Make*: "Jackson does not dispute that Clinton was ambitious, but he attributed it to a 'consuming, burning desire to obtain power. I don't think what he did with it was the objective.

I think it was the obtaining of it.'"[454]

Journalist Ambrose Evans-Pritchard extends this thought to even scarier lengths. "They [Bill and Hillary] have no conviction, no ideology, no guiding purpose. Driven by raw ambition, they will make any compromise necessary to advance their interests."[455]

On top of the Clinton phoniness, another problem presents itself. During the late 1960s and early 1970s, the U.S. government created a program called COINTELPRO. According to prolific author and researcher Robert Anton Wilson:

> **COINTELPRO – Counter-Intelligence Program – was an FBI project that involved infiltrating civil rights groups, peace groups, New Left groups and other dissident organizations, in a deliberate attempt to incite violence, destroy the reputation of those opposing the Establishment, and spread paranoia against dissidents.**[456]

Wilson added: "The Watergate investigations revealed that the FBI's 'Cointelpro' Operation did involve *agents provocateurs* and attempts to divide the Left by inciting crime and spreading paranoia."[457]

Naturally, one of the primary targets of such an infiltration program would be the antiwar movement, and Daniel Brandt tells us "that by 1969 a significant sector of the ruling class had decided to buy into the counterculture for purposes of manipulation and control."[458] Brandt continues:

> • **Student leaders James Kunen and Carl Oglesby both report that in the summer of 1968, the organization Business International, which had links to the CIA, sent high-level representatives to meet with SDS**

[Students for a Democratic Society]. These people wanted to help organize demonstrations for the upcoming conventions in Chicago and Miami. SDS refused the offer.

• Tom Hayden [SDS founder and former husband of Jane Fonda] ... was quoted as saying that while he was protesting against the Vietnam War, he was also cooperating with U.S. intelligence agencies.

• Feminist leader Gloria Steinem and Congressman Allard Lowenstein both had major CIA connections. Lowenstein was president of the National Student Association, which was funded by the CIA until exposed by *Ramparts* magazine in 1967.[459]

This information is confirmed in an article entitled *Clinton's Long CIA Connections*: "In 1967, *Ramparts* magazine exposed the fact that the National Student Association had been receiving CIA funds for many years. [Richard] Stearns was international vice president of the NSA."[460] Further, "Allard Lowenstein was a former NSA president ... Lowenstein admitted to [Roger Morris] in 1969 that he had been knowledgeable and complicit in the CIA compromise of the NSA."[461]

At this point, what have we learned thus far? First, there is verifiable evidence that both the FBI and CIA used agents to infiltrate the 1960s anti-war movement. Second, while apparently non-committal to the peace movement, Bill Clinton suddenly became very active after attending a meeting organized by a variety of 'establishment' type figures in 1969. Then, Clinton's actions mysteriously changed.

In a December 3, 1969 letter to University of Arkansas's ROTC director, Clinton recounted, "I went to Washington to work in the national headquarters of the [anti-war] Moratorium, then to England to organize the Americans here [in London] for demonstrations October 15 and November 16."[462]

Despite his initial passivity, "By the time he arrived at Oxford, Clinton had begun to take part in the anti-war movement – even helping to organize rallies and protests."[463]

It is important to keep in mind that Bill Clinton was careful not to get involved with anything *too* radical. "Clinton either avoided or escaped association with the violent Revolutionary Socialist Students organization, which spearheaded many tumultuous protests in the late 1960s. In 1969, however, he did attend meetings of Group 68, a band of Americans backed by the pro-Soviet British Peace Council, and once described by Tariq Ali ... as the 'soft wing' of the hard-line antiwar coalition."[464]

So, let's start honing in on the question at hand. "What was the extent of his [Bill Clinton's] involvement in the planning and execution of anti-American demonstrations in 1969; and how did he manage to finance an extended tour through Europe that took him to several Eastern Bloc countries and he Soviet Union during the 1969-70 Christmas holidays at Oxford University?"[465]

To answer this question, we first need to ask ourselves: what do we know about this situation?

ONE: Clinton would attend Oxford University at age 22 and would study for two years, from 1968 to 1970, as a Rhodes Scholar. [Senator] Fulbright, who had provided the job that helped Clinton afford his studies at Georgetown, had been a Rhodes Scholar himself. Clinton has expressed the feeling that if it were not for Fulbright he might never have won the scholarship."[466]

TWO: In 1968 Mr. Clinton was selected as a Rhodes candidate and was given a scholarship to attend Oxford University in Oxford, England.[467]

THREE: It appears from documents, various interviews, and his own words that he attended Oxford for one full year only and took no degree. There are no public records to support a claim that he registered or attended any classes during his second term. Instead, it appears that Mr. Clinton lived with various friends on or near the Oxford campus and spent his time involved in various anti-U.S. and anti-Vietnam War activities.[468]

FOUR: Investigation reveals that after the winter of 1969, Mr. Clinton embarked on a tour of Europe, and there are suggestions that school officials told Mr. Clinton he was no longer welcome on campus, but that could not be confirmed. Various friends and classmates of Mr. Clinton, however, have reported that he was uninterested in study and was a lackluster student.[469]

FIVE: Investigation has determined that when Mr. Clinton returned to Oxford after the first year, he 'crashed' with various friends and was described as a moocher who never paid for anything and never seemed to have any money to share or to contribute to the cost of his own subsistence.[470]

SIX: During Mr. Clinton's attendance at Oxford, and his subsequent trips around Europe and Asia, he had no apparent source of income aside from his scholarship, and it is unknown how this tour was funded.[471]

SEVEN: It appears that Mr. Clinton's sole purpose at Oxford in the fall of 1969 was to organize student protests against the United States for the Vietnam Moratorium Committee.[472]

EIGHT: Rhodes Scholars such as Mr. Clinton were favorite targets for recruitment [into the CIA]. This caused serious friction with Britain's MI5 because it violated a US-UK agreement that neither country would conduct covert operations or recruit on each other's home territory. 'Because of the sensitivity of the UK, these kids were treated in some ways like high-level agents,' recalled one officer.[473]

In short order, the apathetic student at Georgetown suddenly became not only *active*, but also a highly motivated leader. "Clinton [took] credit for having helped organize the demonstrations held outside the American Embassy in London's Grosvenor Square in mid-October and near London's Grosvenor Square over the course of a weekend in mid-November [1969]."[474]

How did this drastic turnabout develop? Roger Morris, author of *Partners in Power*, does a stellar job probing into this subject. "'Bill Clinton's ties to the intelligence community go back all the way to Oxford and come forward from there,' says a former government official who claims to have seen files long since destroyed."[475]

This blockbuster information is confirmed by political journalist/author Michael Collins Piper in a 2006 book entitled *The Judas Goats*: "Bill and Hillary Clinton and John Kerry, the 2004 Democratic party presidential nominee – clearly seem to have been prime examples of CIA infiltration of the anti-war movement during the tragic period of U.S. involvement in Vietnam and, in later years, key players in CIA intrigues here at home and abroad."[476]

With this information in mind, the next piece to the puzzle becomes: "how did Bill and Hillary become part of the CIA? The answer is found in a notorious infiltration program called Operation CHAOS.

From 1959 to at least 1974, the CIA used its domestic organizations to spy on thousands of U.S. citizens whose only crime was disagreeing with their government's policies.

This picked up speed when J. Edgar Hoover told President Johnson that nobody would be protesting his Vietnam War policies unless they were being directed to do so by some foreign power. Johnson ordered the CIA to investigate.

In response, the CIA vastly expanded its campus surveillance program and stepped up its liaisons with local police departments. It trained special intel units in major cities to carry out "black bag" jobs (break-ins, wiretaps, etc) against U.S. "radicals."

In 1968, the CIA's various domestic programs were consolidated and expanded under the name Operation CHAOS. When

Richard Nixon became president the following year, his administration drafted the Huston Plan, which called for even greater operations against "subversives," including wiretapping, break-ins, mail-opening, no-knock searches, and "selective assassinations."[477]

It goes without saying that it is strictly illegal for the CIA to operate domestically – to spy on its own citizens – *within* the United States, yet clearly that didn't stop Operation CHAOS. The Agency's excuse for this program was, of course, blamed on *foreign powers.* "The Central Intelligence Agency's infamous Operation CHAOS of the 1960s had been directed at uncovering some discrediting foreign hand in antiwar activities at home and abroad, to the point of recruiting American student informants and placing provocateurs among the demonstrators."[478]

One of these "agents" was none other than Bill Clinton, for there were "later allegations of CIA collusion by and around Bill Clinton at Oxford. One former agency official would claim that the future president was a full-fledged 'asset,' that he was regularly 'debriefed,' and thus that he informed on his American friends in the peace movement in Britain. Similarly, he was said to have informed on draft resisters in Sweden during his brief trip there with Father McSorley."[479]

Bill Clinton was not only a draft-dodger, but a *snitch* that ratted out other peace activists while being a clandestine spook for the CIA. Morris explains his betrayal. "One more CIA retiree would recall going through archives of Operation CHAOS at Langley headquarters – part of an agency purge amid the looming congressional investigations of the mid-1970s – and seeing Bill Clinton listed, along with others, as a former informant who had gone on to run for or be elected to political office of some import, in Clinton's case, attorney general of Arkansas. 'He was there on the records,' the former agent said, 'with a special designation.'

Still another CIA source contended that part of Clinton's arrangement as an informer had been further insurance against the draft. 'He knew he was safe, you see, even if he got a lottery number not high enough and even if the ROTC thing fell through for some reason,' the source said, 'because the Company could get him a deferment if it had to, and it was done all the time.'"[480]

Daniel Brandt provides even more documentation:

> **The CIA's domestic operations were first exposed by Seymour Hersh in _The New York Times_ on December 22, 1974. Within two weeks President Ford created the Rockefeller Commission to look into the matter, and their report was issued the following June. It detailed the CIA's mail intercept program for mail to and from the Soviet Union, described Operation CHAOS (the CIA's domestic spying program that was headed by Richard Ober) ...**
>
> **The Rockefeller report stated that "during six years (1967-1972), Operation CHAOS compiled some 13,000 different files, including files on 7,200 American citizens. The documents in these files and related materials included the names of more than 300,000 persons and organizations, which were entered into a computerized index."[481]**

Former prominent CIA Russian analyst Victor Marchetti lends even more credibility to these claims: "The time that Clinton was supposed to have gone to Moscow was the time when the CIA was very active recruiting American students and other students to go to Moscow ... Without revealing any secrets as to how I came to this conclusion, I would not be surprised to find out that Clinton was actually kind of working for the CIA."[482]

Mike Piper doesn't hedge his bets in the least. "*The Spotlight* (on August 16, 1993) was the first publication ever to outline evidence Bill Clinton had been a CIA asset since his days in the anti-war movement at Oxford."[483]

Roger Morris provides further information. "Several CIA sources would agree nearly a quarter century after the events that there indeed had been several informants among the Americans gathered at British universities at the end of the 1960s, young men who went on to prominence, if not the Oval Office. 'Let's just say that some high today in the U.S. government began their official careers as snitches against the antiwar movement.'"[484]

One individual who would have been very aware of Clinton's status as a CIA informant – and one who was also in a position to expose it, yet didn't – was former President George Bush Sr. But during their 1992 campaigns and debates, Bush didn't utter a peep. "In 1992, Bush ... and his re-election campaign actually had very little to say about Bill Clinton's effort to dodge the draft. In fact, in 1992 – and in the years that followed – some suggested that the very reason that former CIA Director George Bush (then running for reelection against his Democratic challenger Bill Clinton) did not actively take on Clinton and call him a 'draft dodger' was precisely because the former CIA Director knew that Clinton – as a college student – was almost certainly working as a CIA asset, infiltrating antiwar groups in Britain and elsewhere."[485] Stated differently, one CIA agent (Bush) would never implicate another CIA agent (Clinton). Further, Bush's own son – George W. – also pulled quite a number of strings to avoid his own military service; so I'm sure both sides felt that if one hand washed the other and if they let sleeping dogs lie, each would benefit. As you'll see later, the Bushes and Clintons have been working as teammates for decades.

In closing, if we reduce this scenario to its simplest terms, "Clinton evidently had found a way to avoid military service, but still get an 'in' with the power elite in this country: acting as a student sleuth for the CIA."[486] Such an appalling lack of conviction on Clinton's part lends more weight to an earlier claim that he was certainly anything but an extremist or subversive. "No attack by his reactionary opponents later would be more unde-served than the charge that young Bill Clinton was 'radical'."[487] Clinton wasn't a radical. He was a CIA rat.

BEHIND THE IRON CURTAIN

Regarding Bill Clinton, thus far we have learned that "the bearded, disheveled Rhodes scholar was recruited by the CIA while at Oxford – along with several other young Americans with political aspirations – to keep tabs on fel-low students involved in protest activities against the Vietnam War."[488] We've also ascertained that "the program, known as Op-eration CHAOS, would offer informants a wide range of induce-ments: a little cash on the side, taking care of draft problems, and promises of future help."[489]

Regrettably (but not surprisingly), "In the mid-1970s the CIA shredded its archives on Operation CHAOS. One of those in-volved in the purge of records ... had seen Bill Clinton listed as a former informant who went on to run for political office. 'He was there in the records, with a special designation.'"[490] To add further intrigue, due to the violation of an agreement between the U.S. and British intelligence agencies, "according to former White House FBI agent Gary Aldrich, Clinton is told by Oxford officials he is no longer welcome there."[491]

The rabbit hole spirals even deeper. In the previous section we learned that via an FBI program called COINTELPRO, many organizations such as the National Student Association had been on the payroll for years. The international vice president for the NSA was none other than Richard Stearns; who, it seems, has di-rect ties to Bill Clinton. In fact, "By running Clinton's Oxford classmates through NameBase, another curious CIA connection pops out: Richard Stearns, who may have handled Clinton's CIA recruitment. On September 9, 1969, Clinton wrote to Stearns agonizing over his draft situation."[492]

As we'll see in the next section, Bill Clinton went to excessively great lengths to avoid the draft, and at this time – the late 1960s – "Stearns had all the CIA connections anyone would have needed at that time, and the CIA was in the habit of securing exemptions for its assets."[493]

So, at least on Bill Clinton's part, we have the means, opportunity, and motive to sell-out his fellow students and activists to the CIA in return for favorable treatment in avoiding the draft. Stearns even "played a major role in placing Clinton in the McGovern campaign, thereby nurturing Clinton's political ambitions." In politics, it never hurts to have friends in high places. Furthermore, when we're dealing with a vast moral abyss such as that exhibited by Bill Clinton, "ambitious young men don't 'just say no' when the CIA comes calling. The CIA knows how to plant stories, spin the media, and set up scandals that can sink a candidate."[494]

But all the benefits to Bill Clinton didn't come without a price; he had to give something in return, and soon he was serving as a snitch, narc, turncoat, and infiltrator against his fellow classmates and legitimate activists who wanted to end the disastrous Vietnam War. Hence, the first question rolling off everyone's tongue should be: what specific function did Bill Clinton serve as a CIA asset?

Well, with avoidance of the draft still a top priority in his mind, "Within days of posting a guilt-purging letter to Holmes [his ROTC officer at the University of Arkansas], Clinton took off on a forty-day tour of Scandinavia, the Soviet Union, and Eastern Europe."[495] Without much fanfare at the time, "he was ready to undertake one of the full-length grand tours, to Russia and back – five weeks by train moving in a circle north, east, and then west, with extended stops in Oslo, Helsinki, Moscow, Prague, and Munich."[496]

Amazingly, Bill Clinton's luck seemed to still be on a hot streak, for how many college kids get lucky enough to take a month-long vacation to Europe? As always, Clinton appeared to have fortune smiling in his direction. But if we delve a little deeper into this situation, things aren't quite as straightforward as some pro-Clinton biographers want us to believe.

First of all, this epic quest occurred over Christmas break, 1969 – a time when Bill Clinton, who had been away from home at Oxford for many months – would have normally ventured back to Arkansas to spend time with his family. Remember, Bill Clinton was (and always has been) a mama's boy, and he would have done just about anything to have his mother fix him home-cooked meals, do his laundry, and generally dote on him – especially when he'd been 'roughing it' for so many months in the United Kingdom. But instead of being nestled at mama's bosom, Clinton zipped off to Europe and Russia – in the dead of winter – all alone. Does such a scenario sound plausible, especially when Clinton was treated like returning royalty in Hot Springs?

Next we have the matter of money. As stated earlier, Clinton's time in England was marked by a perpetual lack of funds. The *only* job he'd ever had was a summer stint in the mail room as an intern for Senator Fulbright; but beyond that, he lived the lackadaisical life of a student. But out of the blue, Clinton embarked on a forty-day trip across Europe and into the Iron Curtain. "It is unclear how he managed this feat when, according to former girlfriends, he was always broke."[497] "Mr. Clinton's financial standing during this time is also a matter of conjecture. It has been reported that his family was of modest means. Nevertheless, aside from his Rhodes scholarship and [volunteer] work on the McGovern campaign and other political activities, there is no record of student employment, loans, or grants."[498] Another writer notes, "Clinton did not have a job, was not earning money, and, by his own admission, was always low on funds."[499] The situation is so pathetic that, "there is no documentary evidence that Mr. Clinton ever secured a place of residence on his own behalf."[500]

So, how did Clinton finance what would have undoubtedly been a very expensive jaunt across a variety of different countries? After all, he simply didn't wander over to Paris for the weekend. His trek extended forty days across Europe and all the way into Russia – a country that at the time was America's staunchest enemy (i.e. the Cold War). Where did the money come from? "Detractors suggest that his expenses were paid by unidentified segments of the peace movement or, in the extreme, by the Soviet government."[501] To this day, no answers have been forthcoming except for one more Clinton tall tale. "He said he footed the bill out of his own pocket. That explanation created a contradiction that he himself caused by what he said so many times in the past – that he 'had no money when I was at Oxford.'"[502] It seems yet again Bill Clinton wants to have his cake and eat it too; just keep in mind that the CIA has always had deep pockets when such "black budget" projects are involved.

Nonetheless, Bill Clinton's anti-war protest phase began. But before embarking on his European 'vacation,' he organized two protests in the U.K. In his own words: "I went to Washington to work in the national headquarters of the moratorium, then to England to organize the Americans here for demonstrations October 15th and November 16th."[503]

Father Richard McSorley, one of Clinton's Jesuit professor-priests at Georgetown, confirms this information. "As I was waiting for the ceremony to begin, Bill Clinton of Georgetown, then studying as a Rhodes Scholar, came up and welcomed me. He was one of the protest organizers."[504]

It seems remarkable that only a year earlier, Clinton was an uninvolved student in D.C. that had *never* taken part in an anti-war protest. Then, coincidentally, he was summoned to a symposium at Martha's Vineyard with some highly influential individuals, and all of a sudden he's not only attending protests, he's *organizing* them as well. It smells a little fishy to me ... as if he were on a "mission" of some sort.

The peculiarities continued with his trip abroad, with one stop being Oslo, Norway where he became reacquainted with his Jesuit instructor, Father McSorley. Their meeting was supposedly a quirk of fate. "They met by coincidence,"[505] David Maraniss naively writes. "Clinton tagged along with McSorley because he was an insatiably curious fellow who liked companionship."[506]

But is that all there was to it? Soon, Clinton's true objectives became clear. "McSorley carried a calendar from the War Resisters League listing the important peace groups in each European community. He had annotated his copy with advice from the Quaker peace activists in London. Their first stop was an old Victorian mansion near the University of Oslo that housed the Institute for Peace Research, where they met several young Norwegians who were conscientious objectors."[507]

McSorley recounts how Clinton clearly initiated their joint sojourn. "When I got off the train in Oslo, Norway, I met Bill Clinton of Georgetown University. He asked if he could go with me visiting people."[508] Soon, Clinton was directly in the midst of individuals associated with the British Peace Council, World Peace Council, Committee on Nuclear Disarmament, and the International Committee for Disarmament and Peace.

McSorley further explains, "We met three conscientious objectors working there [at the Institute for Peace]. They objected to Norway's role in NATO ... The conscientious objectors were but three of several hundred Americans who sought asylum in Norway, Sweden, and other northern European countries to escape military service during the Vietnam War."[509]

Obviously, information on such individuals would be of great value to certain American intelligence agencies, especially when Clinton visited "several peace centers operated by so-called pacifist organizations that one Clinton critic has described as so far to the Left that even the mainline Communists had to apologize for some of their outrageous antics."[510]

So, although Clinton tried to fit in by playing the role of a long-haired anti-war activist, not everyone was convinced of his motives. "'Theirs was a temperate revolt against the establishment,' Alessandra Stanley wrote of her Oxford years. 'He was not some extraordinary rabid organizer,' said fellow Rhodes Scholar Christopher Key. 'It was not a Jane Fonda-going-to-Hanoi deal.'"[511] In

addition, "Several, in fact, saw Clinton and his circle as self-serving, opposed to the war on their own terms and never carrying
their principles far enough to jeopardize their futures in the system. 'They all hung out together, and they all played it very safe
at the moratoriums, having it both ways,' said Dell Martin, an antiwar leader at Oxford in 1968-70 who knew Clinton, Talbott, and
their colleagues. 'They were conservative, and frankly I had no
patience with them. I felt they were careerists – making a place
for themselves in a society that had caused this war to happen.'"[512]
Clinton persevered with his mission, stopping along the way in
Prague where he "stayed four days with his Oxford classmate,
Jan Kapold, and his family."[513] But this wasn't just any ordinary
household. "Jan's grandmother on his mother's side, Maria Smernova ... was a founder of the Communist Party in that country
after World War II. She was its first president, a position she still
held when Clinton visited Prague in 1970. Maria's husband, Jan
Smerva, was an intimate of Czechoslovakia's first president Premier Klement Gottwald, who took office after the first post-war
elections on May 26, 1946, which put the Kremlin-controlled
party in power."[514] Lastly, Marie Smernova's daughter, Jirina
Kopoldova, "is a registered STB agent [State Security Service] with
the code name 'Jirka'."[515] Do you think information on this family
would have been of great interest to the CIA – an agency that was
teeming with hard-core Cold Warriors? You better believe it, and
what better way to obtain this data than through the guise of a
traveling "anti-war peacenik" like Bill Clinton!

At any rate, the highlight of Clinton's tour behind the Iron Curtain was his stay in the Soviet Union. To set the stage, let me remind you one last time that during his Oxford years, Bill Clinton
was, by his own admission, broke all the time. Yet well into his
forty-day extended trip, he "boarded a Soviet Airlines Aeroflot jet-
liner ... for a flight to Moscow."[516] Upon landing – "New Year's
Eve found Clinton in Moscow"[517] – the young student stayed at
"the city's premier hotel, the National, where a room had been reserved. It can't be established who made the travel or accommo-

dation arrangements for Clinton."[518] His stay in a swanky hotel just off Red Square was even questioned in Clinton's home state. "The booking at the National for the usually impecunious student from Hot Springs would raise eyebrows when it became known even back in Arkansas. 'Arguably the best accommodations in town,' a Little Rock columnist wrote later of the expensive Soviet hotel."[519]

Let's pause again and assess this situation. Bill Clinton is a "starving student," he's broke, and he's known as a moocher. But then he flies into Russia and stays not at the equivalent of a Motel 6 or Comfort Inn, but the Soviet-version of the Crown Royal Plaza in Times Square. Right on Red Square! Does anyone find this arrangement so out of the ordinary that something more had to be going on?

What we need to now determine is: what was Bill Clinton's mission in Moscow? After checking into the National Hotel, "he encountered a delegation of Americans who were negotiating with various Vietnamese, French, and Russian officials for an exchange of American prisoners of war in North Vietnam."[520]

Now we're getting somewhere! New Year's 1970 – POW's in Vietnam were of huge interest to the American government, especially the CIA. If negotiations were taking place *anywhere* on the planet, you better believe the CIA wanted to know about it. Is the picture becoming clearer?

Enter our CIA student spy. According to David Maraniss, Clinton soon became acquainted with the American delegation of POW negotiators at the National Hotel on Red Square.

Late one night Clinton went into the hotel bar and encountered Charlie Daniels, a plumbing contractor from Norton, a small town in southwestern Virginia. Daniels was in Moscow seeking information on American servicemen missing in action in North Vietnam and Laos. He invited Clinton to have a

drink with him and one of his associates, Henry Fors, a chicken farmer and the father of a missing pilot. Daniels later wrote in his diary: "We were joined at our table by Bill Clinton, a young giant of a man sporting a full beard, who introduced himself as a Rhodes scholar whose home was in Hot Springs, Arkansas. Bill was majoring in political science at Oxford, and had decided to visit Russia to get firsthand knowledge of Communism. Bill's knowledge and ability to explain the inner workings of Communism kept Henry and [me] avid listeners until the bar closed at 2:00 am. Our 'one for the road' turned into a whole bevy. I'm sure glad we had only a few stairs to climb to reach our rooms and a spinning bed."

Before they fell asleep, Daniels and Fors spent a minute talking about Clinton. "We thought he might be a spy – this big fellow, friendly, constantly jabbering," Daniels says. "I'm just a dumb plumber. Henry's a chicken farmer. Bill could talk about anything. When we left him and were alone in our room, I said, "Henry, this guy, I don't know what to think of him, do you?"[521]

The duo had reason to be suspicious, for their POW mission was well-planned, high-level, and had even caught the attention of Ross Perot. They were also joined by attorney Carl McAfee.

McAfee was with Daniels and Henry Fors now in Moscow in the effort to track down some MIAs. They had planned the trip for a year, working through their contacts in Lions

International and gaining support from the State Department. They had met with H. Ross Perot in Dallas earlier in the fall, and now found it ironic that they were in Moscow with their visas and Perot was stuck in Copenhagen with no way in. Clinton attached himself to the Daniels entourage.[522]

Before proceeding, let's tickle our curiosities for a moment and query: why was the CIA so concerned with POWs in Vietnam? The answer finds us venturing even further into the rabbit hole, for due to the CIA's widespread involvement in drug trafficking and drug exporting from the Golden Triangle (Laos, Burma, Thailand and Vietnam), they were wary of what returning POWs would tell the American media, especially since many of them had firsthand knowledge of the Agency's nefarious practices. [One of the best books on this subject is Professor Alfred McCoy's *The Politics of Heroin: CIA Complicity in the Global Drug Trade*.] In addition, as many POW-MIA activists will tell you, their brethren have been horribly betrayed by influential forces within the U.S. government, and to have this closed case surface again would have horrible ramifications for how citizens view our nation's leaders. Thus, as was par for the course with so many other CIA-related scandals, they most certainly didn't want this can of worms reopened again.

With this brief overview in mind, let's return to Bill Clinton and the suspicions he raised in Moscow.

"You wonder why Bill gravitated to us? He's twenty-three and we're on top of the best story in the world," Daniels said later. "We're driving the Russians crazy, the North Vietnamese crazy. When he finds us, he stays with us ... For the next two days he was sure to appear whenever it was time to eat or

when he knew the group would gather to discuss the day's events. There were, said Daniels, "no big secrets, we let it all hang out. We knew our vehicles were bugged. We knew our rooms were bugged. So when someone wanted to say something private, we'd give a signal and go outside. Bill was part of the action. If I went out, most of the time when I came back, Bill would be there. If we went outside to eat, he went with us."[523]

Bill Clinton was another "bug" that they were referring to ... a mole, another ear and eye spying for the CIA on this highly-threatening CIA-POW contingent in Moscow. Whatever the other surveillance methods weren't able to obtain, student spy Bill Clinton did. That's one of the reasons why he was in Moscow over the holidays. He was an unabashed operative for the CIA that was obtaining information on the highly volatile POW situation. The other reason involved a much more sublime project.

During his Moscow trip, Clinton was involved in a much bigger operation than spying on his college buddies: the appropriation of former Soviet leader Nikita Khruschev's papers for the CIA. In fact, Clinton's Oxford friend, Strobe Talbott – later appointed to a State Department post by Clinton – is known to have played a role in the CIA's acquisition of the Khruschev papers.[524]

[Note: Years later, this information (provided by *American Free Press* columnist Michael Collins Piper) was confirmed, for Talbott was indeed the translator and editor of Khruschev's memoirs. Clinton's trip to Moscow was one crucial step in obtaining these documents.]

DRAFT-DODGER

O ne of the benefits that Bill Clinton derived from his recruitment into the CIA (albeit a rather insignificant one
if you look at the whole scheme of things) was his ability
to have some strings pulled so that he could avoid the
draft. Clinton was frantic about the possibility that he'd have to
fight in Vietnam, so he tapped into every resource available (including his CIA connections) to keep himself out of the South-
eastern Asian jungles.

Prior to giving an overview of how Bill Clinton – the chosen
one – received an inordinate amount of preferential treatment,
let's first lay out a brief timeline that reveals how he was able to
maneuver through the system.

ONE: When Bill Clinton graduated from Georgetown University in 1968, all graduate school deferments had been abolished.
His college deferment having expired, Mr. Clinton was declared
1-A ("Ready for duty").[525]

TWO: Bill Clinton was inducted into the armed services with
his pre-enlistment physical on July 28, 1969. He was given notice
that he was to report for duty on August 18, 1969.[526]

THREE: Clinton's views at this time reflected many of his
peers. "From my work I came to believe that the draft system itself is illegitimate ... No government really rooted in limited, par-
liamentary democracy should have the power to make its citizens
fight and kill and die in a war they may oppose, a war which even
possibly may be wrong."[527]

FOUR: Despite these views, Clinton continued to play the
system – for one very specific, self-serving reason. "I decided to
accept the draft in spite of my beliefs for one reason: to maintain
my political viability within the system."[528]

FIVE: On August 6, 1969, less than two weeks before Bill Clinton was to report for active duty, he managed to pull off another
escape from the draft. Bill Clinton went to the University of
Arkansas and met with Colonel Eugene J. Holmes, the com-

manding officer of the ROTC program.[529]

SIX: On August 7, 1969, Clinton signed the formal letter of intent to join the University of Arkansas ROTC.[530]

SEVEN: On September 9, 1969, little more than a month after signing up for ROTC, he [Clinton] wrote a letter to fellow Rhodes scholar Rick Stearns [see previous CIA section] that [Strobe] Talbott characterized as full of "articulate ambivalence ... confusion, self-doubt, even self-recrimination."[531]

EIGHT: September 12, 1969 – Clinton writes an unsent letter to the Hot Springs draft board where he confesses "he had 'no interest in the ROTC itself' and had only been trying 'to protect myself from physical harm.'"[532]

NINE: On September 20, scarcely a week after his unsent letter to the draft board, President Nixon announced that there would be no new draft calls for the remainder of 1969.[533]

TEN: The White House announces "a wholly new conscription system planned to begin December 1, 1969 – the draft lottery.[534]

ELEVEN: December 1, 1969 – Bill Clinton draws "number 311 in the selective service lottery – more than a hundred places away from the cutoff for current or even anticipated draft calls. The next morning he jubilantly sent off an application to Yale Law School.[535]

TWELVE: With his lottery luck, Bill Clinton no longer needed the protection that he got from the University of Arkansas ROTC program, even though the program had saved him from reporting to duty that was less than two weeks away.[536]

THIRTEEN: Clinton informed Colonel Holmes at the University of Arkansas ROTC program that he would not be going through with his promise to attend Arkansas and ROTC next fall.[537]

FOURTEEN: In this letter to Holmes, Clinton *thanked* Holmes for "saving me from the draft," then explained that he 'opposed and despised' the war in Vietnam.[538]

FIFTEEN: In response, "Holmes angrily canceled Clinton's

ROTC enrollment. He sent no reply to the young Arkansan in England at the time, though his remarks to the press decades later still reflected his reaction. 'Bill Clinton was able to manipulate things so he didn't have to go in,' the retired colonel told a reporter. 'Ethically, I think he should have stayed in ROTC. He'd given his word and was backing out.'"[539]

SIXTEEN: Holmes added, "I believe that Bill Clinton purposely deceived me, using the possibility of joining the ROTC as a ploy to work with the draft board to delay his induction and get a new draft classification."[540]

In a nutshell, here is what we have. In the summer of 1969, Bill Clinton was supposed to start serving in the U.S. military. At that same time, he attended a moratorium at Martha's Vineyard, where more than likely he was recruited into the CIA. Certain strings were immediately pulled, and soon Clinton avoided the draft – instead traveling across Europe and the Soviet Union as a spy for the CIA. The actual mechanics of the above outlined process were obviously more complicated, but two factors – as usual – persisted: Bill Clinton's overriding deceit, and his reliance upon a network of connections to help him beat the system. The most ironic aspect of this scenario is: when Bill Clinton "purposely defrauded the military ... both in concealing his antimilitary activity overseas and his counterfeit intentions for later military service,"[541] he probably didn't even have to lie! Most people don't know that even though Clinton was described as an "energetic draft dodger,"[542] he also had a legitimate medical condition that may have blocked his acceptance anyway. "Given Clinton's very serious allergy condition, it is almost inconceivable that he would have passed an army physical. The will to scheme overcame the instinct for self-preservation."[543]

Therefore, as we pointed out earlier, Clinton "lies when he does not have to lie, and often tells an extravagant lie when a modest fib would suffice."[544] We can thus view his deceit in two ways. First, "the things that make Bill Clinton's lying and maneuvering to dodge the draft particularly despicable are his determination not merely to avoid the hardships and dangers of military service, but also to dodge the draft in such a way that it would not hinder his overriding political ambitions for the future. Rather than be an honest, out in the open draft resister and face the consequences, he decided to lie and outmaneuver the draft – to use his own words – for one reason: to maintain my (future) political viability within the system."[545]

Secondly, in reference to his self-serving correspondence with Colonel Holmes, "the letter which Clinton wrote 'captures with shattering clarity a young man learning to rationalize acts of deception and compromise as necessary in the pursuit of doing good – which Clinton now regarded as inseparable from his political advancement.'"[546]

The worst part is: Clinton would have gotten away with this scam if it weren't for a cruel twist of fate. After penning his betrayal letter to Colonel Holmes, Clinton went to great lengths in subsequent years to have it destroyed, for "he realized it must never be allowed to fall into the hands of the opposition."[547] That would destroy all the carefully crafted lies that had been spun on various campaign trails and given to inquisitive reporters. But alas, "Clinton had no idea that there was another copy of the letter in the files of Lieutenant Colonel Clint Jones, an aide to Colonel Holmes."[548] So, for years, as can be seen from the following quote, the Clinton lie machine ran full steam ahead. "On September 2, 1992, Bill Clinton told the *Los Angeles Times* that 'it was just a fluke' that he had not been drafted. 'I certainly had no leverage to get special treatment from the draft board.'"[549] But then the Jones' letter was revealed and Clinton was busted in another lie. But for the time being, remember these words, for yet again Clinton used "a crafty combination of lying, evasion, and using others"[550] to further his political aims.

To avoid the draft, Clinton immediately fell back on a man who exerted a great deal of influence on his early career – his Mob-affiliated Uncle Raymond, who "had important connections to the military power structure in Hot Springs, including the Garland County Draft Board."[551] "'We started working as soon as Raymond got word that Billy was going to be drafted,' said Henry Britt, the car dealer's longtime friend and personal attorney. It was a concerted effort 'to get Bill what he wanted,' Britt would say later, adding, 'of course Billy knew about it.'"[552]

Why did Bill's uncle have such pull in that area? Quite simply it was because, "Raymond Clinton had longstanding ties to the Democratic Party and did business with the gamblers. But Raymond Clinton was known around town for his ability to ingratiate himself with powerful people of all sorts."[553]

As mentioned, another person Uncle Raymond brought into the mix was his pal Henry Britt, who remembers a meeting he had one summer afternoon. "Raymond paid a visit to his Central Avenue storefront office and said, 'Well, we've got to keep Bill out of the draft so he can take advantage of his schooling.'"[554]

A *Los Angeles Times* story says that other people were influenced as well. "Raymond Clinton also personally lobbied Will 'Bill' Armstrong, the head of Hot Springs' draft board number 26, and Lieutenant Commander Trice Ellis, Jr., commanding officer of the local Naval Reserve unit."[555] At this juncture, Uncle Raymond's manipulation became apparent. "Two weeks after Commander Ellis found a spot for Bill Clinton [in the Naval Reserve] he wondered why the young Clinton had not shown up for the pre-induction physical. The Commander called Raymond Clinton and asked, 'What happened to that boy?' Commander Ellis still recalls Raymond Clinton's response. 'Don't worry about it ... He won't be coming down. It's all been taken care of.'"[556]

Other wheels were also being greased. "[Henry] Britt called draft board chairman Armstrong, his close friend, and asked him to 'put Bill Clinton's draft notice in a drawer someplace and leave it for a while. Give the boy a chance.' This is apparently what Armstrong did for several months."[557] The result? Bill Clinton "was the only man of his prime draft age classified 1-A by that board in 1968 whose pre-induction physical examination was put off for 10 ½ months – more than twice as long as anyone else and more than five times longer than most area men of comparable eligibility."[558] And you better believe Bill Clinton knew what was taking place on his behalf. "Later letters that Clinton wrote to friends in which he seemed to have a measure of inside knowledge of his draft fate make it more probable that the nephew did know what his uncle and others were doing for him."[559]

Commenting on this subject, former Hot Springs draft board member Robert Corrado said, "Bill Clinton's treatment was unusual. The only explanation for the long delay would be some form of preferential treatment."[560] Henry Britt smugly added, "The draft board was handled successfully."[561]

But who could mount such pressures? "According to [George] Carpozi, Mr. Corrado claimed Senator Fulbright himself called the board and asked for their cooperation in keeping Clinton from being drafted."[562] There's more. "Other strings were being pulled for Bill Clinton. Raymond Corrado, member of the Hot Springs draft board, told the *LA Times* that an aide to Senator J. William Fulbright – the senator [for] whom Bill Clinton had previously worked – called to ask Mr. Corrado to 'give every consideration' to keep Mr. Clinton out of the draft. Mr. Corrado was annoyed 'something terrible' by what he regarded as a request for special treatment."[563]

Corrado wasn't the only one to have their arms twisted by Fulbright's people. "Colonel Clinton D. Jones told the *Washington Times* in a 1992 interview that he received calls from Senator Fulbright's office, from the governor's office, and from the state Selective Service office. Colonel Jones told those people who called in support of Clinton to have Bill come see him."[564]

Still, Clinton continued to bend the truth. "I did what my local draft board told me what the procedures were and I followed them."[565] He also denied any assistance from the esteemed Arkansas senator. In December 1991, Clinton declared, "I am positive I never asked anyone [on the staff of then-Arkansas Senator William Fulbright] for that help in avoiding the draft. No. Never."[566] Yet then, only nine months later in December 1992, campaign spokesman Dee Dee Myers revealed, "Governor Clinton talked to the Fulbright people about what his options were."[567] Lieutenant Eugene Holmes, the ROTC director that saved Clinton's hide, weighed in on this subject. "There began a concerted campaign of phone calls to him on Bill Clinton's behalf. Hot Springs draft board members themselves were telephoning to say that 'it was of interest to Senator Fulbright's office that Bill Clinton, a Rhodes Scholar, should be admitted to the ROTC program,' Holmes remembered, and 'that Senator Fulbright was putting pressure on them and that they needed my help.'"[568] [Please note that Bill Clinton considered enrolling at the University of Arkansas – and even gave his word – so that he could join Colonel Holmes' ROTC program, which was one option available to him at the time to avoid the draft. Yet once Clinton was in the clear, he stuck the knife in Holmes back without batting an eye.]

This special treatment extended all the way to Washington, DC! "Lee Williams, Fulbright's chief aide ... had several contacts there and worked the telephone from his Capitol Hill office trying to arrange Clinton's enrollment. His papers indicate that he contacted the director of the ROTC program, Colonel Eugene J. Homes, on July 16."[569]

Indeed, Bill Clinton and his handlers (governors, senators, military men, and political high rollers) would go to any length necessary to avoid having Bill inducted into the Army, and Clinton possessed an arrogance which conveyed a sense of entitlement – as if he were too *privileged* for military service.

Opal Ellis, the Hot Springs executive secretary and 20-year veteran of the selective service, recalled Clinton saying that "he was too well educated to go to Vietnam, [and that] he was going to fix my wagon and pull every string he could think of"[570] to avoid the draft.

Clinton certainly left no stone unturned, even resorting to assistance from his old globalist-Rhodes scholar buddy, Strobe Talbott, who "traveled to Arkansas in early August [1969] and stayed at the Clinton house in Hot Springs for several days."[571] But these two weren't merely chit-chatting during the visit. "[Fellow Oxford classmate] Cliff Jackson later claimed that Talbott was 'one of the chief architects of Bill Clinton's scheme to void his draft notice' and avoid reporting to the scheduled July 28 induction. Jackson said he had a 'crystal-clear recollection' of Talbott and Clinton visiting him at Republican Party headquarters in Little Rock and discussing their plan of action."[572]

But to insure that he remained free of the draft board and the Vietnam War, Bill Clinton's handlers brought in Arkansas' biggest head honcho-figurehead of the time, Governor Winthrop Rockefeller. To show Clinton's influence (even back then), during one vacation home from Oxford University, "he managed to get himself invited to Winrock, the Rockefeller estate."[573] Ask yourself: how many kids coming home from college get invited to the governor's mansion, especially when that man is a Rockefeller! These men didn't simply exchange pleasantries, though, for "Clinton, it turned out, had maneuvered mightily to avoid the Vietnam War. He had pulled influence with his local draft board – recruiting help from Arkansas Senator William Fulbright and even Governor Winthrop Rockefeller's office – to avoid being called."[574]

As Fulbright's entourage was throwing their weight around, "At least one inquiry came from the office of Governor Rockefeller, according to Holmes's top assistant, Lieutenant Clint Jones. Jones later recalled that both Fulbright's office and Rockefeller's office asked him essentially the same question – could we do something to help young Bill Clinton?"[575]

Finally, it was one of Governor Rockefeller's hand-picked henchmen who had the responsibility of getting Clinton his deferment. "[Cliff] Jackson asked his boss, Van Rush, who was then head of the Arkansas Republican Party, to arrange a meeting for Jackson and Clinton with Willard A. (Lefty) Hawkins, the head of the state Selective Service System, who had been appointed to that position by Governor Winthrop Rockefeller. It would take Hawkins's approval to kill the draft notice in exchange for alternative military service."[576]

But please don't forget: according to Bill Clinton, he didn't receive *any* special treatment from anybody in this matter! Wonder of wonders, he even had the GOP going to bat for him – and he was a Democrat! In the end, he never served a single day in the military. As we said before, not too shabby for a poor kid from the Arkansas boondocks.

HILLARY: CIA "CONTAINER"

While Bill Clinton was "organizing" protests for the CIA, infiltrating student organizations across Europe, and lurking behind the Iron Curtain; Hillary Rodham was also obtaining information for the Agency on a number of groups such as the Black Panthers and the Communists. In addition, due to her campus access to feminists and the anti-war crowd, she was in a perfect position to monitor their activities as well. To really understand how this arrangement worked, the CIA's main intent was not to *prevent* protest from elements which they deemed radical; only to *contain* them. This point is crucial to understand, for the CIA realized that they couldn't entirely stop dissent; but if they could keep it from boiling over and threatening the status quo, then they would be successful.

This containment process is where Hillary Rodham enters the picture. After the powers-that-be were satisfied with Hillary's commencement speech "performance" at Wellesley, they got to see her work firsthand at Yale as a leveling influence on the anti-war agitators. Remember, in the late 1960s and early 70s, student protests against the Vietnam War had become increasingly violent, and they posed a serious problem to the establishment. What the CIA and other similar organizations needed was an *insider* that could pose as a radical, yet keep the pressure cooker only simmering instead of boiling over or erupting.

Hillary Rodham fit the bill perfectly. Similar to her husband-to-be, Hillary was merely playing a role. On the surface she laid forth all the proper rhetoric (i.e. destroy the system, down with the war, Big Business sucks, etc), but in secret she served a different function as one of the CIA's inductees into Operation CHAOS.

What follows is an apt description of her role while at Yale University during some very violent times in the early 70s. "Throughout the melee, Hillary Rodham, a first-year law student, was in the forefront – as leader, compromiser, agitator, counselor. When interviewed, Professor Abraham Goldstein of the law school recalled standing in the back of an oversize lecture hall and watching, impressed as Hillary ran the school's largest protest meeting."[577]

Before proceeding, ponder the following scenario. Who would the CIA rather have at the helm of a potentially explosive student protest – a legitimate, honest-to-goodness radical that was intent on lighting fires and smashing windows; or one of their own who – in the guise of an agitator – actually was put in place to keep the entire affair under control? The answer is obvious, and that's precisely what Hillary did in New Haven.

Martin L. Gross writes, "The students overflowed into the aisles as Hillary, seated on the edge of the stage in blue jeans, skillfully directed the arguments. Soon she was named to negotiate with the administration."[578] How convenient, especially since she was negotiating with officials at Yale University – long a hotbed of CIA recruitment and home of Skull & Bones. Hillary, the compliant *agent provocateur*, was in a perfect position to appease the university while also containing the protesters.

"Hillary was in the forefront again, walking among the angry students, checking with the young marshals, trying to keep order …"[579]

Why was Hillary able to play this dual role? Once again, it all reverted back to her infamous speech at Wellesley, which was quite possibly the most crucial event in her life. "Hillary could only play the leadership role at Yale so early because she had already gained celebrity status. *Life* magazine had run a story about her angry Wellesley commencement speech and the young pundit was often the center of attention holding informal court in the lunch room."[580]

Since the CIA controlled many news rooms and mainstream publications under Operation Mockingbird, it was essential that a *legend* be created for Hillary where she was seen by her peers as a rebellious outsider. But in reality, her outburst against Senator Brooks was merely part of a wider play to augment her myth as a radical.

Here is another description of how Hillary quelled the irate anti-war mob at Yale. "Surrounded on the podium by upperclassmen, Hillary stared at each speaker intently as he or she spoke. Then, like a translator turning tortured legalese into compassionate English, she took their angry words, stripped them of jargon, disarmed them of rhetoric, and spoke them back to them, prefacing, 'What I think I hear you saying is ...'"[581]

Hillary wasn't there to overthrow the system; she *was* the system – a deceptive CIA infiltrator that calmed the fires and took any edge off of *reality* by turning it into a passive, controllable situation. This technique is how operatives work. It isn't something flashy and over-the-top like James Bond movies; they simply shimmy beneath the radar wearing a mask and quietly doing their master's bidding.

Most surprising of all, Hillary has *always* been a tool of the establishment. As the old saying goes: once CIA, always CIA. This adage is true, for if we fast-forward past her college years, we still see Hillary serving the Agency and its war machine. "Even Hillary Clinton was a Cold Warrior of sorts. Described in Roger Morris's book as 'a closet Contra supporter,' she quietly aided Contra fundraising in Little Rock. She also used her influence in U.S. liberal circles to undercut the legitimacy of peace activists and pro-Sandinista church groups opposed to President Reagan's policies in Central America."[582] So, whenever you see Hillary parading around as an anti-war proponent; don't be fooled by her disguise.

WATERGATE

The defining political moment of the mid-1970s was un-doubtedly Watergate and Richard Nixon's removal from the office of presidency. The CIA had an immense amount of interest in this case, especially what was withheld on Nixon's infamous tapes. Because Nixon was well aware of the Agency's long history of criminal activities, including his knowledge of their role in the JFK assassination and CIA drug trafficking in Southeast Asia, the spooks at Langley were horrified of what might be revealed if these tapes became public.

Although many people aren't aware of it, Hillary Rodham played an integral part in deciphering and investigating what was on those tapes. Could she have been the CIA's eyes and ears – a "planted" insider who monitored what took place behind closed doors? As you'll see, it's a very real possibility, for Hillary "served on the staff of the House Watergate committee, a controversy in which the CIA played a major part. Some have suggested Hillary may have kept watch on the committee for the CIA, especially considering Hillary's activities in later years through the Rose Law Firm."[583]

Hillary's very inclusion on this committee raises questions because "she had been with the Children's Defense Fund less than six weeks when she was recruited by John Doar,"[584] hardly a qualifier for the most coveted, historic position in Washington at that time. Furthermore, "she was at the lowest rank among forty-four lawyers, who were joined by some sixty investigators, clerks, and secretaries. Most of the attorneys, both junior and senior, came from corporate practices in Doar's circle in New York and Washington."[585] As an individual on Doar's staff commented, "This was a very conservative, gold plate-law firm kind of group."[586]

Why then would a supposedly hippy radical attorney fresh out of law school with virtually no experience except with the Children's Defense Fund be selected to this highly coveted position? Yet "the House Judiciary Committee invited twenty-six-year-old

Hillary Rodham to join the select team of lawyers probing the Watergate scandal for possible causes of impeachment."[587] Such an appointment defies logic unless, of course, we examine some of the hidden machinations that seemed once again to fall into place for the Clintons. Or, as Joyce Milton writes, "From advocating children's rights to working on the first presidential impeachment of the twentieth century was a huge leap; but Hillary had the right connections."[588]

To begin our analysis, let's connect a few dots. "John Doar, who had been hired as special counsel on the House Judiciary Committee ... was a good friend of Burke Marshall at Yale."[589] So, right away we have another Yale connection to set the wheels in motion. Burke Marshall, it turns out, was an insider with the Martha's Vineyard crowd and "is best remembered as one of the first to receive a call from Ted Kennedy after the senator weaved off the Chappaquiddick Bridge and needed help explaining how and why he had left Mary Jo Kopechne to drown in his car."[590]

Hillary, by her own admission, already "had met Doar at Yale,"[591] but there were also even deeper ties. It appears that Doar had originally asked another CIA operative to join his committee *before* asking his then-girlfriend. According to Hillary's biography:

> **One day early in January [1974], while I was having coffee with Bill in his kitchen, the phone rang. It was Doar asking him to join the impeachment staff he was organizing. He told Bill that he had asked Burke Marshall, his old friend and colleague from the Kennedy Justice Department's Civil Right's Division, to recommend a few young lawyers to work on the inquiry. Bill's name was at the top of the list, along with three other Yale classmates: Michael Conway, Rufus Cormier, and Hillary Rodham. Bill**

told Doar he had decided to run for Congress, but he thought the others on the list might be available."[592]

Again, the Clinton insider network was in full swing, but the tangled web didn't end there. It seems "Doar had also worked with Burke Marshall and Peter Edelman under Attorney General Robert Kennedy."[593] Edelman was not only the husband of Marian Wright Edelman, with whom Hillary worked at the Children's Defense Fund in Washington, D.C. – but he was also the gentleman Hillary was sitting with when she first met her primary handler and fixer, Vernon Jordan. Within no time, "In January 1974, Hillary was chosen for a prized staff position at the House Judiciary Committee during the Nixon Watergate impeachment inquiry."[594]

Last but not least, one of Hillary's "close associates was Bernie Nussbaum, then a right-hand man to Doar, who was later rewarded by Hillary with his appointment to become White House counsel to President Clinton."[595] Nussbaum was later instrumental in covering-up the murder of Vince Foster, as well as ransacking his office of all incriminating files relating to Whitewater, their taxes, and beyond. Isn't it funny how these plum little assignments keep falling into the Clintons' lap? But if we're to believe Bill and Hillary, all of these events simply happen by chance.

Once she became a member of the Watergate investigative committee, Hillary wasn't simply window dressing or a wallflower. She stepped right to the forefront. "Hillary Rodham played a prominent role from the beginning. While other staff attorneys were scarcely ever seen by members of Congress, Hillary usually accompanied Nussbaum and Doar to meetings with committee members, and she was given a number of important responsibilities."[596]

Remember, Hillary was only twenty-six years old at the time with virtually no experience, which makes the next facet of this case even more incredible. While serving on this panel, Hillary was one of the few people alive on the face of the earth who got to hear the uncensored, hidden Nixon tapes, especially one called *the tape of tapes*. Does just *any* twenty-six year old punk kid straight out of college get put in such a position, or do strings beyond our wildest imagination have to be pulled?

According to Hillary, "'I was kind of locked in this soundproof room with big headphones on, listening to the tapes,' she told the *Arkansas Gazette*. 'There was one we called the tape of tapes. It was Nixon taping himself listening to the tapes, making up defenses to what he heard on the tapes.'"[597] Hillary realized the import of this situation. "It was surreal, unbelievable."[598] Also, please be cognizant that what is of utmost importance isn't what Hillary is telling us she listened to on the Nixon tapes, but what she *isn't telling us she heard*. That's what the CIA was interested in! Anyway, let us repeat so that the message is clear. "In her capacity as a researcher, she was one of a select few to hear the Nixon tapes,"[599] and "as a result, she had access to the confidential executive sessions of the full Judiciary Committee as one of the very few staffers who accompanied Doar to the confidential executive sessions."[600] Pretty heady stuff for someone still wet behind the ears!

Consequently, we have to ask: why was it so imperative that the CIA placed one of their own in that room to hear the Nixon tapes? Primarily, it revolved around information, and information sources. Considering that Watergate was the hottest ticket around, the chief counsel had to be extremely diligent in preventing leaks. Therefore, the CIA had to find other means to access this data.

Hillary tells us herself, "John Doar was allergic to publicity. He enforced a strict policy of total confidentiality, even anonymity. He warned us not to keep diaries, to place sensitive trash in designated bins, never to talk about work outside the building, never to draw attention to ourselves, and to avoid social activities of all kinds."[601]

Due to these restrictions, curiosity was killing the Agency, and they wanted to know precisely what that committee was uncovering, and what they intended to do with it. "Doar turned the staff's floor of the hotel into a grated, guarded, wired fortress, sealing off the mounting evidence of the inquiry ... 'We're so damned secretive,' complained one Missouri congressman on the Judiciary Committee, 'that we're going to impeach Nixon in secret and he'll never know it.'"[602]

To compensate for the news blackout and the restrictions on their other customary methods of information retrieval, the CIA needed a mole. The secrecy was so pervasive that "after Doar finished reading the report, he turned to Hillary and warned her never to discuss it with anyone, not even with Doar's boss, Peter Rodino, the chairman of the House Judiciary Committee. The report, he said, must remain top secret."[603]

What specific document was Doar referring to? Answer: "This was the report prepared under Hillary Rodham's supervision by C. Vann Woodward and a team of twelve scholars. Their report left little doubt that previous presidents, including John F. Kennedy, had engaged in immoral and unlawful abuses of power that were as bad as those perpetrated by Richard Nixon."[604] Anyone with even the slightest familiarity with the CIA's illegal activities from the 1950s to the 1970s knows that the Agency's disregard for the law was far more criminal than *any* perpetrated by our commanders-in-chief. Now can you see why they needed an insider to keep a lid on this information.

Hillary was no angel herself, for even a little taste of power at that time created what would later become a monstrous thirst for total information control – *at her sole discretion*. As Lord Acton wrote in a letter to Bishop Mandell Creighton in 1887, "Power tends to corrupt, and absolute power corrupts absolutely. Great men are almost always bad men." Hillary became the epitome of *bad*, and as you'll see later in this book, she became something far more criminal and corrupt than Richard Nixon could ever dream of being. Hopefully, the irony that she was investigating Nixon in 1974 is not lost on the reader.

Anyway, for the moment, let's examine Hillary's actions during the Watergate investigation.

> **Jerry Zeifman, who was chief counsel to the Judiciary Committee proper, had several run-ins with Hillary and felt that on numerous occasions she lied or withheld information about her work. He came to regard her, Doar and Nussbaum as "somewhat less than honorable lawyers." On May 4, 1974, Zeifman wrote in his diary: "I have been mulling over the events of the past week, and I am incensed with Doar and some of his top assistants such as Joe Woods and Hillary Rodham. It seems to me that [Nixon aides] Haldeman and Ehrlichman are crude amateurs at arrogance in comparison to the more polished and sophisticated arrogance and deceit of some of Doar's assistants."[605]**

William Dixon, also a member of the Watergate Judiciary Committee, went even further. "Hillary paid no attention to the way the Constitution works in this country, the way politics works, the way Congress works, the way legal safeguards are set up."[606]

These accusations are very explosive, but once you read section two of this book, perhaps you'll agree that they are well-founded and justified, for this lack of respect for our Constitution and laws is precisely the CIA's *modus operandi*. What, we may wonder though, were Hillary and her associates trying to conceal? One explanation returns again to the Kennedy family. "[Jerry] Zeifman concluded that Hillary Rodham, Doar and some other staffers were part of an effort led by Burke Marshall to hamstring the Judiciary Committee. The goal, he believed, was to protect Ted Kennedy's political future by making sure that information about his brother's misdeeds did not surface during the debate."[607] I don't think Mr. Zeifman took his analysis far enough, though, or quite possibly he suffered from partisan political myopia. The CIA didn't give a damn about Ted Kennedy's future presidential ambitions. Believe me; he was already tainted beyond repair after the Chappaquiddick debacle (which is another whole story in itself). The CIA *was* – on the other hand – extremely concerned with what Richard Nixon may have muttered about their role in the assassination of John Kennedy. That information was at the heart of their mission to infiltrate the Watergate committee.

Whatever the case, Hillary performed her duties well and the CIA emerged relatively unscathed (except for information brought forth by the Church Committee). One thing which can be gleaned from this affair (and others included in this chapter) is that Hillary Rodham went from supposedly being a far-left communist anti-war radical in 1969 to – only four and a half short years later – becoming part of the establishment itself! Then, only two more years later, Hillary was the first lady to the "Arkansas attorney general in 1976 and then governor in 1978."[608] Or, as Laura Ingraham so eloquently writes, "Gone was her talk of evil corporations and the need for economic and political realignment. Now Hillary was the establishment – the governor's wife."[609]

What a far cry her ascent was from seemingly being an enemy of the state. "For Hillary, landing a plum position on the Watergate Committee meant vaulting over her peers onto a very fast track through the ranks of the political establishment and winning a front-row seat at the defining event of her time."[610]

Yes, Hillary could have legitimately fought the system, but instead she became a part of it. Even more interestingly, "Hillary could have written her own ticket. She had already interviewed with Washington super-lawyer Edward Bennett Williams of the prestigious Williams & Connolly law firm and had received every indication that a position was hers for the asking. Many of her

Watergate colleagues went this route, including Richard Ben-Veniste, an associate prosecutor on the Jaworski staff, and James Hamilton, deputy counsel to the Senate Watergate Committee. Others, like William Weld, the future governor of Massachusetts, returned to their homes and pursued careers in elective politics."[611]

But what did Hillary do? She went to Arkansas.

Where? Arkansas? The 49th out of 50th lowest-ranked states in the union. A virtual third world banana republic at the time. Hillary was going to Arkansas? Why? So that she could marry the future president of the United States! From Arkansas? A guy no one had ever even heard of? From a town (Hope) that was barely even on the map and no one had ever heard of. A poor orphaned boy with a dead bigamist father? He was going to be president? And he was from Arkansas! Only a complete mental patient from the psychosis ward would believe such a fairy tale.

Yet Hillary even *bragged* that this unknown commodity from Arkansas was going to be president.

> **Hillary had already spoken to her colleagues about Bill's race for congress and his ultimate design on the presidency. Bernie Nussbaum tells a story ... about how he used to give her a ride home. She would talk about her boyfriend Bill and Bernie would say things like, "What's going to happen? What is he going to do?" And she said, "He's going to be president." And Bernie thought, "What kind of horse [manure] is this?"[612]**

Now ask yourself: do you think Hillary knew something at that point that the rest of us weren't aware of? Here she was – one of the premier shining stars of her generation – and she went to Arkansas? But by selling their souls to the CIA at a very early age, did Bill and Hillary Clinton receive certain promises that would take them all the way to the top ... all the way to the Oval Office? By going to Arkansas, "Hillary was in fact making a conscious change in her game plan – a calculated decision to cast her lot with the man she was convinced would someday occupy the White House."[613]

Official first-term (1979–1981) gubernatorial portrait of William Jefferson Clinton. Clinton became the 40th and 42nd governor of Arkansas. (Arkansas Secretary of State's Office via Getty Images)

CHAPTER FOUR

A Marriage Made in Hell

BATTERED AND BRUISED

To set her prearranged marriage in motion, Hillary Rodham traipsed off to Arkansas (i.e. Razorback country), and on October 11, 1975 she and Bill Clinton were married. It was a marriage made in hell.

There is simply no other conclusion when we remember that Bill and Hillary's marriage was arranged *before* they ever met by powerful forces that used them to fulfill a certain agenda – ultimately to attain the White House. Since their union was never primarily one of love – but instead political advancement – an undeniable amount of enmity (some would even say hatred) has developed between the two. Their *physical* battles are legendary, as are their betrayals, abuses, and inconsideration toward one another. As a result of feeling inescapably trapped in this marriage (due to overt blackmail in regard to their criminal actions), one half of this couple – Bill – rebels with reckless abandon, leaving chaos and wrecked lives in his wake; while Hillary has been forced to live a life of humiliation while continuing to clean up her husband's messes. Who would wish this life of misery on anyone? Sure, they have fame, wealth, and power; but the price they've paid via a prearranged political marriage has cost them something which no material value can be placed upon – freedom. Bill and Hillary are trapped; shackled to each other and enslaved by a *deal* they made in the early 1970s – a deal with the devil.

Even when the Clintons attained their ultimate goal – the White House – they lashed out at one another with such viciousness prior to Bill's inauguration speech that it's a wonder there

wasn't a murder at 1600 Pennsylvania Avenue that day. As you'll
see, theirs truly is a marriage created from the depths of evil
which has taken ... well, one helluva toll.

"G**d*** it ... you bastard ... it's your f***ing fault,"[614] Hillary
screamed to President Clinton after receiving some bad news regarding the Whitewater investigation.   "'You stupid f***ing
moron. How could you risk your presidency for this?' Hillary
glared after the Monica Lewinsky scandal became public in January 1998. 'Motherf**ker, c**k sucker,' are some of Hillary's
more choice words for her husband."[615]

In response, Bill has nicknamed Hillary "The Warden;"[616] while
"at other times, he referred to her as Hilla the Hun."[617] This observation came from Clinton's longtime mistress, who "allowed
herself to imagine that his marriage was an experiment that had-
n't quite worked out."[618] In her own words, Gennifer Flowers described how she perceived their relationship. "I usually tried to
discourage conversations about Hillary, especially during such
intense nights as the one in Fort Worth. Nevertheless, he often
felt the need to talk about her, and most of what he had to say was
derogatory."[619]

Another unflattering term for Hillary was "the Big Girl – as
members of her inner circle called Hillary Rodham Clinton."[620]

As we ease into this discussion of Bill and Hillary's epic battles,
we first need a frame of reference. Who was this Warden, or Hun,
as she was called? Well, Hillary was, at her core, filled with "deep-
seated insecurities about her looks ... though Hillary was the pro-
totype of a smart, successful woman who had it all, her physical
appearance had always been something of an Achilles heel."[621]
The result: "Despite her other youthful accomplishments, there
seems to have remained a kind of empty place or well of insecurity in Hillary. As a young girl she felt clumsy and unattractive."[622]
To make matters worse, she *knowingly* married a serial adulterer
who mocked the difference in their outlooks on life. One time
Bill very aptly quipped, "I was born at sixteen and I'll always feel
I'm sixteen. And Hillary was born at age 40."[623]

So Hillary had to perpetually fill the role of watchdog ... of the *adult* who had to bail her husband out of yet another scandal, reminiscent of a trapped adolescent rebelling against those who controlled him (i.e. Hillary herself, and those who arranged this marriage). As Dr. Paul Fick writes in his psychological analysis of the Clinton presidency, "He had a rollercoaster candidacy with many highs and potential campaign destroying lows; he was faced with repeated embarrassing disclosures abut his personal life; he responded to these disclosures with a glaring tendency to lie; he appeared indecisive and waffled on significant issues; and he was energized by the self-created chaos."[624]

This point is vital in understanding the Clinton marriage. Because he felt forever locked into a loveless political marriage, Bill Clinton's only escape – the only way he could feel *alive* – was through rebellion – to create so much *self-inflicted* turmoil that his overlords, so to speak, would be forced to come in and clean up his messes (sort of like a petulant child deliberately spilling their food). But in this case, Clinton was spilling his seed in as many women as he could physically handle.

The consequences created an unbelievable amount of strife in their relationship, which resulted in a plethora of knock-down, drag out fights. Even from the start, their time together was contentious. As David Maraniss writes [notice the first sentence]: "Pressure was building on the pair to marry or separate. Should Clinton marry Rodham? He told friends that he wanted to get married and that it was Hillary or nobody: but he also realized that while their partnership was intellectually invigorating and politically complementary, their personal relationship was stormy. 'All we ever do is argue,' he confided to Carolyn Yeldell Staley, his high school friend."[625]

Yes, "Both Bill and Hillary had volatile tempers, which they didn't hesitate to inflict on each other. To longtime observers, it was an essential dynamic of their relationship, and the fights were often followed by reconciliation that seemed loving and tranquil."[626]

But the fights were bad ... very bad.

• Soon after Bill and Hillary's residency in the White House began, a secret serviceman reported that during a somewhat high-strung family dispute, the first lady hurled a lamp at the president. And *she had a smile on her face when she let go.*[627]

• After Hillary threw the lamp, she seemed mortified when she realized she had been observed by a security officer. Shortly thereafter, Secret Service agents were permanently moved out of parts of the residence.[628]

• Early in the Clinton administration, the Big Girl had a fit when stories began appearing in the press saying that she had thrown a lamp at Bill and called him a "stupid motherf***er." Another time, it was reported, she had burst into a room looking for her husband, and shouted at a Secret Service officer, "Where's the miserable c***sucker?"[629]

• There is at least one account of Hillary beating Bill with her fists in the face, and clawing him in the jaw, leaving a prominent mark. Close Clinton friend Linda Bloodsworth-Thomas told author Gail Sheehy that it was great that Hillary had "smacked Bill upside the head."[630]

• Comments regarding a scratch on the president's chin. April 5, 1993: "The President cut himself shaving." (Press Secretary Dee Dee Myers). Same day: "He was playing with Chelsea, and I guess he just got scratched." (Communications Director George Stephanopoulos).[631]

• Ever since the Clintons appeared on *60 Minutes* to assure the world of their marriage's incomparable normalcy, tales of their marital friction had circulated through Washington. In the second week of April a two-inch claw mark appeared on the president's right cheek, adjacent an inflamed right ear. The ever-game Dee Dee Myers attributed the damage to a shaving nick, an alibi plausible perhaps if the president shaved with a chisel.[632]

• After Bill Clinton discovered that he lost an Arkansas election. "Telephones and books sailed across the room, smashing windows."[633]

• "Politics, not sex, is what really got Hillary worked up," Paul Fray said. During one argument at campaign headquarters, Hillary picked up a book and flung it at Bill, catching him in the ribs. "She was frightening – she liked to yell, and man, did she like to throw things."[634]

• William Bell, a former member of the White House detail, recalled yet another pitched battle as Bill and Hillary rode together in a limousine – he in the front, she in the back. Once again, an enraged Hillary flung a briefing book at Bill, inadvertently hitting the agent behind the wheel in the back of the head.[635]

• Over the years, the President would suffer numerous unexplained bruises and abrasions, including a sizable goose egg on his forehead. His explanation: "walked into a door." Presidential handlers laughed off any suggestion that their boss's wounds might have been the result of anything other than innocent mishap. But privately, they also wondered aloud if Hillary, whose penchant for aiming objects at her husband's skull had been well established, was actually capable of spousal abuse.[636]

• Hillary, when upset, did not pull her punches – she'd let loose with a string of invectives, turning the air blue, going, as one said, straight for the jugular – much like her father did in Park Ridge. "She gets foul fast. They've both got as short a fuse as you've ever been around," said [Paul] Fray ... "He's got that emotional volatility about him and she does, too. They'll both explode."[637]

• Trooper Roger Perry describing a battle after Bill got caught cheating again on Hillary. "They were shouting. Perry left, trying not to overhear, uncomfortable about intruding on their privacy. About two hours later, he went into the kitchen. A cupboard door was broken off its hinges. Food, pots and pans, broken glass were scattered on the floor. Perry cleaned up the glass."[638]

• With several staff members standing just outside the door, the Clintons shrieked at each other to the accompaniment of shattering glass and slamming drawers. When it was over, staff members cautiously pushed open the door to reveal broken glass, smashed dishes, and a cupboard door ripped off its hinges. To be sure, Hillary had continued her habit of hurling objects at her husband – yellow file pads, files, briefing books, car keys, Styrofoam coffee cups … "They'd be screaming at each other, real blue-in-the-face stuff," one of their drivers said, "but when the car pulled up to their destination it was all smiles and waving for the crowd." Other times, they would sit in the car for as long as two hours without ever uttering a word.[639]

• The February 19 *Chicago Sun-Times* reported that Hillary, in a fierce argument with Bill, had smashed a lamp in the family living quarters. "Seems first lady Hillary Rodham Clinton has a temper to match her hubby's," wrote columnist Bill Zwecker, adding, "Just in case you care, Bill and Hillary sleep in separate bedrooms."[640]

• One Sunday afternoon, [Trooper Roger] Perry was standing next to an intercom outside the kitchen when he clearly heard Hillary telling her husband, "Look, Bill, I need to [have sexual relations with her husband] more than twice a year." At one point, Bill's cheating pushed Hillary over the edge. After learning that her husband had led the daughter of a major contributor to believe he would marry her, Hillary had what some described as a nervous breakdown. She began hyperventilating, and an ambulance rushed Hillary to the hospital for observation.[641]

• The troopers seemed to feel that Bill was justified in slipping out of his marital bed at night to prowl the streets of Little Rock because they saw Hillary as an undesirable, foul-mouthed harridan who had brought the mistreatment and neglect on herself.[642]

• Hillary Clinton on her husband's campaign tactics in Arkansas: "For God's sake Bill, don't be an a**hole. If you want to lose this election because you're too chicken****, then go ahead!"[643]

• Now the president is on the phone with Senator Bob Kerrey, screaming, "F**k you!" Soon a conservative wins an off-year election and Clinton is saying, "Its Nazi time out there – we got to hit back." Thinking about the man he helped put in the White House, Stephanopoulos judges him to be mercurial, weak and prone to tempter tantrums. Now the president is screaming – an outburst, a roar marked by purple rage and eruption of a resentment. Now, worst of all, the president is doing the silent scream, in which he silently rages and refuses to say why.[644]

• Bermuda, June 1979, when daughter Chelsea was conceived. "After a few more beers, Bill Clinton – who normally was not a heavy drinker, and was clearly feeling no pain – made an announcement. 'I'm going back to my cottage to rape my wife,' he said. [The next morning fellow vacationers visited the Clintons' hotel room.] When we get there, the place looks like World War III. There are pillows and busted-up furniture all over the place. Obviously, Hillary's got pissed off at Bill, and threw a few things across the room. I guess that's the price he paid for going back to his room and taking the initiative and demanding sex."[645] [Note: "At the time of Chelsea's birth, Bill Clinton was carrying on a sexual relationship with Dolly Kyle Browning, a woman he had known since high school."[646]]

• George Stephanopoulos trying to cover up for another mark on Bill Clinton's face: "He, he was playing with Chelsea, and I guess he just got scratched ... I didn't get all the details, minute by minute ... It was, was just, just some confusion ... It looked like a shaving – I mean, I just wasn't there." From the White House staff the rumor leaked out that "Bill and Hillary had recently had some rip-roaring rows, during which Mrs. Clinton ... threw things at her husband. One of the missiles mentioned was a lamp. Later in December when the Arkansas troopers came forth with testimony of the Clintons' rocky marriage, the reports of husband abuse in the White House circulated again."[647]

• First, the Bible-throwing story made its way into print. Then, more disastrously for the Secret Service, the *Chicago Sun-Times* and *Newsweek* reported that Hillary and Bill had one of their knock-down, drag-out fights in the residence, with the first lady throwing a lamp at the president.[648]

• The confidential memo written by David Watkins about the travel office gives the maternal image a Joan Crawford twist; portraying the first lady as a scary "Mommie Dearest."[649]

• After Hillary's father suffered a massive stroke. "[Barbara] Streisand spent the night in the Lincoln Bedroom. Hillary was upset that her husband was spending time with one of Hollywood's biggest stars while she kept a vigil at the bedside of her dying father. The day Hillary returned to Washington, a steward who had been summoned to the second floor made a hasty retreat when he heard shouting and the unmistakable sound of slamming doors. At the following morning's news briefing, reporters peppered Press Secretary Dee Dee Myers with questions about the wounds clearly evident on the President's face and neck. Before she ever saw the claw marks, Myers told reporters that Clinton had simply cut himself shaving. 'Then I saw him,' Myers later admitted, alluding to the fact that the First Lady was clearly disturbed by Streisand's presence alone with her husband in the family quarters. 'It was a big scratch, and clearly not a shaving cut.'"[650]

• The Clintons and the staff did *not* have a reputation for being good listeners, but they *did* have a reputation for losing their tempers. The president and Mrs. Clinton, especially, were frequently observed flying into rages at each other or at staffers.[651]

We could continue with plenty of other examples of the Clintons' *loving* marriage, but instead we'll close with a quote from Peggy Noonan's *The Case Against Hillary Clinton*: "These people are not quite stable. They're not completely mad, they don't wear tin foil hats and talk to chairs, but they are extreme in their actions and behaviors."[652]

INAUGURATION DAY MELEE

A perfect illustration of the abysmal Clinton marriage can be found on Inauguration Day, 1993. As I described earlier, Bill and Hillary were bound by a prearranged "contractual" political marriage, and each was made *sick* by it (in a variety of different ways). Their battles were epic – physically violent, verbally abusive, while Bill cheated on Hillary too many times to count (not to mention Mrs. Clinton's tryst with Vince Foster, which we'll cover later). The couple eventually became slaves to this arrangement, but at least they had won the presidency. [And we literally mean *they*, for theirs was a co-presidency.] The Clintons had finally grabbed the brass ring. They'd reached the Promised Land ... their Shangri-la. Now everything should have been better.

But it wasn't; not by a long-shot. In fact, the first couple actually entered meltdown realm on what should have been one of the happiest days of their lives. They'd been working all their adult lives to reach this summit; and in all honesty, they *had* done it. Even with their CIA sellout and a plethora of connections, who would have thought it possible? Bill and Hillary had co-opted the White House. They defied the odds and emerged on top. Victory is the sweetest revenge, and they now had their hands on the throttle of power (sort of).

But these two couldn't allow themselves to bask in the sweet glow of such triumph, for they couldn't rise above themselves. Rather than appreciating what had been accomplished, they instead tore into one another yet again. Theirs is the ultimate tragedy; two self-absorbed monsters so consumed by ambition, narcissism, and self-indulgence that nothing can exist beyond their madness.

The day immediately began on the wrong foot.

Right up to the moment the Clintons departed for the inauguration, Hillary was faced with reminders of her husband's infidelities. On the day of the flight to Washington, state trooper Larry Patterson was assigned by Clinton to pick up one of his former lovers and bring her to the airport, where a group of friends had gathered to see

the Clintons off. Hillary spotted the woman as soon as she arrived, and threw a fit. "What the f*** do you think you're doing?" she screamed at Patterson. "I know who that whore is. Get her out of here." Clinton stood by, saying nothing, and Patterson did what he was told.[653]

So, even on this day of days, Bill couldn't help himself. He had to get one more rush by bringing a floozy to the airport where maybe he could get a quick feel or sneak a quick kiss. Worse, he had to rub Hillary's nose in it by deliberately and blatantly flaunting one of his mistresses and his habitual adultery. With her buttons pushed full bore, Hillary naturally flipped out and allowed the bitch persona to emerge – the abusive, shrieking shrew. The plane ride from Little Rock to D.C. must have been a joy!

In Washington, the scene deteriorated considerably as a brutal power struggle ensued between Bill and Hillary. What follows is FBI agent Gary Aldrich's account:

Other warning signs were more ominous. The Clintons, for instance, had been late for their own inauguration. A case of jitters or understandable last-minute fussing?

No, not according to extremely reliable sources who have spoken to me and who, for obvious reasons, must remain anonymous. One of the reasons the Clintons were late was that Vice President Gore had just found out that the West Wing office usually reserved for the vice president was instead going to be occupied by the first lady.

Network news cameras, trained on Blair House the morning of the inauguration recorded a glimpse of the president and first

lady screaming at each other. Sources I consider very reliable affirm that Clinton told Hillary that if she didn't back down from her plans to unseat Gore, Gore would go public with his anger and perhaps resign. Hillary shouted at him that as far as she was concerned, they had a deal – a deal that dated back to the campaign, when Lloyd Cutler had convinced her to stand by Clinton despite the allegations that he'd had an affair with Gennifer Flowers. The matter had already been decided, she said, and she had no intention of backing off; Gore was bluffing.[654]

The scene continued to get uglier. "'G**damn it, Bill, you promised me that office!' she screamed. Hillary was furious because Bill had reneged on his promise, part of their power-sharing agreement, to give her the office that traditionally goes to the vice president."[655]

Others were affected by the confrontation, including President George Bush. "That morning, there was an embarrassing delay at Blair House, where the Clintons were staying. The Clintons kept the Bushes waiting for twenty-seven minutes before arriving for coffee then rushing off for the constitutionally mandated noon swearing in on the steps of the Capitol."[656]

Hillary's barrage continued. "'You f***ing a**hole!' – more encouraging words from Hillary on Inauguration Day to the newly sworn-in Bill Clinton ... 'You stupid motherf***er.'"[657]

The incident soon spilled out onto the street.

In the morning, at Blair House across the street from the White House, the TV cameras captured Clinton on the front stairs, looking impatient, apparently waiting for his wife Hillary. He stopped, looked up toward the

door and said some word the microphone didn't catch ... But it wasn't exactly all hugs at Blair House, according to a park police officer who was standing in close proximity to the Clintons that morning, who witnessed the scene and overheard Bill as he came out of Blair House saying, "That f***ing bitch!" When Hillary came charging out after him, she was saying, "You stupid motherf****r!"[658]

Joyce Milton confirms this report. "Clinton had referred to his wife as a 'f***ing bitch,' while she came charging out the front door calling him a 'stupid motherf***er.'"[659]

Others were shocked by this crass display of vulgarity. "Standing on the steps of Blair House on Inauguration Day, 1993, Bill Clinton yelled at his wife through the cold morning air. 'F***ing bitch!' he screamed, causing Secret Service agents and well-wishers to cower. 'Stupid motherf***er,' was the reply from our first lady."[660]

Even after Bill Clinton was sworn in while holding his hand on the Bible, Hillary's confrontation with him continued.

After taking the oath, Bill and Hillary Clinton were taken to a holding room in the Capitol building. Minutes passed while everyone waited for Bill and Hillary to emerge to commence the inaugural festivities. A Capitol Hill police officer was ordered to inform the Clintons that everyone was ready and waiting.

The policeman knocked and opened the door of the holding room. He immediately shut it, beating a hasty retreat. Hillary Clinton was screaming at her husband in what was described as "uncontrolled and unbri-

dled fury." Apparently, the matter of office space was *not* settled. The Capitol Hill police and Secret Service quickly conferred about intervening if it appeared the president's life might be threatened by the first lady! The question before them was, "How much physical abuse is too much physical abuse?"[661]

Hillary Clinton: husband beater and physical abuser. Forget about stalkers, lunatics, and assassins. On Inauguration Day, 1993, the president's biggest worry was that his life may have been endangered by his own wife!

So much for life in paradise. From day one, there was turmoil, resentment, jealousy, and hatred in the White House between Bill and Hillary Clinton.

POLITICAL MARRIAGE

As I've written previously, practically every person who knew Hillary Rodham in the mid-1970s was not only amazed that she 'threw everything away' by moving to Arkansas, they were also aghast. Why would this star on a meteoric rise to success ruin her life by moving to one of the most backward, least attractive economic locales in the United States? Hillary was certainly no dummy, which made her relocation seem even more preposterous.

But Hillary *knew* something that nobody else knew. "She had mentioned to Bernard Nussbaum as early as 1974 that her boyfriend was going to run for president one day."[662] Everyone laughed and sneered; and even Hillary must have had moments of doubt when waking up in Razorback country, for "Hillary was often lonely. She had no close friends in town, social events in Little Rock were invariably organized for couples, and the problem, recalls [Webster] Hubbell, was that 'of course Bill was never around.'"[663] Still, Hillary dove in with both feet because, amazingly, "Bill made it very clear, he was going to be president."[664] [And never forget, for *Hillary* to be president, first Bill had to be president.] Even during the days following their marriage, something so bizarre took place that it defied description. As sympathetic biographer Gail Sheehy wrote, "Hillary took her family along on their honeymoon. Father Hugh, brothers Hughie and Tony, and Mother Dorothy all went off to Acapulco and stayed in the same hotel with the newlyweds. It was all so prudish, almost like an arranged marriage."[665]

This was the type of seemingly inexplicable situation that Hillary had gotten herself into. But for the normally cautious and calculating woman from suburban Chicago, she couldn't stake her future on just anybody. She wanted a ticket to the top. "Hillary had little patience with weakness, and no interest in being paired with a loser."[666] Indeed, Hillary had to take charge of her destiny by becoming the main *driver* of the relationship. "She was more the architect, he the builder. She's the planner, he's the contractor on site, relating to everyone."[667]

However, let there be no mistake; theirs was a political marriage, pure and simple. Hamilton Jordan, Jimmy Carter's former Chief of Staff, had the following to say. "The Clintons are not a couple but a business partnership, not based on love or even greed but on shared ambitions. Everywhere they go, they leave a trail of disappointed, disillusioned friends and staff members to clean up after them. The Clintons' only loyalty is to their own ambitions."[668]

This statement is where the real rub comes in because ultimately, it was Hillary who had to diminish her *self* to keep the Clintons' star on the rise. Barbara Olson couldn't have said it more clearly. "In order to keep her husband's chances alive, Hillary had to sublimate her ambitions, even her identity, to his. In time, she could no longer be Hillary Rodham."[669]

That's why Hillary was so enraged on Inauguration Day. She was supposedly promised the vice president's office; yet Bill reneged. Plus, as you'll see, she had to give up her name for his, her career, and where she lived. Then, Bill cheated on her at every turn. Laura Ingraham gives an opinion which was shared by many. "I wondered how a woman so impeccably educated and credentialed and prepared for independence could have made such a devil's bargain ... What a story of irony and tragedy – a woman, once so promising, now finally trying to collect her just reward, one she clearly expects to be as grand as the humiliation she has been forced to endure. Was this the promise of feminism? Were women now to submit to any indignity, even a sham marriage, for access to power and fame?"[670]

Hillary: the governor's wife, first lady, congresswoman, and maybe president of the United States. For what? A devil's pact? The entire scenario, conceived by others far beyond the Clintons' relatively humble roots, knew that for this prearranged marriage to work they needed a *fighter* who was in it for the long run ... and that adultery was part of the agreement – something to be overlooked.

Family friend Helen Dowdy emphasized the contractual crux of their partnership. "Bill and Hillary had to have an agreement. I absolutely, positively feel like that, one-hundred percent. An agreement where the wife would say, do what you need to do as long as you don't bother me and don't get caught. I just think that's the kind of marriage they have."[671]

So, it wasn't Bill's pathological womanizing that grated on Hillary, it was his deliberate disregard and carelessness. In other words, "In the years to come, it would be noted frequently, she [Hillary] reserved her true anger for the times he had strayed from the path of political viability. That was to her the true infidelity."[672] To Hillary, infidelity wasn't adultery; it was being untrue to their "cause." Even after Bill Clinton appeared on every network imaginable and admitted his immature affair with Monica – humiliating Hillary to no end – she was still fighting for the team. Sydney Blumenthal observed, "Hillary was at peace with her ithyphallic husband just forty-eight hours after his nationally televised press conference of August 15 ... I could hear the President and Hillary bantering in the background ... they were still working as a team."[673]

Yes, Hillary always was out for number one – but number one wasn't simply Hillary, but Bill and Hillary. Once their names were signed on the dotted line, the two became one; despite how little Hillary trusted her husband. Another family friend lamented on Hillary's willingness to invest in this political union. "Even then, the pattern of her lack of trust in him was set. It wasn't just me. There were others she was suspicious of. But that pattern was set long before they got married. And she still decided the most important thing was that political partnership, that goal they'd set, rather than taking care of their personal life, or being confident, or having a trustworthy relationship. I'm just amazed, as a woman, at her thought process. To be so smart and allow that to happen ... to go for politics over personal life and love and happiness. They had all these rules, but he kept breaking them. And he's still breaking them."[674]

Sadly, by the time they rose to prominence, Hillary didn't *have* any choice but to stay with Bill. Why? Because the powers-that-be that arranged this deal deliberately lured Bill and Hillary into illegal acts which will be outlined later in this book. It was quick money for the Clintons – a lucrative payoff, like Hillary turning a $1,000 investment into $100,000 – but highly illegal. Their future acts would have surely brought jail time; and the Clintons knew it. They were trapped; they had to play the game or spend an indeterminate amount of time behind bars (or far worse, as those familiar with the Clinton Body Count know). The result was truly bizarre. "Bill and Hillary not only complemented one another in a remarkable way; over time they came to seem eerily necessary to one another, as though neither can really exist or succeed on their own. Rather than two-for-one, the truth is more two-*as*-one."[675]

Helen Dowdy's husband Oscar agreed. "It just seemed like a marriage of convenience because they were both headed in the same direction politically, that was the goal; that was the deal."[676]

Democrat Hamilton Jordan is especially direct in his analysis. "'The Clintons are not a couple but a business partnership, not based on love or even greed but on shared ambitions. Every move they make is part of their grand scheme to claw their way to the very top.' Jordan saw the Clintons as tawdry, unprincipled, opportunistic, taking advantage of anyone weak enough to fall for their stories."[677]

Gennifer Flowers, who knew Bill intimately as his mistress for a dozen years, puts it even more blatantly. "It is now common knowledge that Bill's relationship with Hillary is nothing more than an arrangement between two partners in power."[678] She continues, "I firmly believe that Bill and Hillary had forged this contract long before we met. Apparently Hillary was willing to put up with her husband's cheating, but she never would have tolerated his leaving her without trying to exact some revenge. And, frankly, I wouldn't have blamed her."[679]

So, one Christmas when their daughter Chelsea was unwrapping presents, she asked, "Mommy, why doesn't Daddy love you anymore?"[680] She had no way of knowing that her parents didn't have what would commonly be seen as a typical 'loving' marriage. No, "Hillary, it seems, long ago accepted Bill Clinton as someone who could advance her goals, as a necessary complement to her more intellectual cold-blooded pursuit of power."[681] Likewise, "for better or worse, Hillary Rodham is the woman Bill chose, to be his helpmate. And, like most other aspects of their rise to power, it was a carefully calculated choice."[682]

The only problem with this analysis is: they didn't select one another; they were simply pawns on a much larger chessboard being moved about by individuals with power they could only dream about. Even as first couple, Bill and Hillary were mere tools to the real power brokers. One writer – Dr. John Coleman – gave the following account of what happened on one occasion when Hillary became so disenchanted with Bill's overt womanizing that she decided to leave him. To salvage their investment, the power brokers stepped in.

> **It was shortly before Clinton was approached by Pamela Harriman and Jay Rockefeller that he found himself without his wife. This was a bad setback; obviously, a man with marital troubles was not suitable to occupy the Oval Office. Harriman made a beeline for Hillary and explained the situation: if she returned to her husband, she could count on being the next "first lady." Never one to pass up an opportunity for advancement, Hillary agreed to mend relations with her spouse, on condition that there would be no more extramarital affairs.[683]**

Well, we all know one part of that supposed agreement wasn't adhered to, and even when confronted with further betrayal and humiliation, Hillary told Betsey Wright "that she was not willing to abandon the partnership. She had invested too much in Bill Clinton and was determined to see it through."[684] The word "partnership" was substituted for "marriage" and that the word "investment" was used instead of "love"; but what is one to expect? "The marriage is a very cosmopolitan arrangement, more typical of European jet-set society than of America. It is a playboy marriage."[685]

The end result is what we see today of the Clintons – a couple that spends very little time together. "Bill and Hillary Clinton have built largely separate lives – partly because of the demands of their distinct career paths and partly as a result of political calculations"[686] [And partly because they hate each other's guts.]

Stated differently, Hillary had to deliberately distance herself from Bill after he left the Oval Office because of the political dangers he posed to her. She knew that their partnership was seriously jeopardized because one party – Bill – appeared to rebel against it more than the other participant – herself. A fitting example was Bill's aborted presidential run in 1988. The machine was gearing up, feelers were being sent out; and then they got hit with a whammy: the Gary Hart factor. On the surface, the Colorado Senator's flirtatious rendezvous with Donna Rice was a major scandal, but as you'll see, I feel he was nothing more than a sacrificial lamb; the guinea pig in a much larger scenario that once again benefited Bill Clinton.

Anyway, top Clinton aide Betsey Wright compiled a list of all the women Bill had slept with. "She started listing the names of women he had allegedly had affairs with and the places where they were said to have occurred."[687] The result was disastrous, for if the press ever got a load of Clinton's harem, especially on the heels of Gary Hart, he would be sunk forever. In the end, the whole matter was a blessing in disguise for Clinton because by 1992 the public had become desensitized to the adultery issue and the Clintons could say it was old news.

In addition, Hillary now had time to prepare a better strategy for the obvious questions which would be asked of her. "Hillary seemed to emerge from that experience with a coldly calculating new perspective: instead of making sure that Bill changed his ways, she realized that she must keep his recklessness out of the public eye if either of them wanted to make it to Washington."[688]

Hillary was the *driver*; the person who kept the wheels on their three-ring circus of a marriage. But the resentment borne of this responsibility certainly took its toll. After one particular incident where Bill strayed off course yet again and threatened his reelection, Hillary blew up. "His face was turning bright pink, said one present, and Hillary was leaning into him and screaming. The message was: Hillary was sick and tired of saving his [rear end] every time he [messed] up, and he better start taking [his career and his future] seriously."[689] After all, "The Clintons marked off their married life in terms of electoral cycles."[690]

The vicious cycle became Hillary's cross to bear; part of her "duties" agreed upon when the pact was formulated. "Throughout their marriage, it had always been Bill who screwed up and Hillary who came to the rescue."[691] Hillary had to know everything; she had to be in control, the one with her finger squarely on Bill Clinton's pulse. That's why so many people in the know *knew* Hillary was lying when the Monica Lewinsky scandal broke. Here was "a woman who interviewed potential White House appointees, oversaw the President's daily schedule, and ran many important White House meetings; a woman who deployed a legion of loyalists to keep an eye on her sex-addicted husband."[692] Hillary was (and still is) an unabashed control freak and information junkie. It's inconceivable that this "all-seeing, all-knowing, all-powerful woman had been unaware of the existence of Monica Lewinsky,"[693] especially when they were fooling around right in the Oval Office.

But understand; Hillary feigning ignorance was the only way she could perpetuate the illusion that their marriage was genuine, and not a sham. Hillary had to yet again play the role of a humiliated wife who was *angry* at her cheating louse of a husband. "The estrangement was vital, wrote political consultant Dick Morris, for it helped substantiate the idea that they had a real marriage to begin with."[694]

Think about how pathetic this situation really is. Even the feminists, one of Hillary's longest and staunchest supporters, were appalled. "Many women said they couldn't stand her because she was willing to tolerate abuse from her husband in order to stay in power."[695] That's what it all boiled down to. Hillary was "married to a ravenous sexual predator at best – a brutal serial rapist at worst ... She could have forced Bill into counseling and therapy under pain of divorce. She could have withheld her public support – as Lee Hart did in 1988. ... [Or] the very least she could have done was to see that her husband's victims were somehow taken care of. But there was a problem. Any measure of honesty in this regard – even the slightest hint that Mr. Clinton had acknowledged to a therapist that he was a sexual predator – would sink any chance the Clintons had of ever reaching the White House. Rather than sacrifice her personal ambition, Hillary Clinton chose to sell out every one of her feminist principles – and along with them, the interests of every woman in the world."[696]

The above passage defines what it means to sell one's soul. "Hillary had done a lot of heavy lifting for her husband, most of it, such as the various bimbo eruptions, that required her to hold her nose. She's sustained repeated public mortification and personal humiliation. She had to cover for her husband and lie."[697] As you'll see in the following chapter, Hillary absolutely knew about Bill's affairs, so even the supposed public humiliations weren't real. They were more akin to an actor filling a role – like Anthony Hopkins playing Hannibal Lecter. He wasn't actually a killer, and Hillary wasn't actually embarrassed. She only had to *pretend* she was! Or, as Gennifer Flowers wrote, "Hillary Rodham Clinton is far too smart a lady to be fooled. Let's face it; she'd have to be a moron not to know she's married to a philanderer. Hillary certainly knew about me, and I'm sure she still has ways of keeping tabs on old Billy boy."[698]

Please don't get the wrong impression, though, that Hillary is a doormat or a victim, for her sufferings do lead to payoffs. "'Her stoic exterior,' Dick Morris observed, 'masks enormous pain.' This latest act of betrayal [Monica Lewinsky] had left her deeply scarred emotionally. But it's also true, Morris would point out, that Hillary 'is never happier than when she can rescue him.' The reason: 'Because then Bill invests her with even more authority and the balance of power shifts in her favor.'"[699]

The scenario gets even creepier, as we saw with the rape of Juanita Broaddrick, because Hillary Clinton has been a long-time *enabler* of Bill Clinton's horrific actions, especially in regard to his abuse of women. "In order to keep her marriage going, Hillary had compromised her own ambitions, accepted her husband's chronic infidelities, and taken on the role of protecting him from the consequences of his often self-destructive behavior."[700]

This regrettable choice flies in the face of Hillary Clinton, champion of women's rights and feminist supreme.

> **Many commentators, and Hillary Clinton's biographer Gail Sheehy, have dubbed Hillary her husband's "enabler." I'm not trained to make a psychological diagnosis, but whatever you call his behavior, it's a big step backward for women. To put it simply, Hillary has succeeded in making the country safer for infidelity by letting Bill get away with it time after cheating time. Hillary shows millions of young women across the country that it's okay, that some things are more important than trust and honesty. Whatever Hillary may personally think of adultery, her unflagging allegiance to our commander in cheat puts her squarely in the role of doormat wife of the olden days, who knows of her husband's affairs but chooses to look the other way.[701]**

This observation is crucial, for it illustrates one of the most tragic aspects of the Clinton presidency. The Monica Lewinsky affair increasingly blurred the line between right and wrong and created more of a 'gray area" without absolutes. It is this type of moral confusion from which our country is still struggling to recover.

That's one of the reasons why Hillary is so dangerous. She represents hypocrisy to the "nth" degree, for how can a Gloria Steinem superwoman permit such repeatedly egregious behavior by her husband? To make matters worse, Hillary became Bill's No. 1 cover-up artist. "Former Arkansas state auditor Julia Hughes Jones said that Hillary was not only aware of Bill's womanizing, she enabled it. 'Every time he was out and Hillary knew where he went, she would call behind him to see what she needed to do to take care of it.'"[702] Undoubtedly, "Hillary's knowledge of her husband's cheating has been the oldest running theme of their relationship."[703]

It's one thing to turn a blind eye, but when Hillary actively and deliberately engages in a slash & burn vendetta against the women Bill cheated with when they threaten their political viability, then her decisions become inexcusable. "George Stephanopoulos depicts Hillary leading the war room smear campaign against Gennifer Flowers, whose audio tape of Bill coaching his former lover to lie to the press put such a scare into the Clintons' first presidential campaign. Bill's coaching Gennifer, caught on tape, would be echoed five years later in Monica Lewinsky's testimony. Lewinsky described how President Clinton coached her to lie and obstruct justice during his 2 a.m. call from the White House."[704]

Dick Morris stressed the ugliness of this arrangement even more forcefully. "Defending your husband in public is one thing. Declaring war on the prosecutors, witnesses, and reporters investigating him is something very different. The tactics she used to defend Bill drew out the absolute worst of Hillary Clinton. Hiring private detectives, releasing opponents' confidential personnel files, stonewalling the investigation, and outright lying to save their joint political career, this woman who had helped impeach Richard Nixon came more and more to resemble her former target."[705]

But that's how this political marriage operated, for "the marriage had never been a separate entity; without Bill's career, without the cause, the race to the top, the marriage itself was empty, a drained vessel."[706] Here again, Hillary was the driver, for "the reality involved the game plan, and here Hillary held all the cards. She was convinced she was the only one in the world who could get him [Bill] where he wanted to go – and he believed her."[707]

The conflicting messages of this complex marriage are mind-boggling, for on one hand Hillary was the controller, rescuer, enabler and attack dog; still, "her political power was doubly derivative: dependent on both Bill's tenure in office and the survival of their marriage. If either should capsize, her power would disappear."[708]

Bill has already been president. He's grabbed the brass ring;

Hillary hasn't. Thus, in this sense, Bill himself is the driver, and he knows it, as he once confided to a professor prior to Hillary's arrival in Arkansas.

> **"Because she's so good at what she does, she could have an amazing political career on her own," Clinton said. "If she comes to Arkansas, it's going to be my state, my future. She could be president someday. She could go to any state and be elected to the Senate. If she comes to Arkansas, she'll be on my turf."[709]**

This basic fact stated above is another harsh reality. Until her 'selection' to the New York senate in 2000, "Hillary owes everything to Bill. For all her feminism, Hillary has never learned to stand on her own."[710] But before you get the impression that the deck is now stacked in Bill's favor, "If Hillary had walked out in January 1998 [during the Monica Lewinsky disaster] instead of taking to the airwaves to denounce the 'vast right-wing conspiracy,' what little there was of the Clinton legacy would have been obliterated."[711] The same applies today. If Bill turned the tables on Hillary and she spilled the beans, the fantastic Clinton legacy would turn to horse droppings in a minute.

So what we have is a symbiotic, parasitic relationship where each partner depends upon, feeds off, and ultimately fears the other. If one goes down, both go down.

When Peggy Noonan interviewed a political insider well familiar with Hillary, here is how she described the Clintons after showing Noonan a book entitled, *Borderline Conditions and Pathological Narcissism* by Otto Kernberg, M.D. "The key to understanding both Hillary and Bill Clinton, she began, is that they are narcissists. I said that this has been said before, and she answered that a big point has been missed: they are, together, a particular kind of narcissist, and they have done a particular kind of mind-meld."[712]

What type of mind-meld would she be referring to? "Cynics like to say that Bill Clinton and Hillary Rodham had one thing in common: they were both in love with Bill Clinton. That belies the compatibility of their mutual aspirations. He wanted political success. She wanted political power."[713]

To accomplish these goals, the Clintons had to repeatedly fool one collective entity: the public. Again, from Peggy Noonan's book, *The Case Against Hillary Clinton*: "Their relationships with other people are clearly exploitative and sometimes parasitic. It is as if they feel they have the right to control and possess others, and to exploit them without guilty feelings, and behind a surface which very often is charming and engaging, one senses coldness and ruthlessness."[714]

What she's referring to is you – the voting public. To the Clintons, you're nothing more than another obstacle which must be overcome to reach their ultimate goal. Any lie or manipulation is acceptable if the end justifies the means, just as it is with each other. Clearly, despite their differences, Bill and Hillary are more similar to one another than dissimilar. During their epic quest to attain the White House, the battle naturally wore on the duo – but they still remained intact because of an inherent lack of humanity. "The worn repetition tended eventually to expose less their differences than what they always had in common: contempt for the public audience; an overweening arrogance rather less disguised in her than him; constant faith in their capacity to manipulate opinion; an underlying glibness and shallowness beneath their practiced, polished surface."[715]

These people can't even stand or trust each other; how do you think they feel about you? They cheat and lie and obfuscate their entire lives with each other. To them, you're simply fodder; votes in a vast machine that is viewed in terms of victories along a charted course. They are, in fact, so un-substantive and shallow that even the crux of their marriage – faithfulness – is dismissed as insignificant. "Gail Sheehy describes how Hillary 'told herself that adultery was a very small, unimportant part of her husband's life – a pastime, like when he'd get up in the middle of the night and go down to the basement and hang over the pinball machine for hours.' In no way did she see a connection between his sexual escapades and their relationship."[716]

Adultery as unimportant ... a mere pastime which was to be capitalized on for political gain or to derive the upper hand in a marriage power struggle? Could this scenario possibly be all the Clinton marriage is about? "'Like the moon,' ex-advisor Dick Morris wrote in his memoirs, 'Hillary only shines or – one suspects – receives affection, when her husband is most luminous. She seems most brilliant when Saturday-night Bill has strayed, gotten caught, and needs his wife to rescue him."[717]

BILLARY

The image is both mesmerizing and horrifying as Hillary Clinton appears on the cover of *Time* magazine. Like Medusa drawing a man in before turning him to stone; or Helen of Troy, a face that launched a thousand ships. Hillary has inexplicably become an inspiration to some; but to most others, she's a horror – the ball-buster, the bitch, the doppelganger entity that assumes control of the host's body. Or, as David Brock opines with literary brilliance, "The *Washington Post* reported that *Time* magazine's excerpt of the Stewart book features a cover photo of Hillary Rodham Clinton looking like a Gothic fiend. At first glance, she's a vampire – ghastly white skin, scarlet lips, teeth slightly bared – coming at us cloaked all in black. In that eternal cliché of suggested guilt, her glance is averted. But study the image for a minute and you'll notice that the red 'M' in 'TIME' forms two perfect horns on the first lady's head. This is no mere bloodsucker; it's Satanella."[718]

A more comical slant can be derived from a cartoon in R.W. Bradford's *It Came from Arkansas* where Bill Clinton holds his scowling wife above his head at a baseball game. A meek-looking bald man standing beside him says, "Um, sir, you're supposed to throw out the first *PITCH*."

Bill and Hillary: Billary. The moniker has been around for over two decades now. "The term 'Billary' was first used by me in '86, said [Frank] White's campaign consultant, Darrell Glascock,"[719] and ever since it's been the subject of jokes, late night comedy skits, and was even lampooned in a song by Ted Nugent called *Kiss My Ass*.

But the reality of this union – where Hillary assumed so much control of their relationship that the term had to even be coined in the first place – is much starker. In fact, there hasn't even remotely been another political couple in history that has required such an invention; not even Napoleon and Josephine or Franklin and Eleanor Roosevelt.

Hillary, perpetually aware of public opinion, would actually prefer the "Billary" jokes to continue, for if people ever saw her real persona without the spin and gloss, they'd be mortified. Dick Morris, well acquainted with this couple, nails Hillary's genuine motives.

> **Both of the Clintons are masters of subterfuge. But Hillary's deceptions and disguises are very different from Bill's. Bill Clinton deceives himself, and fools us in the process. He pretends, even when he is alone, that he is not doing what he knows he is doing. He never tells his right hand what his left hand is up to.**
>
> **By contrast, Hillary knows full well who she is and what parts of her must never be exposed to public view. She reminds herself consciously, day after day, which parts of herself to hide and which to expose. Where Bill's instinct for deception is neurotic, Hillary's is opportunistic. He wants to hide his private life from our eyes; Hillary seeks to conceal her character from our view. But the things that Hillary hides are inte-**

**gral to her political essence. They are who she is
and what makes her tick. Her trickery is designed to hide her most basic character and instincts from all of us.**[720]

In essence, Hillary *is* the Clinton political machine. Here is
the way Webb Hubbell – a longtime Clinton crony – was introduced to the couple. "A friend explained to Hubbell that Bill Clinton was a Rhodes Scholar and Yale law graduate. When he asked
who Hillary was, his friend laughed and said, 'the rumor is, she's
his brains.'"[721]

Lieutenant Colonel Robert Patterson lays it out even more
succinctly. "When Hillary was with us, she ran the show. She
was the power behind the throne, and her priorities came first."[722]
During his Arkansas gubernatorial campaigns, opponents would
often taunt Bill with his lack of real world experience. "Clinton
lacked business sense because he never had to meet a payroll or
live on a budget in his life. 'Is there any record anywhere of his
ever having drawn a salary from any source except a government
agency?' Orval Faubus was still asking several years after his own
ill-fated comeback effort against Clinton in 1986. By and large,
the criticism was valid. Until Clinton assumed the presidency
his wife was the chief bread winner."[723]

There's a funny story which illustrates how Hillary was
clearly the hands-on driving force of this partnership. One day
when Chelsea was at school and the nurse wanted to give her an
aspirin, she quipped, "Call my dad; my mom's too busy."[724] Let
there be no doubt, as longtime confidant John Peavoy remarked,
"Hillary was destined to run the show from the beginning."[725]

Destiny ... as in prearrangement. Hillary was the one *selected*
for Bill Clinton because "she was his Bobby Kennedy, his hatchet
man, she was the one who could handle the nasty situations, and
who actually seemed to get a real kick out of charging into the
fray."[726]

If it weren't for Hillary the Fixer, Bill would probably still be back in Arkansas working as a hack at some boring bureaucratic job eating watermelon and paying child support to three different women. But Hillary was his driver; the one who lit a fire under his feet each day. "It was Hillary who seemed to supply most of the energy. When Hillary was in residence at the White House, she would talk to Bill in the evening and get him pumped up for the next day's fight. When she was away, his attention tended to wander."[727]

In essence, Billary was actually Hillary, with Bill filling the role of figurehead and mouthpiece. But it was his wife who was pulling the strings behind-the-scenes (as well as right out in front). She kept their train on a track which had already been mapped out for them. Here is how a former campaign aide described the dynamics. "She *is* his closest advisor. She's terribly well organized and always pushes him to more decisive action. Part of his deliberate process is to keep everything open as long as he can. Everyone realizes they have to keep Hillary informed and posted, and they do that. If they don't, he'll always ask for her opinion anyway. It's not that she forces her way into the process. He invites her into the process."[728]

A close friend continues this thought of Hillary being Bill's right-hand man. "They probably have one of the most multidimensional marriages I know because they turn to each other for virtually everything ... they don't do anything with each other without tremendous emotion behind it. They scream and yell at each other ... It's a very taxing relationship because it's so enmeshed and emotional."[729]

This intense emotion often led to intimidation and fear, particularly on Bill's behalf in regard to his wife. A prime example of how the president quivered in the presence of Hillary is seen in this story about health care. As most people know, this issue became one of the huge disasters of the Clinton presidency, with Hillary taking most of the blame because it was her pet project. Bill realized what an albatross it had become, and most certainly wanted to distance himself from it. Hillary had blown it, but he didn't want *her* to know it. Joe Klein lays it all out.

> **At the end of the conversation in which the
> President and I discussed the great health care
> disaster, Mrs. Clinton suddenly appeared and
> asked me, with a smile, how she had fared. "He
> ripped you up," I told her, also with a smile.**
>
> **The President fairly leaped from his chair,
> crossed the room, put his arm around Mrs. Clin-
> ton, and kissed her several times on the fore-
> head. "I told him," he said, hugging her tight,
> "that health care was all my fault."[730]**

Imagine, the President of the United States – supposedly the
most powerful man on earth – sniveling at his wife's feet like a
pusillanimous jellyfish. Hillary was the iron lady; a dominatrix
who cracked her whip and brought Bill to his knees. Lieutenant
Colonel Patterson describes this incident when he was in an elevator with the Clintons, two secret service agents, and a doctor.
"Every vulgar word you've ever heard poured from her mouth:
'G**damnit,' 'you bastard,' 'it's your f***ing fault.' On and on and
on. What grabbed my attention was not so much that she was
saying these things but the way the president reacted. He looked
like a beaten puppy. He put his hand down and didn't try to fight
back. He said, 'Yes, I understand. Yes, dear, I know.' The rest of
us weren't supposed to make eye contact anyway ... I witnessed
several incidents like this; and while I got used to Hillary's wrath,
her ability to turn it on and off amazed me."[731] State Trooper Larry
Gleghorn, who served on the Clinton's security detail, offered
similar words about Hillary's combative personality. "She was a
bitch day in and day out. She always screamed we were taking
the wrong route when we drove her to an event. She was a die-
hard anti-smoker and most of us smoked. She hated it if we wore
cowboy boots with our uniforms. It made her furious. On official
trips, you'd go to their rooms and tell her, 'We need to leave in fif-

teen minutes,' and she'd snap, 'We know it.' Then they'd be late and she'd give us a good cussing. The troopers mocked Bill's dependence on Hillary and his evident inability to stand up to her ... I think he feared her. He was always telling me that she was smarter than he was."[732]

Billary wasn't founded in love; it was based on good old-fashioned fear-mongering. It almost appeared as if Bill was nothing more than a Silly Putty bumpkin in his spouse's tight-fisted grip. Even things Bill didn't seem capable of comprehending, Hillary was apparently on top of. "He took her opinions about people very seriously. Journalist John Brummet, a political columnist and author of *High Wire*, recalled one instance when Bill was governor. 'We were talking about a female journalist who'd really been tough on him. And he said Hillary had told him never to be alone with her because what she really wanted was to be with him, or to compromise him in some way.' That had never occurred to me, or to him. But he said Hillary knows this kind of thing. That's largely the dynamic of the relationship – almost a good-cop bad-cop marriage."[733]

Hillary was the hard-edged, suspicious, keenly aware, always *on* half of the relationship; leading her babe in the woods naïve husband through the slings and arrows of their political minefield. It's peculiar, because Bill was raised around mobsters and con-men in Little Rock. You'd think his radar would be more fine-tuned; yet Hillary was assigned as his handler. She had the laser eye, misanthropic paranoia, and tough-as-nails perception that he didn't adequately possess.

And when they needed to *flip* an enemy or badger an opponent, Hillary could just as easily turn on the charm and use her feminine wiles to accomplish the task.

After Bill was elected governor of Arkansas in 1978, he lost his 1980 campaign. The blow was devastating, so the duo reassessed every angle for their 1982 race, with Hillary ultimately being the one to save the day.

As the 1982 election neared, it was time for some fine-tuning. Bill, Hillary, and their consultants had spent weeks analyzing every barrier to success, and [they] came up with a big one: the conservative managing editor of the *Arkansas Democrat*, John Robert Starr.

Starr had been on Bill from the beginning, like white on rice. [Ernie] Dumas remembered getting a call from Betsey Wright, early in the 1982 campaign. Bill, she said, was worried about Starr – how could he run, how could he serve, if the conservative *Arkansas Democrat*, a statewide newspaper, was going to continue to harass him nonstop?

"It was true, too," said Dumas [a longtime political reporter]. "Everybody had been savaged, all his aides, there'd been cartoons drawn about them, editorials, the whole resources of the paper were turned against him. Bill said, 'How can I ask anybody to serve in my administration if we're going to be hammered like that?' Was it possible to neutralize the *Democrat*? And they'd figured out it was Starr, he dominated the paper, everybody imitated Starr, all the headline writers and commentators took their cue from Starr."

So the obvious answer had to be – fix Starr.

Dumas thinks Hillary was probably the one who figured out how to do it.[734]

And just like that, within weeks, "He [Starr] came totally around, and the paper really was neutralized. There was no more harassment."[735] How did Hillary do it? Earlier we mentioned her 'feminine wiles,' but let us clarify, for Hillary wasn't especially known for her velvet touch. When Hillary walked into the editor's office that day, let's just say she had a little *muscle* behind her. Here's how the conversation *may* have gone:

> **John, there are some powerful people who have a vested interest in Bill Clinton becoming governor again. Sure, they let him get bounced after one term to teach him a lesson ... and I must say; we've learned our lessons the hard way. But John, your newspaper is putting a real crimp in our plans with its never ending negative stories; and in all honesty, it's making certain people very upset. I hate to drop names, but how about Stephens Inc., Don Tyson, Wal-Mart, Senator Fulbright, the Rockefellers, and the Rose Law Firm. If you don't believe me, you can pick up the phone and call them yourself. They all have a stake in Bill's success, and if you don't start playing ball, they're intent on leveraging you out of business by making sure that a significant portion of your advertising dollars are withheld. And John, we all know a newspaper can't stay afloat without ad money. It's been done to other newspapers and magazines in the past, and it can happen again. So, John, whatta ya say?**

If you're not convinced, an Arkansas insider explains how high-rollers manipulated the press. "I knew Clinton controlled the local media. Why? Because it takes advertising revenue to run a paper. Clinton's people, the Stephens, Tyson, and others, owned the businesses that did 80 percent of the adverting. So with that in their favor, they were able to muscle the local media into not touching this stuff."[736] I'll bet John Starr was fuming, but just like that he did a dramatic turnabout, and soon his paper was firmly behind Arkansas' native son, Bill Clinton. It's called economic blackmail, and the public would never have known a thing about it. Plus, who better to be the hit-man than Hillary? She knew how the game was played, and she wasn't afraid to crawl into the mud and bring the hammer down.

Hillary's presence was so strong that she even set the stage for the mood of an entire room. A member of Bill Clinton's secret service detail recounted the difference in atmosphere with and without Hillary. "The president's mood greatly depended on the presence or absence of Hillary. When she wasn't around, he had more fun. He played golf and played cards ... He'd stay up to all hours of the night smoking cigars and talking to anyone who'd listen. When she was along, he toed the line. He was on time and he'd go to bed. He feared her, it seemed."[737]

This same individual continued, noting the extreme differences in setting when Bill was present, or when Hillary was away. "Events and trips without her were akin to a frat house. It was hard to know which was better – the Nazi-like edge that emerged when she was around or the pseudo-Animal House atmosphere that emerged when she wasn't."[738]

Yes, Hillary was the taskmaster, the tyrant who could – potentially – reduce her husband to the most infantile of states. What follows is without doubt the most striking illustration of BILLARY at its most peculiar, bizarre, and downright creepy. It is an image presented by none other than George Stephanopoulos – a Clinton insider – and if true, it will permanently and forever change the way we view this off-their-rocker couple. Hillary as not only Bill's guide, protector, and slayer of demons ... but Hillary Clinton was Bill's very own mother-figure.

After more than twenty-five years of marriage, Hillary surely knows Bill Clinton better than anyone else. David Maraniss, Roger Morris, Dick Morris, R. Emerett Tyrrell and others have tried to unlock the mysteries of the forty-second president. Now the former FLOTUS [First Lady of

> the United States] will have her turn. She can ex-
> plain, for example, whether, as George Stepha-
> nopoulos described, she would feed Bill lemon
> slices dipped in honey, and he would call to her
> in baby talk, "Hee-a-ree, Hee-a-ary."[739]

Bill Clinton, former President of the United States, suckling at the bosom of Mama Hillary. Lord help us all.

DIVORCE?

We've seen Bill and Hillary at their most cruel, vicious, hurtful, vindictive, and strange. We've even seen them morph into some type of grotesque caricature known as Billary. But was it ever possible that the star couple could be no more? Yes, the Clintons discussed and contemplated the Big D on numerous occasions. "After several terms as governor, Bill's humiliation of Hillary was so public and so flagrant that they almost divorced."[740]

Veteran Clinton staff member Betsey Wright recalled an especially turbulent time in the couple's marriage. "She concluded that he [Bill Clinton] was going through a severe midlife crisis. She said that he was having a serious affair with another woman, and was not even being discreet about it. Everyone knew, she said. She knew, the troopers knew, Hillary knew. There were great screaming matches at the mansion. Once a counselor was called out to mediate. Clinton was broaching the subject of divorce in conversations with some of his colleagues."[741]

It seems that after Bill lost his first gubernatorial reelection race, something serious happened. Rudy Moore wrote in 1992, "As I look back, it is more evident that Bill Clinton was not the same person psychologically in 1980 that he had been before or that he has been since. It must have been something personal, perhaps in his relationship with Hillary, but he was ambivalent and preoccupied."[742]

John Robert Starr, editor of the *Arkansas Democrat*, is more specific. "My theory on Bill Clinton's love affair is that in the term when he was out of office, or certainly when he was defeated, he thought he had fallen in love. Not with Gennifer Flowers. And I don't think it was a casual, one-night deal."[743] Starr continued, "I have concluded that he fell in love with somebody, it was relatively brief, and because he referred to it in the singular when he offered to tell me about 'it,' I don't think there was more than one."[744]

Around this same time, it was Hillary's turn to contemplate this issue, especially in light of Bill flaunting his indiscretions. "During the summer of 1985, Hillary confided to friends outside of Arkansas that she'd had enough and was about to file for divorce."[745]

Her decision followed a particularly humiliating episode with Bill's longtime mistress. "[Gennifer] Flowers and Hillary crossed paths at a fundraiser held in the Capitol Club. This time, Hillary tried to draw her husband away from a conversation with Flowers, saying, 'Bill, I'm going over to the bar for a drink. Will you come with me?' Even this modest power play failed. Clinton brushed her off, saying, 'You go ahead,' while Flowers crowed silently. 'It was a showdown,' she [Flowers] had observed, 'and I had won.'"[746]

A few years later, after Clinton's first aborted run for the presidency due to questions that would have to be answered about his adultery (on the heels of Gary Hart's crash & burn), the topic of divorce arose again. "By 1989, the Clintons were considering divorce. David Maraniss describes how 'Clinton was broaching the subject of divorce in conversations with some of his colleagues, governors from other states who had survived the collapse of their marriages.'"[747] Another source confirms that at this time in the late 1980s, "both Clintons did some private muttering to friends about the possibility of divorce."[748]

"Visibly upset, even humiliated, by her husband's decision not to run; Hillary was especially distraught about the painful reason for it. Her friends say Hillary questioned many of the decisions she had made in her life and seriously considered divorcing Bill in the wake of his announcement. In conversations with him and her ... this was the first time she acknowledged knowing of his extramarital affairs."[749]

This account is not entirely accurate, for as we'll see later, it was actually Hillary's decision not to have Bill run in 1988. With Gary Hart's promiscuity so fresh in reporter's minds, Clinton's entrance into the race would have been disastrous, and Hillary knew it. Granted, in private she was distraught over not knowing if Bill would ever get his act together, but in public she had to yet again play the victimized wife. For this reason, I'm sure, she fretted about the decisions she'd made in life (i.e. signing on the dotted line to a prearranged marriage).

Then, of course, the Monica Lewinsky media circus was unleashed with a potpourri of details regarding Bill's torrid affair with a young intern. Hillary was yet again backed up against the wall – at least according to her very well-oiled propaganda machine. In reality, Hillary was well aware of Monica before the press ever broke this story. What really torqued her jets was the disclosure of Bill's sickeningly brutal rape of Juanita Broaddrick, especially when NBC's *Dateline* broadcast an interview with Ms. Broaddrick on February 24, 1999. This information was truly damning, and not something she could so easily squirm out of. Hillary "could no longer dismiss Broaddrick as just another disgruntled groupie or a tool of her husband's right-wing enemies."[750] Even the tepid National Organization of Women was turning up the heat against pro-abortion Bill Clinton. "A statement by Patricia Ireland of NOW put the White House on notice that the feminists would no longer tolerate such antics, and Hillary couldn't defend Bill Clinton without alienating the very friends whose support she was counting on in her future endeavors."[751]

The result? "She and Bill were once again discussing divorce, and as their political interests diverged, it became more difficult to imagine how they could find a common ground to repair their battered partnership."[752]

But they did. It all boiled down to one thing: their pact ... their Devil's deal ... their political marriage. Yes, both participants in this arrangement wanted out, "but in the end, nothing happened. The basic deal remained intact. The other women remained, on the outside, an enormous distraction and the source of great pain and immense risk, but ultimately used and discarded."[753] But why would Hillary stay? Bill didn't cheat on her dozens of times, or hundreds of times; but thousands! Nobody in their right mind would consider Hillary a pushover or a doormat; just the contrary. She honored their 'pact' for one reason: "only by staying married could Hillary have a husband who could win power and would be willing to fully share power with her."[754]

Imagine, if you will, the humiliation involved in staying true to this sordid little deal. Hillary has a healthy ego, and certainly a fair share of pride. But *everyone* knows she's a cover-up artist for a cheating louse and that their marriage is a sham. For Hillary "to admit otherwise would raise the question of why a woman who had by that time become a feminist icon had put up with so much humiliation."[755] Worse, Bill's cheating went on for what seemed like forever. By the late 1980s, "Clinton took less trouble than ever to hide the evidence of his affairs. He was already the inspiration for 'governor jokes,' which were understood to refer to Clinton even when told in neighboring states."[756]

Psychologically, even with a tough bird like Hillary, the pressures of such a devious arrangement must have taken an enormous toll. "The pain felt by the First Lady undoubtedly goes much deeper than that experienced on a public or political level."[757]

What remains is a woman *scarred*, and regardless of how competent or tough Mrs. Clinton is, one has to question her judgment. A fitting example of how deeply these infidelities can cut is found in the following passage.

There can be no doubt, of course, that Hillary knew that something had gone on be-

tween Lewinsky and her husband. In addition
to a copy of *Leaves of Grass,* one of the gifts he
was said to have given Monica was a brooch –
and Clinton's interest in collecting antique
brooches, some of which ended up as gifts to
various women, was well known in Arkansas.
Monica, in turn, knew Clinton well enough to
be aware of his penchant for frog-related knick-
knacks. These gifts told the story of a relationship that had been affectionate at times, even if
one-sided. For a woman who still cared about
her husband, this had to be far more hurtful
than any allegation of a quick grope or sexual
encounter.[758]

By the way, Bill Clinton was said to have given Hillary a copy
of *Leaves of Grass* on their second date, too. Not only does he
stick the sword in, but he gives it a good twist to really let Hillary
know what a cruel man he is. Even then, "Hillary could not
admit that she had known about Bill's escapades with Monica
Lewinsky. That would have only confirmed people's worst suspicions that her marriage was a political arrangement rather than
a true love match."[759]

Even the lesbian aspect of Hillary's life was aired yet again
during the Monica Lewinsky debacle. "In an appearance on
KABC radio in Los Angeles, [Dick] Morris volunteered his opinion
that Hillary was a lesbian, or at least frigid – a suggestion that
blamed her for a pattern of behavior that Clinton had followed
even before his marriage."[760]

These embarrassments were like a barrage of punches in a
prize fight – heavy, damaging, and non-stop – for decades.
Hillary was scorned, beaten-down by adultery, publicly humiliated, and laughed at. She became not a symbol of feminine
strength and pride, but an object of denigration and derision ...
what a woman *shouldn't* become – a doormat that is stepped on

and tolerates abuse for the mere sake of political advancement.

Yet not once has she pulled the curtain back to reveal the illusion. She's the ultimate magician, never letting the audience in on what the trick really is. Why? It's not only due to her pact with Bill; Hillary also fears being thrown in prison or even killed if she lets the cat out of its bag. Her very life depends on it. The Clinton Body Count is a reality, and Hillary darn well knows it! She's seen others (many others) take the fall (six feet under), and there's no doubt whatsoever that their overlords would have no compunction whatsoever arranging an accident for her, like Princess Diana or John F. Kennedy Jr. Or, it could be an inadvertent *suicide* like poor Vince Foster. I can see the headlines now: *Hillary can't handle pressure, offs herself.*

Hillary's words to political strategist Betsey Wright are still haunting to this day. "She was unwilling to abandon her partnership. She had invested too much in Bill Clinton."[761] Some people – like the Arkansas state troopers charged with protecting the first couple – sneer that this 'investment' is so twisted that "she wouldn't divorce him if that sumbitch did it right in front of her. She wants the power."[762] Put even more crassly, "Hillary has stayed in the marriage out of pure self-interest – for the power and status. In other words, she's a traditional wife who ignores her husband's catting around because he's a good provider. Bill's more than a paycheck – he's her ticket to political power. Either way, Hillary is no model for modern womanhood. She's either a dupe who loves her man so much she's willing to sacrifice all dignity for his sake, or a Machiavellian who craves power so much she'll do anything to keep it."[763]

Similar to how we proved earlier that Hillary was not a radical; likewise she's also not a feminist. Quickly, the myth is being eroded, and what we find beneath all of Hillary's fabrications is the hollow shell of a vulgar opportunist with no principles whatsoever. Love, gender, faith, the sanctity of marriage, and doing the right thing obviously don't matter to her, for "time and again through more than two decades of married life, Bill Clinton has made up for his private failings by awarding Hillary with public power."[764]

Similarly, Bill's viability depends upon Hillary keeping up the charade. "If Hillary left him, he would be dead meat, just like he would have been dead meat ... if Hillary hadn't stood by him."[765] That means no more glitzy Clinton Foundation, no more lucrative speaking engagements, seats on powerful corporate boards, status within the Democratic Party, and especially no more cherished Clinton legacy (which, inexplicably, some people still buy).

When voters examine the world and throw their hands up in desperation because our political leadership seems so hopeless, the Clintons are one of the primary examples of why we're in such a mess. So, to answer the question of whether or not they'd ever get divorced, "As long as the plan was alive, divorce was, and would continue to be, unthinkable."[766]

At this stage of their lives, a split would only occur if the plan expired; and even then it's doubtful – for certain obvious reasons. The Clintons are magicians ... illusionists ... and they can't let their *Wizard of Oz*-type secrets be revealed. In addition, who else *could* they be with on a functional basis? They've reached the major leagues of symbiotic sickness. Everyone else pales in comparison. They haven't scaled the mountains, soared to the heights, or plummeted to their depths. They'd be *bored* with anyone else. The Clintons feed off each other. They're vampires, and the blood of their sickness is each other's evil ... an evil that resulted from making that pact in 1975 when their souls were forever sold. It was – and is – a marriage made in hell, and the by-product of such a union is what we've seen in their lives and how they treat each other. Hatred: it's the only thing that lasts forever; and a sentence that only the most heartless and depraved can endure.

Being married to Bill has aged Hillary "like a president." (Getty Images)

CHAPTER FIVE

Bill & Hillary's Sordid Sex Lives

RAPIST AND REPEAT OFFENDER

In the opening pages of this book, Bill Clinton's violent rape of Juanita Broaddrick was recounted in all its grisly detail, along with Hillary Rodham's extensive efforts to cover up the entire matter. As veteran reporter Lisa Myers stated on NBC's *Dateline* in 1999, "The explosive new allegation tonight is that President Clinton sexually assaulted a woman twenty years ago in Arkansas. It involves an alleged encounter at this Little Rock hotel in the late 1970s between the attorney general Bill Clinton and campaign worker Juanita Broaddrick. In court documents today, Paula Jones' lawyers claim Clinton quote 'forcibly raped and sexually assaulted' Broaddrick, then quote 'bribed and intimidated' her to remain silent."[767]

But this tragic incident is only one in a vast repertoire of depravities that constitute Bill and Hillary's sordid sex lives. In the following sections you'll read more about rape, violence toward women, cross-dressing, drug use, homosexuality, abortion, perversion, and rampant adultery.

But for now, to show just how extensive Bill Clinton's womanizing was, let's name some names that have been linked to this man.

• Judy Gibbs, a model and call girl who appeared in *Penthouse* magazine [and] runs a popular house of prostitution in Fordyce with her sister Sharon.[768]

• Marilyn Jo Jenkins, "an executive with the Arkansas utilities company Entergy [who is] connected by marriage to one of Arkansas's wealthiest families."[769] During an especially low point

in the Clinton marriage, "the heartsick governor confided that he
loved both Hillary and Marilyn Jo. Corporal [Danny] Ferguson
later testified that Clinton had told him, 'It's tough to be in love
with both your wife and another woman.'"[770]

• Deborah Mathis, a female broadcaster who was later named
as a Clinton paramour in a lawsuit filed by a state employee,[771]
and who later originated the label "Hillary the Hun" in a feature
story she wrote about his wife.[772]

• Marsha Scott, the daughter of Miss Arkansas 1945 and Clyde
"Smackover" Scott who played football for the Philadelphia Ea-
gles.[773] She talked openly about her affair with Bill Clinton and
bragged about her comforting labors on the night of [Vince] Foster's death. "I spent the night in his bed. I had my head on his
lap, and we reminisced all night long."[774]

• Catherine Cornelius, an attractive blonde in her early twen-
ties who had handled the Clinton campaign account for her travel
agency.[775] She was only nineteen when she joined the White
House travel office, [and] not only accompanied the President
when he traveled without Hillary but had unusual access to the
Oval Office.[776]

• Debra Schiff, formerly a flight attendant on Clinton's campaign plane [who] later turned up as a West Wing receptionist.[777]

• Robin Dickey, a former administrator of the Governor's
Mansion in Little Rock and the mother of Helen Dickey, who was
Chelsea's live-in nanny.[778]

• Regina Hopper Blakely, Miss Arkansas 1983.

• Lencola Sullivan, a former Black Miss Arkansas who had
won the swimsuit competition in Atlantic City and came home to
work as a reporter for KARK-TV.[779]

• Beth Coulson, who was appointed by Clinton to the state
court of appeals.[780]

• Sally Miller Perdue, a former Miss Arkansas whose alleged
affair was kept under wraps until July 17, 1992, halfway into the
presidential campaign. She stated, "Bill's driver would drop him
off in a park near my condominium and he'd sneak through the

back patio to have it with me for an hour, two hours, three hours."[781]

- Elizabeth Ward, a former beauty queen and Miss Arkansas who was also crowned the winner of the Miss America pageant in 1981.[782]

- Susie Whiteacre, the governor's press secretary.[783]

- Sheila Lawrence, the wife of a major Democratic fund-raiser.[784]

- Susan McDougal, wife of the Clintons' Whitewater partner. Jim McDougal explains how he eavesdropped on one of their phone calls. "Susan and Bill Clinton were talking [on the telephone], an intimate conversation filled with giggles and sexual innuendo. Dispirited, I quietly hung up. I was left with no doubt that Susan and Bill were carrying on an affair."[785] When confronted, his wife confirmed these suspicions. "Rather than lying clumsily, Susan acknowledged her relationship with Bill."[786]

- Dolly Kyle Browning, a purported high school girlfriend who claimed to have an extended affair with Clinton.[787] Browning assessed Bill's lack of regard for his wife. "He didn't talk about Hillary. She was not an issue when it came to dealing with me, or any of the other women for that matter. She is not a factor – not a factor in his emotional life, anyway. They made a deal a long time ago. That's pretty obvious. She does not figure in his thinking *at all*."[788] Bill's icy lack of regard for Hillary during this time was confirmed by others. One campaign volunteer said, "I never heard him refer to Hillary as his fiancée. Not once. In those instances when she accompanied him to public events, she was shoved into the background and basically forgotten."[789]

- Cyd Dunlap, who claimed Clinton propositioned her in 1986.[790]

- Susan Carpenter-McMillan, who confirmed Paula Jones' claims about Clinton's irregular penis ("Well, you know, his penis isn't necessarily straight").[791]

- Sherry Wright, owner of the Something Special Boutique.[792]

• Beverly Lindsey, an Arkansas Democrat and state coordinator of Walter Mondale's 1984 campaign.[793]

• Susan Coleman, who was completing her sophomore year at the University of Arkansas when Bill Clinton taught a criminal law class on the Fayetteville campus.[794]

• Ghislaine Maxwell, daughter of the late British Press lord Robert Maxwell.[795]

• Charlotte Dawson, statuesque blond host of Australian television's top-rated *How's Life*.[796]

• Saffron Burrows, socialist, feminist, and former model who was married to fifty-three year old film director Mike Figgis [and who was] an outspoken bisexual who went on the record years before she met Bill saying she had a crush on Hillary.[797]

• Patricia Duff, ex-wife of billionaire Revlon chairman Ron Perelman.[798]

• Lisa Belzberg, thirty-eight year old wife of Seagram's heir Matthew Bronfman.[799]

• Kristy Zercher, a former flight attendant on the Clinton 1992 campaign plane.[800]

The list goes on – with many of Bill's dalliances being nothing more than anonymous one-night stands – while other names will be mentioned throughout this chapter. Also, remember what I wrote earlier: Bill Clinton hasn't cheated on Hillary dozens of times, or even hundreds of times; but *thousands* of times. Often, Clinton used those in his own security detail to procure women for him. In an article for the *American Spectator* entitled *His Cheatin' Heart*, David Brock tells how "nearly a dozen Arkansas state police troopers were used as *pimps in uniform* to feed their boss's insatiable sexual appetite."[801] One trooper, L.D. Brown, "alleged that he solicited over a hundred women on behalf of Clinton."[802] This misuse of state resources was so brazen that Clinton "used the troopers to transport him to assignations, procure women Clinton had spotted or get their phone numbers for him, deliver gifts to the women, guard him while he was having sex with them, and cover up his activities from his wife."[803] To insure their silence, "Clinton offered the troopers jobs in exchange for re-fusing to cooperate with the reporters nosing around about his past sex life."[804] One of them, "Buddy Young, once Clinton's chief bodyguard, [was] ensconced in a comfortable FEMA office,"[805] a job which paid him, "$92,300-a-year."[806] The frat boy atmosphere was so pronounced that Party Boy Bill would even share his booty. "When there were extra girls Clinton was known to invite his security people to party with them."[807]

Clinton's unbridled philandering reached such out-of-control proportions that prior to one gubernatorial campaign, "two of his closest backers met with him privately at the mansion ... when Hillary was gone. They carried a list of some of the women most widely known to have been involved with the governor since the late 1970s. It was a precursor of what would be called inside the 1992 campaign the 'Doomsday List,' a later and longer enumeration of Clinton's affairs or other sexual episodes, with each woman assessed and action recommended according to the potential for exposure or betrayal."[808]

The list was so long that "he didn't even recognize some of the names of women we knew he'd done, said one advisor. He just got red in the face and waved his arms and said, get this G**damned paper out of here. Hillary doesn't know any of this. What good is this G**damned paper?"[809]

Of course Hillary *did* know plenty about these affairs, but Bill Clinton liked to play a pathetic little game of denial when his misdeeds were exposed. Worse, all of these flings weren't of the sweet and gentle variety. Similar to Juanita Broaddrick, Bill Clinton raped, bit, and assaulted other women too. Before recounting these incidents, however, let's examine Mr. Clinton's attitude toward women. Like Hillary, he portrays himself as a champion of women's rights and a supporter of their cause. In reality, women to Bill Clinton were (and still are) nothing more than sex objects to be used for his own personal gratification.

Those assigned to protect Bill Clinton during his tenure as Arkansas governor witnessed his demeanor firsthand. "The re-

peated testimony of the troopers would show the undisguised
Clinton rating women as objects, 'ripe peaches,' as he called them,
'purely to be graded, purely to be chased, dominated, conquered,'
according to L.D. Brown. The governor had been predatory even
toward one of the trooper's wives and toward another's mother-
in-law."[810]

"One former agent interviewed by *Capitol Hill Blue's* Doug
Thompson complained that Clinton would greet female voters
with a display of boyish charm, then turn away and speculate
under his breath about whether they gave good [oral sex] or
not."[811] Likewise, "[L.D.] Brown said he and Clinton frequently
rated women on a ten-point grading scale."[812]

Even cruder was Clinton's reaction when a woman seemingly
betrayed him or a fellow philandering candidate. After Gennifer
Flowers went public with their twelve-year affair, Clinton spat,
"What does that whore think she's doing to me? ... She's a f***ing
slut."[813] When Susan McDougal of Whitewater fame crossed him,
Clinton sneered, "Have you heard what that f***ing whore Susan
has done?"[814] In the same vein, "Bill Clinton displayed his famed
sensitivity to others' pain as he discussed Ted Kennedy's 'accident' at Chappaquiddick – He couldn't get a whore across a
bridge."[815]

Even Clinton's favorite choice of gratification – the oral sex –
was based on a thought process so twisted that it defies logic.
"Clinton told him [trooper Patterson] how, after having researched
the subject in the Bible, he had concluded that oral sex did not
constitute adultery."[816] Further, "Clinton had insisted that oral
sex was the safest sex because stomach acids would neutralize
the AIDS virus."[817] Clinton even bragged to another trooper that
Gennifer Flowers was proficient at oral sex[818]

Yes, this is the same Bill Clinton that's a darling of the hypocritical National Organization of Women ... the same Bill Clinton
who boasted about a pickup truck he used to drive in the 1970s.
"It was a real sort of Southern deal. I had Astroturf in the back.
You don't want to know why, but I did."[819]

Should we be surprised? Bill Clinton is a rapist, and Juanita Broaddrick is not the only example of his sickness. Elizabeth Ward Gracen, a former Miss Arkansas, was another one of his victims. "According to Gracen, several days later [after they had met] they had sex in her apartment – rough sex, during which he bit down on her lip and caused it to bleed. The painful encounter, so reminiscent of his attack on Juanita Broaddrick, would leave Gracen feeling frightened and confused."[820]

Others confirmed her story. "Judy Ann Stokes stated under oath at her own deposition that when Gracen had privately confided in Stokes about the encounter with Clinton, Gracen had been 'tearful,' and had said the sexual encounter was not something she had wanted."[821] When Stokes was asked if she thought Clinton raped Ms. Gracen, she replied, 'Absolutely. He forced her to have sex. What do you call that?' Stokes was totally convinced it was rape."[822] *Newsweek's* Michael Isikoff tells virtually the same story. "Clinton flirted with her – then invited her to the apartment of one of his friends at the Quapaw Towers [coincidentally, where Gennifer Flowers also lived]. They had sex that night. It was rough sex. Clinton got so carried away that he bit her lip."[823]

Although Gracen admitted that the sex was initially consensual, it developed into something far more sadistic than she had originally bargained for. "I think Clinton is a very dangerous, manipulative man, and I've had to be very careful."[824]

But Juanita Broaddrick and Elizabeth Ward Gracen aren't the only two that lip-biter and rapist Bill Clinton has capitalized upon. "A young woman lawyer in Little Rock claimed that she was accosted by Clinton while he was attorney general and that when she recoiled, he forced himself on her, biting and bruising her."[825] Similar to Juanita Broaddrick, Clinton was yet again confronted by his victim's husband, this time at the 1980 Democratic Convention. "'If you ever approach her,' he told the governor, 'I'll kill you.'"[826] Thus, "both Broaddrick and the young lawyer in Little Rock had described biting during forced encounters."[827]

Commenting on Clinton's appalling history of sexual violence toward women, Cynthia Alksne, a sex crimes prosecutor, *Wall Street Journal* columnist, and former host of MSNBC's *Equal Time*, took the gloves off. "When I was a sex-crimes prosecutor, rapists often got at least eight years of public housing – in jail, not the White House. If these allegations are true, jail is where Mr. Clinton belongs."[828]

There are yet more accounts of similar deviant behavior. An acquaintance of Bill Clinton was invited to the White House in 1996. "When she entered the Oval Office, Clinton immediately ushered her into his hideaway annex – the same place he took Lewinsky for their romps together. The two old friends chatted at first. But then, Clinton started getting physical, trying to kiss her, touching her breasts. She was stunned. She had no idea how to respond. I've never had a man take advantage of me like that, she confided ... finally, he gave up and turned away. 'What happened next?' Michael Isikoff asked. 'I think he finished the job himself.'"[829]

As you'll see later, shades of Kathleen Willey are unmistakable, as is the *modus operandi* of this sexual predator. "Bill Clinton had, like John F. Kennedy, become an aggressive, out-of-control womanizer, someone who aspired to be both married and enjoy his charm and sexual magnetism by indulging in "quickies" in a backseat, a basement, or a room off the Oval Office. [But] Bill Clinton went beyond the wildest rumors of JFK – to being credibly accused of sexual harassment and forcible rape."[830]

What follows is another incident relayed by Lieutenant Colonel Robert "Buzz" Patterson.

> **I received a phone call in my office from Lieutenant Colonel Mark Donnelly, presidential pilot and commander of the Presidential Pilot Office.**
>
> **"Buzz, we have a problem," he said grimly. "One of my female stewards claims she was approached and touched inappropriately by Pres-**

ident Clinton and she's upset." ...

"Where did this happen, Mark?"

"In one of the galleys on Air Force One on a recent trip. Apparently, he cornered her."

...

Two weeks later, Kris [Engskov, the president's personal aide] walked into the compartment where I was seated on Air Force One. He said quietly, "We got them together. The president apologized. She seems fine with it." ...

I brooded over the fact that if our commander-in-chief had been actually serving in the armed forces, he would have been jailed.[831]

SEX GALORE!

A number of Clinton apologists over the years have protested, "Why is everyone so concerned with Bill and Hillary's sex lives? That's personal. Let's worry about *real* issues." My response: rape, especially for repeat offenders, *is* a serious issue, especially when a spouse uses her political influence to help cover it up. Likewise, rampant adultery and a sham political marriage are equally important topics which should be laid on the table for all to see. The only reason why those who help operate the Clinton spin machine want to divert attention away from Bill and Hillary's sex lives is because it shows – in graphic detail – what truly depraved and immoral people they are (not to mention the embarrassment factor). On top of that, it illustrates how unfit they are to serve the public, for if these two are so debased and have such little regard for vows they made to each other, how could they possibly give a hoot about any promises made to us – the citizens and taxpayers? Bill and Hillary's sex lives *are* an issue precisely because it is a reflection of far worse crimes which they have committed, all of which you'll learn about in part two of this book series.

What follows below is a sampling of Bill Clinton's sordid fornication practices. By the time you've finished it, be ready to take a shower.

• Sally Perdue tells of a "four-month affair with Clinton that began not long after he returned to power in 1983, [with] reports fixed on her colorful details of the governor parading around her apartment in one of her black negligees playing his saxophone, using cocaine."[832] "According to Purdue ... state troopers regularly brought Clinton to her condominium at Andover Square. They'd pull up in a wooded area about thirty-feet from the house and wait there. Clinton would flick a patio light to summon the police car when he was leaving. Purdue revealed Clinton's typical routine: he'd drink a few Budweiser beers, and then Clinton would begin playing the clown. She described Clinton as a showman and a brilliant actor ... I still have this picture of him wearing my black nightgown, playing the sax badly; this guy tiptoeing across the park and getting caught on the fence. How do you expect me to take him seriously?"[833] To keep these details hush hush, "She was promised a federal job if she remained silent about the affair. The offer was overheard by a witness, who also heard the accompanying threat that 'we can't guarantee what will happen to your pretty legs' if she declined the offer."[834] So, not only is Bill Clinton a closet transvestite, but then he sends his thugs to physically threaten those who pose a threat with regard to potentially disclosing his little secrets.

• The following FBI-Arkansas state police transcript reveals how convicted drug dealer Roger Clinton (Bill's brother) would take women over to the governor's mansion for all types of debauchery.

Rodney Myers: Hey, Rog, did you ever take women over to your brother's place to [have sex]?

Roger Clinton: Yeah. There was the mansion and the guest house. Oh, they love it. Just

> f***ing love it.   There's so [many available
> women] in this town. Too many [woman's sex
> organs] in this town.
>   Rodney Myers: Good Lord. That's a f***ing
> good life. Get over to the G**damn governor's
> mansion and f*** yourself to death.[835]

The Clinton boys seem to have a particular distaste for
women, with Bill calling them 'whores' and 'sluts' while Roger
refers to them using the derogatory term 'cunts'. These are our
sensitive males? Here is another account of the bacchanalia
which took place at the governor's mansion.

> Another source reported that Roger and
> his visitors had all-night [sex] sessions with
> alternate partners and X-rated cassettes run-
> ning on the TV all the while to keep them
> aroused and stimulated for non-stop sex.[836]

When asked if they were doing any drugs other than marijuana, Roger Clinton admitted to rampant cocaine use. "Like it
was going out of style. Snort, snort, snort – all night long!"[837]

> "Where were the state police? Didn't they
> do anything to stop the illegal behavior?"
> "Hah," laughed one insider. "The visitors
> were bringing broads for the cops."[838]

Lastly, if you think Bill and Hillary were unaware of these antics, don't be fooled. Visitor logs "show that Roger Clinton stayed
at the mansion or guest house no fewer than thirty-six times between February 7, 1983 and January 13, 1985."[839]
   • Then there is the troublesome case of Susan Coleman, a
"student in one of Bill Clinton's classes at the University of
Arkansas Law School who became pregnant and purportedly

committed suicide."[840] The following information is reported in
George Carpozi's *Clinton Confidential*.

> **Susan and her husband Dalton Coleman left
> Little Rock abruptly in the summer of 1976
> (shortly before Bill Clinton was elected State At-
> torney General) ... Bill Clinton by then had
> been married barely a year to Hillary Rodham.
> A short while later, Susan learned she was preg-
> nant. Coleman said the baby couldn't be his
> and left his wife ... On February 15, 1977, in the
> seventh month of her pregnancy, Susan Cole-
> man is purported to have put the muzzle of a
> shotgun into her mouth and pulled the trigger.
> Her life ended just five months after her
> twenty-sixth birthday.[841]**

The above information was contained in a letter which was
circulated to many news agencies, and the *CBS Evening News*
even did a segment on it. Correspondent Eric Engberg read the
letter, which included this poignant line, "Susan Coleman's suicide fifteen years ago followed a love affair with her law professor,
Bill Clinton, that left her pregnant."[842]

Finally, the letter concluded, "The affair had cost her [Susan
Coleman] her husband, her family, her self-respect. Her heart
was lost to the lover who rejected her and her baby. A mistress
with child wouldn't fit in with his political ambitions – and his
ambitions were large scale. His ambitions were of a national
scope. His name was Bill Clinton."[843]

Is this letter and scenario legitimate, or a cruel hoax? Please
reserve judgment until you read the chapter entitled "Clinton
Body Count." Also, during an investigation by former Arkansas
state employee Larry Nichols, "One woman Nichols did not identify but merely described as a member of Clinton's staff, also allegedly became pregnant and had an abortion as a result of an

affair with Bill Clinton."[844] As you'll see, Bill Clinton *never* wore a condom, and in the next section you'll learn how Gennifer Flowers also had to endure the trauma of aborting a child after becoming pregnant by Bill Clinton.

• Because Bill's philandering became so uncontrollable, he and Hillary visited a therapist. "The Methodist marriage counselor apparently worked wonders; Hillary emerged after several emotional sessions to proclaim that she and Bill had recommitted themselves to the marriage. She had no inkling that almost immediately Bill would be back on the phone to [Marilyn Jo] Jenkins, and over the course of just three months sneak her into the basement of the Governor's Mansion no fewer than four times."[845]

• "Jim McDougal [of Whitewater fame] was convinced his wife Susan was having an affair with Bill, and though she [initially] denied it, Bill confided to L.D. Brown that they were lovers."[846] At the time, Jim McDougal was Bill Clinton's business partner and one of his closest pals. With friends like Slick Willie, who needs enemies?

• McDougal's wife wasn't the only one Bill Clinton moved in on. "A young Governor Clinton had attended an engagement party for the nephew of a wealthy supporter. No sooner had he arrived than Bill took the shocked host aside and announced the twentyish bride-to-be 'hot.' That night, Bill seduced the young woman in front of her fiancé, broke up the engagement, and over the course of several months led her to believe he intended to divorce Hillary and marry her."[847] Hillary refused to do anything about it.

• After the disastrously embarrassing Monica Lewinsky affair, Bill Clinton still didn't change his tomcat ways. "According to one witness who declined to be identified, he [Clinton] even made a pass at an attractive woman during one of his public appearances, unfazed by the reactions of witnesses, who were gasping in amazement."[848]

• An account by Larry Nichols of Bill's modus operandi while governor: "Several times I saw him come out of the governor's mansion jogging. He'd go for about half a block and a state police car would be behind him. As soon as he was out of sight of the mansion, he'd get into the car to go to an apartment complex nearby. He'd be in there for about forty-five minutes, then come out, get into a police car, be dropped a block from the mansion, then run back in."[849]

• "Christine Zercher's encounter with the then-candidate Clinton was scary enough to her. In 1992, Zercher was a stewardess aboard Clinton's campaign plane, Longhorn One. By all accounts, a party atmosphere prevailed as Clinton continually flirted with the all-blonde flight attendant cadre. ... For forty-five minutes late one airborne night, Zercher sat frozen after Clinton awoke, plunked himself down next to her, and casually began caressing her breasts – as Mrs. Clinton slept all the while just feet away."[850] "Christy Zercher, a regular crew member, later told tales of Clinton's lewd behavior; he dipped his finger in his tea and sucked on it, mimicking oral sex, and invited her to join him in the lavatory."[851] Afraid that she would blow his cover, the Clintons retaliated. "Zercher's house was burglarized at two a.m. while she lay asleep in an upstairs bedroom. The thief left behind jewelry, money, and other valuables. Zercher later told the *Star* that the only items taken were her diary and most of the photographs she had from the days on the crew of Longhorn One."[852]

• "In 1984, [Trooper L.D.] Brown accompanied Clinton when he attended an Arkansas-SMU football game in Irving, Texas. After the game, Clinton went to a strip joint near the stadium and was shoving money in the dancers' G-strings. Brown also recalled another trip when he accompanied Clinton to a disco in Boca Raton, Florida. He solicited a girl for Clinton and watched from a distance of ninety feet as she engaged in sexual relations with Bill in a parked car."[853]

• Clinton got fellated in other places, too, like right in the driveway of the governor's mansion. A "woman drove up into the governor's mansion parking lot in a yellow and black Datsun or Nissan pickup truck and asked to see Clinton. The governor came out of the residence and climbed into the front seat of the truck which she parked in an area off the rear driveway. 'This time [Trooper Larry] Patterson said, with a gleam in his eye, he got an even clearer view of the sex act by aiming a remote-controlled video camera with a swivel base mounted on a thirty-foot pole in the back yard of the house right into the truck. The image was projected onto a twenty-seven-inch TV screen in the guard house. He was sitting on the passenger side and she was behind the wheel. 'I pointed the thing directly into the windshield and watched on the screen as the governor received oral sex,' Patterson said. 'As this act was occurring, Chelsea's babysitter at the time, Melissa Jolley, drove into the compound.'"[854]

• Speaking of Clinton's daughter Chelsea, even her elementary school wasn't off limits for daddy's sexual romps. "On the way to an evening reception for the Harrison County Chamber of Commerce at the Camelot Hotel, Clinton ordered Patterson to make a stop at Chelsea's elementary school. When they arrived, one of Clinton's girlfriends, a young woman who sold cosmetics in a Little Rock department store, was waiting. While [Trooper] Patterson guarded the entrance to the parking lot Clinton sat with the woman in her car and, according to the trooper, he saw the lady's head go into his lap."[855]

• How's this for class. Clinton was even chasing women at his own wedding! Ann Henry [wife of state senator Morris Henry] stated that "during the reception one of the guests came upon Bill making out with another woman in one of the bathrooms."[856] Another acquaintance added, "One woman – a member of the Fayetteville contingent who would remain a friend of the Clintons for decades – pushed open the bathroom door and was totally floored by what she saw: Bill passionately kissing a young woman. He was fondling her breasts. I was so shocked I just closed the door quickly and quietly."[857]

• Then, while he was President of the United States, Bill Clinton was "a frequent late-night visitor to the Marriott Hotel in downtown Washington, which has an underground parking garage with an elevator that allows guests to go to their rooms without passing through the lobby."[858] Such a situation is a great cause for concern, because, according to FBI agent Gary Aldrich, "I have been informed by a well-placed White House source that there are times when the president, leader of the free world, is missing – that is, cannot be located by staff – for hours at a time."[859] Supposedly, even Hillary is kept in the dark. *"She* does not always know where the president is, because the Clintons sleep in separate bedrooms."[860]

So, what happens when Bill Clinton sets up these clandestine trysts? "The president's driver is believed to be Bruce Lindsey, a high-level White House staffer and longtime friend of the president."[861] Further, "the president does not have a room in his name; the guest who rents the room is known only to the hotel management. Some information indicates this individual is female and may have celebrity status."[862] Then, with Lindsey driving, "the president gets into the back seat and lays on the seat, covering himself with a blanket kept there for that purpose."[863] In addition, a White House informant has stated that "several other hotel staff members have also seen Bill Clinton at the hotel without any Secret Service agents in attendance."[864]

• Sneaking around late at night in basements is nothing new to Bill Clinton, even after he won the election in 1992 and was still governor of Arkansas. "He would later bring a female Arkansas Power and Light executive to visit him in the basement of the governor's mansion four times *after* his election to the presidency, creeping down to meet her, while a state policeman stood watch against Hillary and Chelsea upstairs."[865]

Further verifiable proof of Clinton's relationship with this woman: "Douglas Frantz and William Rempel, two reporters with the *Los Angeles Times*, wrote that Governor Clinton had called one of his girlfriends, who worked for Arkansas Power and Light, fifty-nine times over a two-year period, calling her eleven times on July 16, 1989, and in August 1989 spent ninety-four minutes on the phone with her after midnight. [Trooper] Roger Perry stated that President-elect Clinton sneaked this woman into the governor's mansion on at least three separate occasions – once at 5:15 a.m."[866]

• Susan McDougal, a former mistress of Bill Clinton, said that the governor even cheated after election victories. "At an inauguration party, Susan had seen Bill Clinton disappear from the party with a tall blond in tow."[867]

• Former right-hand man Dick Morris describes an evening on the campaign trail when Bill met with a 'reporter' at a restaurant. "Of course, she wasn't *really* a reporter. He had met her during the 1980 campaign, when she was an intern for a media outlet. The couple held hands and rubbed knees under the table, not much caring if we watched. Eileen [Morris' wife] and I were amazed that this man, who was desperately seeking reelection, would be so reckless in a public place."[868]

• How about the incident with one of rock n' roll's most infamous fringe figures, Connie Hamzy – "Sweet Sweet Connie" – "a thirty-six-year-old self-professed groupie whose sexual expertise had been immortalized years before in Grand Funk's paean to rock-n-roll superstardom, *We're An American Band*."[869] "On August 31, 1984 Hamzy was sunbathing by a hotel pool in Little Rock when one of Clinton's aides approached and said the governor wanted to meet her. According to Hamzy, 'You're kidding,'' I answered and, looking at my skimpy purple bikini, added, 'I don't have any clothes on.' 'I'm sure that's fine with him,' the aide said, motioning for me to follow him inside."[870]

"Clinton, who had just given a speech to a manufacturer's association, wanted to meet her. Hamzy entered the hotel where, according to her diary, Clinton told her, 'I want to get with you,' pulling her into a dark hallway leading to a hotel laundry room. 'He was feeling me, and he was hard, and we were ready to do it when we heard somebody coming and we stopped.'"[871]

When Hamzy went public with this story in *Penthouse* magazine, the Clinton camp, of course, spun it that *she* accosted him. But, "to prove her version of events, Hamzy later submitted to a polygraph test – and passed."[872] Hamzy added, "I thought they [the public] had a right to know what was coming out. I mean, it's the truth. I didn't expect them to call me a liar ... I might be a groupie and a [lady of low morals], but I'm not a liar."[873]

• "At least one of Clinton's trysts had taken place in the Governor's Mansion since his election to the presidency, making a mockery of his promise on *60 Minutes* to err no more."[874]

GENNIFER FLOWERS ABORTS BILL CLINTON'S BABY

Of all his mistresses, Gennifer Flowers definitely knew Bill Clinton better than any of them. In fact, one of the eeriest elements to their affair was that in *Sleeping with the President* – Flowers' tell-all expose – there is a photo of her in high school that resembles almost exactly Monica Lewinsky many years later. The closeness of their images is too uncanny to be coincidental. Flowers also wrote of their twelve-year relationship, "My affair with the then-governor of Arkansas was an open secret ... truth is, people in Little Rock had been whispering about us ever since we met, yet Bill made little or no attempt to be discreet. On many occasions, he would have his driver pull the state car up to the front door of my apartment building, walk through the lobby, and take the elevator to my second-floor apartment, completely oblivious to certain people who were clocking his every move."[875]

Was Clinton really oblivious, or did he knowingly enjoy a certain *protected* status put in place by those who were guiding his political career? This question seems especially pertinent in relation to Flowers because "both seemed to be addicted to the sexual excitement. Bill was always a risk taker; once he wanted her [Flowers] to make love with him in a bathroom in the governor's mansion while his wife and fifty guests were just a few feet away out on the lawn."[876]

Danger was always an integral part of Clinton's behavior. According to Dolly Kyle Browning, "He is so arrogant he thinks he'll never get caught. And then there's a part of him that wants to get caught because he thinks he can lie his way out of anything. Usually, he can."[877] Others have surmised that it went one step further. "Bill Clinton was never concerned about being caught having a sexual encounter with any woman to whom he was not married. In fact, he actually wanted it to come out and [he] had his damage control planned in advance. He wanted it out so he could get it over with and move on."[878] In this sense, marital infidelity was nothing more than an inconvenient burden that had to be dealt with at some point in his life so he could get on with other more important matters, like getting elected president.

Anyway, before addressing the subject mentioned in the title of this section – Gennifer Flowers' abortion – what follows are a few of the other 'highlights' of their twelve-year affair that didn't get widespread coverage by the mainstream media.

• "According to several of the women involved with him, Clinton flatly refused to wear a condom."[879] As a result, Flowers "began monitoring her health with regular AIDS tests after learning that the Arkansas governor had sex with dozens of different women during the years she shared an intimate relationship with him."[880] Flowers added, "I felt that he had literally put my life in danger because he was having sex with all these people – and I assume not protected sex – and we've all heard of AIDS."[881] Hillary Clinton also feared getting AIDS, so we need to ask ourselves: if Bill Clinton has that little regard for his *own* life and that of his lovers, how much concern do you think he has for *your* life, especially when he was commander-in-chief in charge of our military and nuclear weapons?

• When Bill and Gennifer had sex on her sofa, Clinton refused to let her draw the shades.[882]

• How about Bill's pet nickname for his penis: "Two words were not being spoken much at the Democrat's convention in Los Angeles: 'Monica' and 'Willard.' Monica needs neither introduction nor explanation, but Willard maybe does; it's the name Bill Clinton gave to his sexual organ, according to another of his women, Gennifer Flowers. Clinton's reasoning: 'It's longer than Willie.'"[883]

• Hints of Monica Lewinsky: "Gennifer said Bill wanted to engage in a form of vicarious phone sex. They both would masturbate while talking dirty to each other. Gennifer admits that she usually only pretended to masturbate, because she was not turned on by phone sex, as was Bill. She said it got to the point where Bill wanted to have phone sex every time he called."[884] Flowers noted, "Bill would often try to get me to talk dirty so that he could have an orgasm at the other end of the phone."[885]

• It gets even kinkier. "Over time, Bill's suggestions got wilder. He suggested that Gennifer drip hot wax from a candle all over his body as a prelude to lovemaking, but she got scared and refused. But she did agree to spank Bill during foreplay, and he enjoyed it. On another occasion he suggested that he tie Gennifer to the bed. When she refused, he asked if she would tie him to the bed."[886] Flowers chuckles, "He did get a tremendous charge out of having me slap his behind."[887]

• It's difficult to see Bill Clinton in the same light after this recollection from Gennifer Flowers. "The next time I tied Bill to the bed, he asked me to use a ... vibrator on him. It was exciting to see him getting so aroused, and I couldn't wait to untie him so he could use it on me, which he did."[888]

• Hollywood, eat your heart out. "One time Bill asked Gennifer to wear a short skirt with no underwear and sit opposite him, crossing and uncrossing her legs like the character actress Sharon Stone portrayed in the movie *Basic Instinct*. Gennifer said that this occurred before the movie was released and gave Bill credit for the idea after reading about it in a magazine."[889]

• Gennifer also claimed that Bill smoked marijuana on numerous occasions when he came to her apartment. She added: he did inhale. She also said he confided in her that he had used cocaine, although she admits he never used it in her presence.[890]

• As for their sex: "They did it in every available venue, from Gennifer's condominium boudoirs to a medley of hotel rooms, and almost carried their coupling into the men's room of the governor's mansion, while Hillary prowled nearby corridors, coiled and ready to strike and catch them *en flagrante delicto* in the john."[891]

Bill Clinton "would later confide to Monica Lewinsky that the number [of women he had slept with] ran into the hundreds, and there is no reason to doubt him. By most reports, Bill tended to have several long-term affairs running simultaneously, buttressed by incessant one-night stands."[892]

But when President Clinton had his butt dragged into court to testify, when he appeared on *60 Minutes*, and while addressing the American public on TV, he initially denied *ever* having sex with *any* of the women named in this book. Over time, he was forced to confess his involvement with Lewinsky, Paula Jones, and Gennifer Flowers; but even then he lied.

> **"Did you ever have sexual relations with Gennifer Flowers?" the attorneys asked him.**
> **"Yes," Bill Clinton replied.**
> **"On how many occasions?"**
> **"Once," he said.**[893]

One of the lawyers in the Paula Jones lawsuit, David Pyke, was especially pleased with finagling this admission from Clinton. "Contrasted with his 1992 denials of a sexual relationship between him and Flowers, we thought it conclusively established Clinton as a liar on matters relating to his relations with women."[894]

Coming clean about this matter was especially infuriating to the president. In his grand jury testimony, "Clinton's anger at Flowers seeped into words when he told the prosecutors how he'd 'rather have taken a whipping' than admit to an affair with Flowers 'after all the trouble I'd been through with Gennifer Flowers, and the money I knew she had made for the story she told about this alleged twelve-year affair, which we had done a great deal to disprove.'"[895]

In Clinton's twisted universe, the truth *does* cause a great deal of trouble, particularly when he urged Ms. Flowers on numerous occasions to obstruct justice and lie. More damning for Clinton was that his crimes were recorded on Flowers' answering machine. "On the tapes, Clinton can be heard advising Flowers, 'if they ever hit you with it, just say no and go on. There's nothing they can do.'"[896]

Below are a few other incriminating segments of conversation that Clinton had with Gennifer Flowers.

> **Clinton: If all the people who are named deny, that's all.**
>
> **Clinton: They can't run a story like this unless somebody said, "Yeah, I did it with him."**
>
> **Clinton: I want to run for president. I wonder if I'm just going to be blown out of the water with this. I don't see how they could have overlooked it so far.**[897]

The lengths to which he went were pathetic. "A recurring theme throughout the tapes is Clinton's never-ending scheming to conceal their affair and portray any allegations about it as part of a scurrilous Republican plot. ... 'All you got to do is deny it. Hang tough. Deny everything. The press can't prove anything. As long as everybody hangs in there, we're in the clear.'"[898] When everything was finally laid on the table, it was Flowers – during a press conference at the Waldorf-Astoria Hotel – who put the matter into perspective. "Yes, I was Bill Clinton's lover for twelve years, and for the past two years I have lied about the relationship. The truth is; I loved him. Now he tells me to deny it. Well, I'm sick of all the deceit and I'm sick of all the lies."[899]

Clinton's entire life was a lie, and his criminality went even further when he illegally used his position and power as governor to get a job for Flowers for which she was unqualified. In 1990, with her musical career floundering and increased heat from the press to disclose her involvement with Bill Clinton, Flowers wanted a payoff. Thus, Governor Clinton broke the law and landed her a position as an administrative assistant. "She didn't remotely qualify for the job she applied for – unless the fix was in. If anyone doubts that Clinton pulled strings to get Gennifer Flowers placed on the state payroll at $17,520 a year, these doubts should evaporate after this evidence: Dan Barnes received the initial phone call from Judy Gaddy commanding him to find a job for Gennifer at the appeals tribunal. The order came straight from the governor."[900]

Hereafter is a condensed version of what took place behind the scenes. "Barnes had to override departmental policy and allow outside applicants in addition to those already employed by the department."[901] When Flowers was unsure whether she would be offered the job over those within the department who were more qualified, Clinton told her, "No problem. I talked to Barnes. It's a done deal."[902] One of the women in line for promotion into this position filed a complaint with the State Grievance Review Committee. "The governor's people kicked a supervisor upstairs, denied a position to the employee recommended to take her place, and then reclassified the job so it could go to an outsider."[903]

Proving that she wasn't qualified, evidence at a hearing revealed that "Gennifer had scored ninth among eleven candidates who took the phony merit test given to camouflage what was already a *fait accompli*."[904] Even more embarrassing, "Gennifer, in her own testimony, was unable to name any computer on which she'd worked."[905]

In laymen's terms, such tactics are known as influence peddling, and it *is* a crime! Shirley Thomas, assistant director at the State Health and Human Services Department, summarized, "There was favoritism. It was a serious infraction. There certainly was not an adherence to state procedures."[906] Further, "Clinton's own involvement in the duplicity and lies is incontrovertible."[907]

But why should we be surprised, for Clinton and Flowers often conspired together, even taking a nasty delight in bashing Hillary during the course of their affair. "Flowers laughed when Bill

snickered about fooling 'Hilla the Hun,' and he complained bit-
terly to Dolly Kyle [Browning] about being repeatedly nagged by
'The Warden.'"[908] Similarly, here is an account describing Bill and
Gennifer's opinion of Hillary. "She is vitriolic about Hillary, describing her as 'a fat frump with big thick glasses, an ugly dress
and a big fat butt.' Bill ... referred to her as 'Hilla the Hun' and
'Sarge.'"[909] What we're seeing isn't love between a married couple;
it's an ugliness and undeniable hatred on Bill's behalf. Yet we're
still supposed to believe they have a *real* marriage.

Bill continued to rub his wife's nose in his sordid affairs, like
the time he pulled a JFK-Marilyn Monroe stunt by having Gennifer Flowers sing at one of his official ceremonies. "The beautiful singer, who had come to perform at the gala, was the
mysterious woman all Arkansas had been talking about. ... Coming out of their collective stupefaction after Gennifer Flowers' appearance in a red cocktail dress adorned with a generous splash
of shiny silver beads, the know-it-alls began to wonder: was
Arkansas's first lady unaware of who the guest vocalist *really* was?
Or, as developments soon suggested, was she totally onto the role
Gennifer played in her husband's secret life?"[910]

Gennifer answered the question herself: "I know she knew.
Hillary avoided looking at me all night long."[911] But mere embarrassment wasn't good enough for Clinton; he also wanted a
quickie that would completely humiliate Hillary.

> **"Come on, nobody's in there ... let's go in
> and get a quick one off," Gennifer said Bill
> pleaded with her. They were standing outside
> the men's room.**
>
> **"You're crazy! What if Hillary should catch
> us?"**
>
> **"Oh, you worry too much," Gennifer
> quoted Bill's protest. "She'll never be the
> wiser."**
>
> **Just then, who should come sauntering**

> **along the hallway? It was Hillary. She passed**
> **us with her gaze straight ahead, walking like**
> **a zombie. She didn't acknowledge Bill, and**
> **she seemed to want to regard my presence**
> **even less.**[912]

What type of husband would want to engage in such tomfoolery, especially in a public lavatory; and what type of wife would tolerate such brazen behavior – and then *stay* with this man? Answer: two completely depraved individuals.

But the most crushing details that were conveniently overlooked by the corporate press were those surrounding Gennifer Flowers' abortion of Bill Clinton's unborn baby. "By December 1977, Flowers realized her period was late and went to a doctor to confirm her suspicion that she was pregnant."[913] More intriguingly, Flowers wrote in her autobiography, "I was pregnant with William J. Clinton's baby."[914]

Gennifer's short-lived joy obviously wasn't shared with a man who could not, by any stretch of the imagination, be burdened with an illegitimate child from his mistress. So, Gennifer lamented, "Bill gave me the two-hundred dollars I needed for an abortion."[915] "A few days later, she informed the baby's father – Bill Clinton – that she intended to terminate the pregnancy. He did not object, and the abortion was performed in late January of 1978."[916] Flowers' naivete was finally quashed by a bitter dose of reality. "I still hoped that he [Clinton] would at least express some regret that we couldn't have a child together, or say how nice it might have been if circumstances were different. But, no, he wasn't going to grant me even that much."[917]

Remember, Chelsea wasn't born until February, 1980. There's not a snowball's chance in hell that Clinton would welcome an illegitimate child into the world that wasn't from his handler wife.

Of course Bill didn't join Gennifer at the abortion clinic, but at least he called her afterward. "'Gennifer, it's Bill. How did it go? Are you okay?' Flowers wrote, I let a moment of heavy silence pass before answering. 'Now that you ask, I feel awful. Killing that baby was the worst experience of my life.'"[918]

But Clinton, ever one to add insult to injury, inflicted even more pain. Flowers wrote:

> **For the next few months, Bill and I went on pretty much like before. Then one night he walked in beaming. He had some big news to share. "Hillary is pregnant. I'm going to be a daddy. Gennifer, isn't it great?" I tried to smile, but I was deeply insulted. There he was, on cloud nine because he was going to be a father. And I'm thinking, "You bastard. I was pregnant with your baby, and that meant absolutely nothing to you."[919]**

What Flowers eventually realized was that she was, and had always been, nothing more than a piece of meat to be used for Bill Clinton's gratification; one of his objects, or "whores" as he liked to call them. Sure, he despised Hillary and found her completely unattractive in a physical sense; but she was part of the *plan*. Therefore, Chelsea was also part of the plan (mostly to dispel rumors that Hillary was a lesbian, and that they had a legitimate marriage, not only a political arrangement). On the other hand, aborting Gennifer's baby meant no more to Clinton than emptying yesterday's trash. It was a disposable fetus that represented scandal, shame, and embarrassment. Clinton even went so far as to lie and say he couldn't have children. "Bill had initially told her [Gennifer] he was sterile because of a bout with the mumps as a child."[920]

As for those who wonder if Hillary was aware of this messy situation, the answer is clear. "According to two longtime Arkansas friends, Hillary knew about Flowers' pregnancy – and was devastated by it. Indeed, they believe it is one of the reasons she seldom speaks of the pivotal 1978 governor's race – one of the

Clintons' notable early triumphs – and went so far as to actually omit it from her memoirs."[921]

Hillary knew—just like Hillary knew *everything* else.

HOOKERS' ROW AND A BLACK LOVE CHILD

Clinton loyalists want you to believe that any possibility of Bill Clinton fathering a black love child is pure tabloid trash. Admittedly, any headline regarding a "love child" does sound sensationalistic; but before dismissing this notion, ignore the rhetoric and instead focus on the actions of those involved to determine if such a scenario is plausible.

In a nutshell, here is what we're dealing with.

> **In 1984, Bill may have had a sexual escapade with a trio of prostitutes in Little Rock's "Hookers' Row." Bobbie Ann Williams, then a 24-year-old prostitute, worked the corner of Seventeenth and Main streets. Williams said that she was paid $200 to perform oral sex on Clinton and that she arranged for an orgy after Clinton offered to pay each of the participants $400 apiece. Williams also alleged that she had late-night sex with Clinton at the Holiday Inn in Little Rock on numerous occasions and that Clinton was the father of her light-complexioned ten-year-old mulatto son, Danny.[922]**

Too bizarre to be true? If you think so, please re-read the previous sections and remember: Bill Clinton is described as a sex and risk junkie who never wore condoms, and was already known to have impregnated at least one other woman. Also, "nearly everyone Bill talked to was aware that he had cheated on Hillary – he went so far as to admit it to several of them. But only a handful knew the magnitude of Bill's faithlessness."[923]

To begin our analysis, we must first return to a woman named Betsey Wright who compiled the first of numerous "Doomsday Lists" which chronicled Bill Clinton's adulterous affairs. "There were at least twelve women on the list, and for the next four hours Wright grilled Bill about his relationship with each of them. She did not even bother to bring up the subject of his many one-night stands, the nagging question of Danny Williams's paternity, and his alleged dalliances with the prostitutes of Spring Street. Wright's inevitable and sobering conclusion: Bill could not run in 1988."[924]

So, even as far back as the late 1980s, the possibility that Bill Clinton not only visited ladies of the night, but also sired an illegitimate child, was on the table *inside the Clinton camp.* One of the women in question, Bobbie Ann Williams, "a young black woman working the stretch of Spring Street known as 'Hookers' Row' ... claimed that she had sex with him [Clinton] on thirteen separate occasions over the next several months, including one evening when she brought along two other prostitutes to fulfill Bill's *ménage a trois* fantasies."[925] Even more strange is the fact that no one took the woman's claims seriously "until she gave birth to Danny Williams in 1985. Williams's son was white, and with each passing year his resemblance to Clinton grew stronger."[926]

Of course, the entire matter could have been resolved with a simple blood test, but this solution remains problematic because Clinton's "medical records remain sealed."[927] If one wades through the Clinton literature, some say DNA tests have proven that the child is not his, while others state the opposite. The fact remains, "Clinton has been repeatedly asked to have a blood test in order to settle paternity allegations, but he has refused."[928] Why did he resist? Could it be that some sources "described sexually transmitted diseases hidden in his medical records?"[929] To further cloud the issue, "Since Clinton's election both mother and son have vanished without trace. Family members refuse to discuss the sordid mess."[930]

But these individuals, and others, have spoken in the past, and here is the story that has unfolded. For starters, "Little Rock's seedy 'Hookers' Row' is the last place that a governor of Arkansas would be expected to visit,"[931] but as we've established, Bill Clinton is no ordinary politician. According to Bobbie Ann Williams, "I was twenty-four in 1984 and was working as a prostitute at the Johnson apartment building on Seventeenth and Main Street when I first met Bill. Me and some girls were walking around Spring Street near the governor's mansion when we saw him come jogging down the street in a tight t-shirt. I was dressed real sexy in this tight little skirt, a halter top nothing under it; and a wig with curls. The other girls were pretty excited. They knew about the governor's jogging trips. He'd pick you up right there on the street. ... Three days later we saw him again. This time, he picked me – and said that he knew a place where we could go have sex."[932]

The story continues. "She said he asked her to perform oral sex on him, which she claimed she did after asking to be paid sixty dollars. When it was done, he gave me two hundred dollars, she related ... then after he was done, he pulled up his pants and ran off jogging."[933] Of special note is this bit of information. "The sex, Mrs. Williams attested, was accomplished without the protection of condoms. Bobbie Ann said Clinton didn't use protection because he 'just didn't like them.'"[934]

Before continuing, let's see if what we've established so far fits Bill Clinton's modus operandi. First, he likes black women (Bobbie Ann Williams); he's a risk-taking sex addict (prostitutes); he used a particular excuse to get away from Hillary (jogging); the proximity was near his mansion (Hookers' Row); he received his preferred form of sex (oral); and he didn't practice safe sex (no condoms).

The governor revisited this red-light district and Williams soon thereafter. "A couple of weeks later, he said he wanted to have an orgy. He said he's pay us four hundred dollars apiece. There was me and two friends – and we jumped at his offer."[935]

The wheels were now in motion. Bobbie Ann Williams continues. "We were waiting when this big white car – it wasn't a limo, but it was a big car with tinted windows [Clinton's official state transport, a Lincoln Town Car] – drove up and stopped beside us. The man behind the wheel was a state trooper assigned to guard the governor."[936]

Again, another piece of the puzzle fits perfectly into place – Bill Clinton using state policemen to be his drivers during such occasions.

After "a sixty-mile drive to this little house in the woods,"[937] the festivities began. Bobbie Ann picks up the story. "He liked looking at us. We all three crawled into bed with him and started playing around. ... He liked using all the dirty words he could think of for the woman's body parts. And we could tell he liked it when we talked dirty to him. He also watched us girls make love to each other. He told us what to do. That really got him turned on. Finally, he was ready for straight sex and tried using a condom, but he took it off."[938] After their little romp was concluded, Williams chuckled, "He surprised all of us with a fifty dollar tip."[939]

Fact or fiction? It would be easy to dismiss this story out-of-hand if it weren't for one detail: the location of where it transpired. To set-up an investigation, five reporters from the *Globe* newspaper first met with Mrs. Williams. "Before we did anything, we had Bobbie Ann take a lie-detector test. She passed it not once, but twice. Then we proceeded from there,"[940] editorial director Phil Bunton declared.

> **"The reportorial team established that the governor indeed had a white car. In fact, all his cars were white. And they were large, long-chassied, eight-cylinder Lincolns. Then our reporters followed Bobbie Ann's directions to the house in the woods," Bunton continued. "They found Barrow Road was the fastest way to get**

to the house she described – and discovered it was the home owned by Clinton's mother."[941]

Bill Clinton's mother owned the house where this orgy with three hookers took place! This cabin "had been purchased in [1980] ... to serve as a retreat for Bill when he was a first-term governor and as a getaway for his mother from her year-round residence, the family's Hot Springs home."[942] [Note: Clinton was so spoiled that his mother bought him his own Arkansas-style Camp David for weekend retreats (and orgies).]

This shocking episode would have probably been buried by the Clinton camp if it weren't for a man named Robert "Say" McIntosh, described as "the owner of a local diner that specialized in barbecue and sweet potato pie and a political provocateur with a flair for street theater."[943] McIntosh became a problem when he started showing up at rallies "distributing handbills featuring a photograph of a boy about seven years old who he claimed was Bill Clinton's illegitimate 'love child'."[944] Soon, "during Clinton's 1990 bid for a fifth term [as governor], detractors showed up at rallies with small glass vials and signs that read, 'Just a few drops, Bill.' They wanted blood samples to prove the paternity of Danny Williams."[945]

McIntosh needled Clinton even further by announcing his predilection for "dark meat." "Bill Clinton has been with enough black women to cast a Tarzan movie. And he's got a little black son out there living in poverty."[946]

The heat was being turned up so high that members of Williams' family were even directly confronting the Clintons. "Bobbie Ann's husband, Dan Williams, who knows the child couldn't be his because he's black, was likewise frustrated when he tried to get relief for Danny. 'He drove up alongside the governor while he was jogging and told him about the boy,' Lucille [Bolton, Bobbie Ann's sister] explained. 'Clinton's reaction was shocking. Dan said the governor pulled out a roll of hundred dollar bills and threw it in the window of the car. Then he just kept jogging.'"[947]

By this point Mrs. Clinton was getting nervous about the adverse publicity, especially since they had their eye on the White House. "In staff meetings, Hillary grew increasingly impatient with her husband's unwillingness to do anything about the rumors. 'This is dangerous, Bill,' she told him. 'People are going to start believing this crap. We've got to do *something.*'"[948]

Lucille Bolton was even able to speak directly with Hillary about this touchy subject.

> **Upset by the publicity and hoping to strike a deal with the Clintons, Bolton called the Governor's Mansion and managed to get through to Hillary.**
>
> **Bolton had expected Hillary to sound upset, but instead she was calm, businesslike. "Is it true," Hillary asked almost matter-of-factly, "that he has this illegitimate child?" When Bolton told her the stories were true, Hillary put her in touch with a private security company that specialized in squelching such talk. "Don't worry," she told Bolton. "These people know how to stop rumors."[949]**

But the idle chatter didn't stop, and this time Hillary wouldn't speak with the boy's aunt. Lucille Bolton said, "I was so furious over the situation that I went to the governor's mansion ... to talk to Clinton about Danny. But I couldn't get past the aides, who listened to my story and then sent me packing."[950]

Even bigwigs in the Democratic Party were getting antsy. "During one meeting with party leaders in Chicago, Clinton angrily denied that there was any validity to the stories. So why not simply provide a blood sample and put the rumors to rest? ... At no point, in fact, would Bill willingly provide the blood sample that supposedly would have established that he was not Danny's biological father."[951]

This controversy was still brewing nearly a decade later (January 1999) – right through the Monica Lewinsky debacle – with some sides claiming that Clinton was not the father, while "other DNA experts contested on the grounds that there was insufficient information in the Starr report to make any valid comparison."[952] Still, "right up to the day the *Star* revealed the test results, the White House failed to issue a flat denial of the allegations."[953]

Even more peculiar are suggestions "that the Clinton camp struck a deal with Say McIntosh in exchange for his silence."[954] Here is what unfolded. In 1991, Say McIntosh filed a lawsuit against Clinton, claiming that the governor had reneged on a promise to pay him $25,000 ... in exchange for his help in stemming 'negative publicity' about Clinton's affairs. Furthermore, McIntosh charged, Clinton had promised to obtain an early release for his son, Tommy McIntosh, who was serving a fifty-year term for cocaine distribution. McIntosh hinted that the money was supposed to have been a bribe from Hillary."[955]

Here's the real zinger. "On January 20, 1993, the day Bill Clinton was inaugurated as President, Tommy McIntosh was pardoned."[956] Here's how it went:

"A few weeks later, Jerry Seper of the *Washington Times* encountered Say McIntosh on a downtown street. McIntosh told Seper that he had struck a deal with Clinton immediately after the election. 'Those who question my credibility should ask themselves, if there was no deal, how did this happen?' he said. 'How did my son get out of prison eighteen years before he was eligible for parole?'"[957] That's the bottom line. "In exchange for no longer championing Danny Williams' cause, McIntosh hinted that Hillary had promised him $25,000 – an amount he would later sue to collect. He also claimed Bill had promised to shorten the fifty-year prison sentence of his son Tommy McIntosh, who had been convicted of cocaine distribution."[958]

Ultimately, the question remains: did Bill Clinton father an illegitimate black child by a Little Rock prostitute? Don't be swayed by the Clinton rhetoric, but instead examine their actions.

- Bill Clinton refused to take a blood test.
- There are allegations of an apparent bribe on Hillary's behalf.
- The Clintons' chief antagonist admitted to being bought off.
- Hillary hired a private detective to squelch negative publicity.
- The antagonist's son was released from jail 18 years before he was eligible for parole.
- Bill Clinton yet again used influence peddling to remedy a sticky situation.

Are these the actions of an innocent party with absolutely nothing to hide?

BILL CLINTON'S CROOKED MEMBER

When allegations surfaced that Bill Clinton had sexually harassed Paula Jones, the Clinton attack machine went into overdrive. Serpentine hit-man James Carville snarled, "Drag a $100 bill through a trailer park, you never know what you'll find."[959] Yet despite all their damage control and character assassination, it has been proven – in court – that Bill Clinton lied about his affairs with Monica Lewinsky and Gennifer Flowers. As a result, he's been disbarred, undergone impeachment hearings, and disgraced the office of the presidency. Further, "The Clintons would pay Jones $850,000 to keep her from appealing the decision"[960] handed down by U.S. District Court Judge Susan Webber Wright. To add further humiliation, "Since Clinton had no savings of his own; Hillary would write a check for the $375,000 portion of the judgment not covered by his insurance."[961] Hillary gets cheated on repeatedly, and then she has to bail her husband out.

But financial hardships weren't the only consequence of Clinton being a sexual predator in the late 1990s. His own daughter "Chelsea was rushed to the Stanford campus hospital no fewer than four times with stress-induced stomach pains."[962] What precisely ailed her? "On May 19, [1998] she collapsed with severe stomach pains and was rushed to the campus hospital. After a battery of tests ruled out appendicitis, ulcers, or pelvic inflammatory disease, doctors came to the inevitable conclusion that the pains were brought on by the stress [of the Monica Lewinsky affair]."[963] Obviously Bill cared more about illicit sexual relations than his daughter. Lastly, to show how vindictive they were – even when 100% in the wrong – "Less than a week after turning down a settlement offer from Bob Bennett, Paula Jones was informed that she was the target of an IRS audit."[964] If you remember correctly, the same retaliatory tactic was leveled against Juanita Broaddrick after Bill Clinton raped her, while others were threatened with physical violence (or worse). As you'll see in an upcoming chapter, all of these strategies can be traced back to Hillary Clinton and her war room thugs who specialize in smearing the women her husband attacked and violated.

Luckily, even though Clinton is sneaky and debased, he's not real adept at concealing his illicit dalliances. In other words, he's not real bright when it comes to covering his tracks (or else he just doesn't care). With Monica Lewinsky, if it weren't for evidence (in this case, semen) that he left on her dress, he'd still be lying about their affair in the Oval Office. Likewise, there was one indisputable factor that led to Clinton's downfall with Paula Jones – the unusual appearance of his penis.

But prior to covering this aspect of the case, let's first examine what happened that fateful day when Bill Clinton propositioned Paula Jones. [And please, I'd like all of the women reading these words to imagine if their father, brother, husband, or co-worker acted in the same manner – how would you feel about that individual?]

"During Clinton's last term as governor, [Paula] Jones was twenty-four years old and working as a clerk at the Arkansas Industrial Development Commission. One day – she later determined it was May 8, 1991 – Jones and a colleague named Pamela

Blackard were working behind the registration desk at an AIDC conference at a Little Rock hotel called the Excelsior. After the governor and his security detail arrived, a trooper named Danny Ferguson stopped to chat with Blackard and Jones."[965] Then, according to Ferguson (in an article by David Brock), "Clinton asked him to approach the woman, whom the trooper remembered only as Paula, tell her how attractive the governor thought she was, and take her to a room where Clinton would be waiting."[966] Once Ms. Jones arrived at his room, "the governor greeted her [and] made small talk for a few moments."[967] "The come-on Clinton allegedly used with Paula Jones, according to her lawsuit [was] 'Don't we make a beautiful couple – beauty and the beast.'"[968]

"After about five minutes, Clinton was standing near the window. He reached over and held her hand, pulling her close to him. Jones withdrew and tried to make conversation. Clinton was listening to her but his face was 'beet red.' He moved closer to her, leaning against the back of a chair, and put his hand under her clothes. She said, 'What are you doing?' and tried to retreat but he was now trying to kiss her neck."[969]

At this point Clinton's sexual predator instincts kicked in. He "then began touching her. Jones rebuffed him and moved to sit down on the sofa. Clinton followed her there, then exposed himself and asked her to perform oral sex."[970]

In her own words, Paula Jones described the scene. "'He took my hand and loosed his tie,' she reported in an affidavit. 'You have nice curves,' Clinton reportedly said. 'I love the way your hair goes down your body.' He then asked her for 'a type of sex.'"[971]

It got even creepier. "When she looked over, Clinton had his trousers and boxers down to his ankles and was sitting there, exposing himself. 'I was literally just scared, shocked,' Jones said. Clinton was 'holding it ... fiddling it or whatever. And he asked me to – I don't know his exact word – give him [oral sex] ... I was so shocked. I think he wanted me to kiss it ... And he was saying it in a very disgusting way, just a horny-ass way that just scared me to death.'"[972]

Clinton even resorted to laying his hands on the unwilling woman. "In her amended complaint, Jones says that before Clinton coaxed her to 'kiss it,' he stroked her hair and complimented her on her curves. She retreated to the couch, whereupon Clinton followed, says Jones, placed his hand on her thigh, and began sliding it toward her pubic area."[973]

Realizing she had to make a break or risk being physically violated, Jones made her move. "'His face was red, beet red. I'll never forget that look,' Paula said. 'I tried to move away. I thought if I started asking about his wife he'd get the message.' He didn't. 'He pulled his pants down to his knees; he had an erection, and he asked me to kiss it. Then he just stood there holding it.' At this point she jumped up from the sofa and said, 'I'm not that kind of girl.'"[974]

Foiled, Clinton pulled up his boxers, then said none too subtly, "You're smart. Let's keep this between ourselves."[975]

The matter did become public due to an article that appeared in the *American Spectator* magazine, and the Clinton cabal would have undoubtedly kept lying about the incident until the end of time if it weren't for one minor detail. In her lawsuit, Paula Jones said she could *prove* that Clinton had sexually harassed her. "It was paragraph 22. There were distinguishing characteristics in Clinton's genital area that were obvious to Jones."[976]

Distinguishing characteristics? What could it be? "In mid-October Clinton was embarrassed when a *Washington Times* headline queried, 'is this the president's distinguishing characteristics?' The article went on to say that the sealed affidavit described a penile condition known as Peyronie's syndrome, which is characterized by a distinct angular bend or curvature of the penis."[977]

What could they be talking about? "The president was suffering from a condition described in 1743 by a French scientist named Francois Gigot de la Peyronie. Now known as Peyronie's disease, it afflicted one out of every one hundred men between the ages of forty-five and sixty and was marked by curvature of the penis."[978]

Paula Jones explained further. "Clinton's penis, she said, seemed to hang downward. She and [Deborah] Ballantine joked that it looked like the leaning Tower of Pisa. Lydia Cathay, Jones' sister, would later say that Jones had talked about it with her as well, describing Clinton's penis as 'crooked' and 'gross'."[979]

Clinton was shamed even further when Paula Jones was questioned in a deposition about his member, describing him in these terms. "He was a really big man and really overweight and it [his penis] seemed like it was real little compared to his weight."[980] Jones also swore in a State of Virginia affidavit, "Mr. Clinton's penis was circumcised and seemed to me to be rather short and thin. I would describe its appearance as seeming to be five to five and one-half inches, or less, in length, and having a circumference of the approximate size of a quarter, or perhaps very slightly larger. The shaft of the penis was bent or 'crooked' from Mr. Clinton's right to left."[981]

Another woman intimately acquainted with Clinton in a physical way was a prostitute that former Clinton employee Larry Nichols interviewed. She told him that "he had a very, very small, almost to the point of what you would call deformed, penis."[982]

THE GROPER STRIKES AGAIN

A friend in need is a friend indeed, or so the saying goes. But with friends like Bill Clinton, who needs enemies (or rapists, or sexual predators)? Just ask Kathleen Willey, a woman who "had come to work as a volunteer at the White House"[983] after Clinton won the presidential election in 1992. But Willey was more than just a mere worker. "Willey and her husband, Edward E. Willey Jr., had been longtime Clinton supporters who had donated $10,000 and worked in his 1992 campaign. In fact, the Willeys were in Little Rock on election night to celebrate the Clinton victory that same year."[984]

Regrettably, the Willeys fell on hard times. "By 1993, Ed Willey, a former lawyer who worked in real estate, had been charged with embezzling more than $250,000 from a former client. In November 1993, both Kathleen and Ed had to sign a promissory note agreeing to pay the money back in two weeks as part of a deal to keep Mr. Willey out of jail."[985]

Not knowing where to turn, Willey decided to call upon an old friend – one who had a little bit of pull, President Bill Clinton – especially "after meeting Clinton many times at Democratic events, she would often be invited to the White House."[986] So, on November 29, 1993 Willey met with President Clinton. "After a couple of minutes of small talk, she was near tears as she told Clinton about her husband's financial trouble. The bottom line, she told the president, is that she needed a job."[987] Stated differently, "Kathleen could no longer afford to work for free."[988]

Willey was distraught, her husband was close to being imprisoned, and the financial woes were devastating to her. At a time such as this, Bill Clinton could have shone like a star by being the upstanding human being he claims to be. But "after Willey told the president of her family troubles, Clinton told her how sorry he was – and then kissed her. This was no social kiss; according to Willey, he put his hands in her hair and up her skirt."[989]

During a *60 Minutes* broadcast, Willey explained her resistance and fear. "I just remember thinking, 'what in the world is he doing?' And, I pushed back away from him, and – he – he – he – he – he's a big man. And he – he had his arms – they were tight around me and he – he – he touched me."[990]

But Clinton would not take no for an answer. "Willey asked if he was concerned about people waiting outside, but Clinton brushed it off, saying he had a meeting but he could be late. Clinton took the coffee mug out of Willey's hand and said, 'I've wanted to do this ever since the first time I laid eyes on you.' He began kissing her again, and his hands were everywhere – on her breast, up her skirt, in her hair. He put one of his hands on her crotch."[991]

Newsweek reporter Michael Isikoff continues the sordid tale.

"Did he put your hands on his penis?"
"Yes, he did," Willey replied. "Was it erect?"
Indeed it was.[992]

Here's where things get very interesting. "Willey told Michael Isikoff she knew Paula Jones was telling the truth because during this encounter Clinton's face was 'beet red,' just the way Paula later described it."[993]

Yes, this intense rush of blood to Bill Clinton's head appears to be an uncontrollable physical reaction when he erupts into sexual predator mode. "Willey said that the president was so out of control that his face was purple, and the veins were showing on his neck and forehead."[994] Such a description is frightening, for it portrays Clinton as almost Frankenstein-like in his need to violate this woman (and others). As Willey later told Linda Tripp, "Clinton's sexual approach came out of nowhere and was forceful, almost to the point of an attack. The president had his hands on her breasts and all over her body."[995] Finally, in Linda Tripp's statement to the FBI, she quotes Willey as saying, "'the meeting ended when someone entered the adjacent office.' That last line is essential, since it reveals that Clinton's assault stopped only when discovery seemed likely – and not because Willey said no."[996]

Any legitimate feminist organization in the world would classify the above incident as a sexual assault, with the perpetrator being categorized as a sexual predator. That definitely, precisely, and absolutely describes Bill Clinton; who, as we have shown, is a repeat offender with a high recidivism rate. He should not have been president of the United States; he should have been in prison.

Prior to Willey fleeing from Clinton's clutches, "she pushed herself away from him and Clinton turned away from her and 'finished the job himself.' The woman said she'd been stunned;

she'd never had a man take advantage of her like that."[997] Then, proving Bill Clinton was in fact scheduled for a meeting and that high-ranking individuals were waiting for him, Kathleen Willey "left hurriedly and saw head of the U.S. Treasury Lloyd Bentsen, chairman of the OMB Leon Panetta, and chairperson of the Council of Economic Advisers Laura Tyson outside the Oval Office waiting to meet with the president."[998]

Shortly after fleeing from this horrible scene, Willey met with someone who – as you will see – keeps surfacing in a variety of Clinton scandals, including the murder of Vince Foster and the Monica Lewinsky debacle. "After leaving the Oval Office, she went to see a friend who worked in the White House counsel's office. Her name was Linda Tripp."[999] Tripp could immediately tell that something was seriously awry. "'Where's your lipstick?' Willey took her aside and told her what happened. Tripp shook her head and said to Willey, 'I could always tell the president wanted you.'"[1000]

It's hard to imagine, but events turned even more tragic. "The next morning, Willey learned her husband was dead."[1001] Here is what transpired.

> **The day before, the stress of their financial situation had become too much for Ed, and he had left their home to stay at a friend's house for the night. By the evening of November 29, Kathleen Willey was upset about her encounter with Clinton, but she was much more concerned with locating her husband. She couldn't contact him. She found out the following morning that at about 5:00 pm the previous evening – a couple of hours after her encounter with Clinton – her husband, then sixty years old, had walked off into the woods and committed suicide by shooting himself in the head."[1002]**

Remember, when Kathleen Willey walked into Bill Clinton's office earlier that day, she pleaded with the president, "There's something going on in my life. Ed has gotten himself into some financial trouble, and I'm really kind of desperate."[1003] But instead of assisting this obviously traumatized woman, Clinton attacked and took advantage of her. Plus, as you'll see later in section three of this trilogy, the apparent suicides and freakish accidents surrounding the Clintons are off the scale as to what would be considered even remotely normal. Was Ed Willey's "suicide" a simple act of a man at the end of his rope, or something more, such as a warning?

Before deciding, let's fast-forward a few years to when Kathleen Willey testified in the Paula Jones hearing. "A few months before her deposition Willey had three tires replaced on her car. 'I remember standing at the tire place on a warm September day, waiting for them to fix my car.' The mechanic approached her saying, 'It looks like someone has shot out all your tires with a nail gun; is there someone out there who doesn't like you?' I can hear the shiver in her voice as she says, 'that really got my attention; that's when I started to get worried.'"[1004]

As you'll discover, the Clinton dirty tricks team used tactics such as these on a regular basis. Luckily, Willey went public on *60 Minutes*, quite possibly saving her life by doing so.

DNA EVIDENCE, CIGARS, & THE BIG CREEP

Americans *en masse* sat around their television sets to watch President Bill Clinton confront the issue of whether he had an affair with Monica Lewinsky in the White House.

He narrowed his eyes and trained a laser-like glare straight in the eye of the news camera. Seven times he jabbed his finger. His forehead was shiny with sweat.

> **"I'm going to say this again. I did not have
> sexual relations with *that woman* ... Miss Lewin-
> sky. I never told anybody to lie. Not a single
> time. *Never.* The allegations are false."**
>
> **It took Bill Clinton just twenty seconds and
> fifty words to tell one of the most blatant lies in
> the annals of modern presidential history.**
>
> **Behind him, dressed in a lemon-and-cream-
> colored suit that picked up the yellow in the
> president's tie, Hillary nodded in approval, even
> though she knew he was lying.**[1005]

Indeed, "The first televised images of the President that day
were startling. For once, this most facile of politicians seemed
flummoxed: He looked tired, blotchy, shifty, nervously parsing
tenses – 'There *is* no relationship.'"[1006]

Presidential aide Dick Morris recalled, "Clinton's whole tone
between the lines was, Oh God, have I f***ed up this time.'"[1007]

Bill Clinton had, without any doubt, screwed up beyond his
wildest nightmares – at least on the surface. As we'll see later, in
the Clintons' twisted world, they actually *applauded* the Lewinsky
scandal because it *saved*, rather than threatened, their dual presidency. But where the rest of the world was concerned – one
that was under the sway of their vast spin machine – "The reality
of the Lewinsky affair was astonishing in its selfishness, crude-
ness, and banality. It had happened in the White House. With
an intern. It involved acts – and the President had now admitted
as much – more exploitative than romantic."[1008]

For anyone unfamiliar with their story, or if you understand-
ably wanted to forget the whole mess, here's a quick refresher.

> **On November 15, 1995 – just four months
> after coming to the White House – Bill and
> Monica had their first sexual encounter,
> sparked by her now-famous panty thong flash**

as the two stood in the chief of staff's office. Later that day after some necking and groping, the intern performed oral sex on her boss – while he talked on the phone to a member of Congress ...

After their initial meeting, and up until March 29, 1997, Bill and Monica had at least ten sexual encounters, usually lasting fifteen to twenty minutes each, frequently in his private study near the Oval Office ... when they weren't together, they had long phone calls filled with sex – ten to fifteen such chats – one of which concluded suddenly when the commander in chief began snoring.[1009]

If nothing else, Bill was a fast worker. "According to Lewinsky, they had met just two hours before their first sexual encounter."[1010] Certainly, Monica wasn't Bill's only intern. Linda Tripp – who pops up again to "sometimes boast that she was the last person to see [Vince Foster] alive – 'I served him his last hamburger,'" – called these gals "The graduates – women employees at the White House who purportedly owed their careers to their sexual relationships with Bill Clinton."[1011] Tripp continued her description, "As for the president's sexual behavior, it was worse – far worse – than anybody realized. There were, she said, a whole bevy of White House staffers known as the 'graduates': women who had had affairs with Clinton and got cushy jobs in the West Wing. Everybody knew who they were."[1012]

Monica Lewinsky found out about Bill's graduates the hard way. "On December 6, 1997, Lewinsky approached the White House gates trying to deliver Christmas presents for Clinton through Betty Currie. She couldn't reach Currie at first and when she did, she learned that the president was in the Oval Office with another woman. This upset Lewinsky."[1013]

But in all honesty, Monica shouldn't have been surprised.

"Clinton pursued Lewinsky for the same reason he had pursued other women – because, presumably, he enjoyed the excitement and the sex, such as it was. These relationships were simply the way he lived."[1014]

While doing so, he seemed to take particular delight in thrashing his wife Hillary in the process. Similar to Gennifer Flowers and his other mistresses, Bill and Monica were likewise cruel to the *other woman*. "Hillary would later learn that Monica had a nickname for her, too: 'Baba,' an abbreviated form of the Russian *babushka*.[1015] [Note: although the word *babushka* refers to a type of head scarf, it is also used in reference to a Russian peasant woman, or a frumpy old grandmother type – precisely what Monica thought Hillary was.]

Bill himself wasn't immune to these monikers: "She referred to him as 'The Creep' [or 'The Big Creep'] because all he wanted was oral sex."[1016] Ms. Lewinsky even made jokes about her own role in Bill's life. "Monica jauntily asked whether she could be 'assistant to the president for [oral sex],' and Bill responded, 'I'd like that.'"[1017]

Hillary, naturally, bore the brunt of Bill's humiliating lifestyle, for 'her husband had admitted to Lewinsky that he had had 'thousands of affairs' earlier in his marriage,"[1018] a fact that emerged during Kenneth Starr's quasi-investigation.

One of the most stinging blows imaginable took place following her husband's 1996 State of the Union speech.

> **Turning to Hillary in the gallery above the House chamber, his eyes moist with tears, the president said, "Before I go on, I would like to take just a moment to thank my own family, and to thank the person who has taught me more than anyone else over 25 years about the importance of families and children – a wonderful wife, magnificent mother, and a great first lady. Thank you, Hillary!"[1019]**

There's only one catch. Shortly after having given this heart-wrenching speech lauding Hillary, Bill soon snuck Monica into the Oval Office and gave her the speech he read from – personally signed by himself.

Here is how it was described. "Two years later, Betty Currie hid beneath her bed some of the gifts that Clinton gave Lewinsky. Among them was an official copy of the 1996 State of the Union address, which was inscribed, to Monica Lewinsky, with best wishes, Bill Clinton."[1020] No wonder Monica called him 'The Big Creep;' the man was heartless.

The reason he gave Monica this memento was obvious: sex, sex, sex.

• One of their most notorious moments became the butt of many jokes. What is Bill Clinton's pet name for Monica Lewinsky? Answer: my hairy humidor! "In another particularly bizarre and now legendary incident, the commander in chief inserted a cigar into his playmate's vagina."[1021]

• On Tuesday, February 3, 1998, the *New York Post* reported that Lewinsky had told a former Pentagon intern, Dennis Lytton, twenty-four, that she was having an affair with the president and that she had 'earned her presidential kneepads,' referring to the position she assumed to perform oral sex on the president.[1022]

• During independent counsel questioning, Monica Lewinsky was asked about her first encounter with Bill Clinton.

> **"Then he touched your breasts with his hands?"**
> **"Yes, he did."**
> **"Did he touch your breast with his mouth?"**
> **"Yes, he did."**
> **"Did he touch your genital area at all that day?"**
> **"Yes ... he put his hand down my pants and stimulated me manually in the genital area."[2023]**

• Monica bragged to her high school friend, Neysa Erbland, about this incident inside the Oval Office. "She told me that she had given him [oral sex], and that she had all her clothes off, but that he only had his shirt off and that she had given him oral sex and they kissed and fondled each other and that they didn't have sex. That was kind of a little bit of a letdown to her."[1024]

• Their activities extended outside the White House, too, such as at Radio City Music Hall. "The young woman traveled to New York to attend a gala fundraiser on the occasion of his [Bill Clinton's] 50th birthday. At this event, Lewinsky contrived to place herself near the president, and then, in the words of one of her FBI debriefings, 'Lewinsky reached behind herself to fondle and squeeze the President's penis.'"[2025]

• On March 29, with the president still on crutches from his knee injury at golfer Greg Norman's house in Florida, Lewinsky once again performed oral sex while, as she put it to Starr's prosecutors, Clinton 'manually stimulated [her].'"[2026]

• One time, after being interrupted in the Oval Office, it seems Bill had to pleasure himself. "Their January 21 session ended with a scene out of a pornographic bedroom farce. When the president, as was his custom, stopped Lewinsky before completion, the couple faced a dilemma because there were visitors waiting outside the Oval Office. ... In order to avoid being seen, Lewinsky tried to leave through the office of Betty Currie, Clinton's personal secretary, but the door was locked. When Lewinsky came back to tell the president that she would have to find another exit, she found him in the office of Nancy Hernreich, Currie's boss, masturbating."

• On another occasion after receiving oral stimulation from Monica, Bill couldn't resist taking another jab at Hillary. "The Starr authors concluded their description with one of the report's several gratuitous and cruel observations about the Clinton marriage. 'And then I think he made a joke,' the report quoted Lewinsky as saying, 'that he hadn't had that in a long time.'"[1027]

• Always a *compassionate* man who could feel everyone else's pain, "On the day of [Admiral] Boorda's funeral Clinton called Lewinsky and they [had] phone sex. Typically, Monica remembers, Clinton called when Hillary was out of town. On one occasion Clinton called her at 6:30 am for phone sex.[1028]

- A real class act. "Monica said in one deposition that her oral sex encounters were quickies. Clinton simply unzipped his pants and did not disrobe. She said on one occasion, as she performed oral sex in a hallway, someone came into the Oval Office and Clinton zipped up real quick and went out and came back in. She added, I just remember laughing because he had walked out there and he was visibly aroused."[1029]

Although Bill and Monica's meetings generally consisted of her performing oral sex on him, Bill's taste for nastiness did not diminish in the two decades since he raped Juanita Broaddrick. "The *New York Post* reported that Linda Tripp, sourcing Monica herself, told the grand jury that Clinton sometimes enjoyed 'rough sex' with Lewinsky."[1030] Tripp continued, "I don't mean abusive, I mean very over the top, out of control, physically powerful, where he would repeatedly say to Monica, 'I'm not hurting you, am I?' And essentially he was, but she didn't say he was."[1031]

Even more peculiar, and potentially damaging, was the possible existence of a sex tape. Michael Isikoff reports, "The next day, November 21, Tripp called me. There was another courier pickup from the Pentagon this morning. Only this time, it was not a letter. It was a tape – for phone sex, she told me."[1032]

After doing some snooping, Isikoff found, "The messenger who delivered it also had to make a delivery to *Newsweek* that morning. I asked him to describe what he had delivered to the White House. It was a package, sort of like this, he said, holding up his hands, sort of like a small box. Like a tape? I asked. Yes, he told me, like a tape. I was once more impressed with the reliability of what Tripp was telling me. And with the strangeness of the information: a sex tape couriered to the Oval Office."[1033]

For the moment, let's pause and review what type of situation we're dealing with. Monica Lewinsky "would meet with the president in a small hideaway off the Oval Office and service him with oral sex, [and] they would have phone sex in the early hours of the morning, with the intern talking provocatively while the president masturbated. [Linda] Tripp recounted conversations in which Clinton had confessed his deep-seated sexual problems, how he had 'hundreds of affairs and was so congenitally unfaithful to his wife that, as a therapeutic device, he circled on a calendar the days he had been good.'"[1034]

The big question is: should the American public be reminded of this information, especially when Bill and Hillary could realistically occupy the White House yet again and lead the 'free world'? Bill's escapades with Monica would have undoubtedly been steamrolled over by the vast Clinton lie machine had it not been for one glaring error on the president's part.

I'm sure you know where we're going. "Though they shared the oral sex experience about nine times, they never had sexual intercourse. Clinton told her ... there was too much of a consequence"[1035] in going any further. Certainly there were, like unwanted pregnancies (which Clinton was well acquainted with), and sexually transmitted diseases.

Monica couldn't quite figure out the seeming quandary she was in. "Lewinsky was baffled by the president's insistence on not ejaculating. The two excuses he always used were, one, that he didn't know me well enough or he didn't trust me yet, she said. So it sort of seemed to be some bizarre issue for him."[1036] But then it happened ... the day of infamy. "During their clandestine meetings, Monica usually performed fellatio, but Bill always avoided climaxing; however, the first time he did ejaculate, at her insistence, he left an indelible mark on her navy blue Gap dress."[1037]

Here it was: physical proof of their affair – "Gap dress, size 12, dark blue, as the FBI report put it."[1038] Without this evidence, Bill Clinton would have lied incessantly about their trysts. Again, Linda Tripp seems to have been the driving force. Tripp must be given this: she was right about the dress.

Many of Clinton's own friends regarded him as so untrustworthy on sexual matters that they believed the president would never have admitted his relationship with Lewinsky if she had not kept genetic proof. Without the dress, the subsequent investigation of the relationship might have come down to a he said/she said contest between Clinton and Lewinsky ... but the dress made Lewinsky bulletproof."[1039]

The Starr investigative team had Clinton dead to rights. "The president provided the blood sample on August 3, and preliminary tests that night showed a match. More refined tests later put the odds at 7.87 trillion to one against the semen on the dress coming from someone other than Clinton."[1040]

Clinton, a pathological liar, could have continued his web of deceit – which would have been even more disastrous for him – had it not been for one of their well-placed moles. A source close to Kenneth Starr reported, "When the stain proved to be Bill's semen, I said to one of the guys, 'Why the hell did you guys announce that match before Bill went into the grand jury? You could have leaked that it was cheese, and the DNA test had come out negative, and then the son-of-a-bitch would have gone in there and lied like hell.'"

The answer was, the test was done in the FBI lab, and the Clintons knew the results before we did. Someone in the Justice Department was leaking to them. The day the FBI got the test results, they trotted them right over to the White House. So, when the President went into that grand jury, he had to know the jig was up."[1041]

Bill Clinton appeared to be trapped, as he lamented to longtime aide Sidney Blumenthal. "I feel like a character in a novel. I feel like somebody who is surrounded by an oppressive force that is creating a lie about me and I can't get the truth out. I feel like a character in *Darkness at Noon*."[1042]

Clinton's denial, self-deception, and overt deceit to Blumenthal are obvious; but on the other hand, *much* more than oral sex in the Oval Office was taking place during Clinton's second term.

In fact, Hillary was partially correct when she spoke of a vast conspiracy against the Clintons. But she was only half right because there were actually *two* conspiracies taking place concurrently – one to expose the president, and the other to protect him.

First, let's examine the pro-Clinton faction that was at work. The most obvious participant – veteran Clinton handler and perennial Bilderberg attendee – was Mr. Vernon Jordan. At various times after this scandal broke, we see Jordan lending his assistance.

• Jordan told her [Lewinsky] to come on over. As soon as she arrived, Jordan called President Clinton. Jordan told Clinton about Lewinsky's subpoena and promised to get her a lawyer.[1043]

• On December 22, Jordan took her in his limousine to see [attorney] Frank Carter.[1044]

• [Literary agent Lucianne] Goldberg relayed to the lawyers what Tripp had said about her taped conversation with Lewinsky: "'Vernon Jordan told her to lie.' ... The question seems to imply Jordan's knowledge of Lewinsky's relationship with the president and at least an implicit sanction for her to conceal it ... still, the allegation that Vernon Jordan was coaching Monica Lewinsky to lie under oath ..."[1045]

• About six p.m., Lewinsky picked up [Betty] Currie outside the White House, and they drove to Vernon Jordan's office in Dupont Circle.[1046]

• He even assisted Monica in her search for employment. "Jordan promised to help her and asked her to send letters to three business contacts he was going to give her."[1047]

• Ms. Lewinsky specifically remembered that "Vernon Jordan told her, 'It doesn't matter what anybody says, you just deny it. As long as you say it didn't happen, then it didn't happen.'"[1048]

• Monica portrayed herself as holding out for a job from Jordan in return for her testimony during the affair. As she told [Linda] Tripp at one point, "I'm supposed to sign, and I'm not signing until I have a job."[1049]

• The situation got so bad that one of the companies Jordan

set Lewinsky up with had to run for cover. *"Clinton Accused of Urging Aide to Lie; Starr Probes Whether President Told Woman to Deny Alleged Affair to Jones's Lawyer* rang the front page headline in *The Washington Post* on January 21, 1998. On the same day, Revlon rescinded its offer of employment to Lewinsky, since Vernon Jordan was now facing investigation for possible obstruction of justice."[1050]

Ask yourself: why would Vernon Jordan, who meets on a regular basis with the most powerful people on earth at the Bilderberg meetings – why would he help a chubby little intern who was known as a 'stalker' within the White House? Why would he lend his assistance in trying to find her employment, as well as a lawyer? Why would this global luminary even *speak* to her? Does he lend such a helping hand to *every* White House intern? Of course not. But he did when Bill Clinton's presidency was at stake, even going so far as to have Monica Lewinsky commit perjury before a grand jury

There were others who also tried to protect the president, such as "U.S. Representative to the U.N. Bill Richardson [who] had offered her [Lewinsky] a job in New York."[1051] Also on the president's side were those members of the media who had for decades concealed his tawdry little trysts, especially in Little Rock.

"Despite widespread talk of Clinton affairs in their newsrooms, the Arkansas press never once broached the subject in print. 'The reporters knew all about it,' said Darrell Glascock, the political operative who ran Frank White's 1986 campaign against Clinton. 'Hell, half of them went out drinking with Bill and Gennifer Flowers.'"[1052]

But Washington, D.C. was a horse of a different color, and there were certainly headhunters out to get Bill and Hillary.

The variable we must address right now is: could Monica Lewinsky – either knowingly or unknowingly – have been used as an agent to ensnare known philanderer Bill Clinton in a messy sexcapade?

For starters, Monica was an ideal candidate, for throughout

her adult life she was known by many acquaintances as being obsessive about men, even to the point of stalking them. Secondly, as is required of any agent, "Lewinsky possessed an extraordinary memory, and her friend Linda Tripp persuaded her to make a computerized matrix of all her contacts with the president."[1053] Third, Lewinsky, who was Jewish, "gained her internship on the recommendation of millionaire businessman Walter Kaye,"[1054] also Jewish. Her lawyer, William Ginsburg, was Jewish; and in fact, many of the other primary exposers were Jewish, including literary agent Lucianne Goldberg, plus two of the first members of the media to break the story: Matt Drudge and *Weekly Standard* editor William Kristol.

On top of that, of special note – especially in this age of victimization – was Lewinsky's lack of resorting to the victim role. "To Lewinsky's credit, she never portrayed herself as any kind of victim to Clinton's advances. Indeed, her own account of that day demonstrated how hard she tried to seduce the president. Her efforts began with a now-famous gesture ... she lifted her jacket and gave the president a quick glance at the top of her thong underwear."[1055]

Such an act is akin to offering heroin to a junkie ... they can't resist. Yes, the tables had been turned. Bill Clinton – the sexual predator – was now being preyed upon by the initiator Monica Lewinsky; almost as if she were on a mission!

Events then moved quickly: "Lewinsky allegedly began her affair with Clinton in the White House on Friday, November 15, 1995. Eleven days later she was converted to a full-time position responding to a congressional correspondence in the East Wing."[1056]

Her stay was short-lived, though, once Hillary and her pit bulls caught wind of what was taking place. "Deputy chief of staff Evelyn Lieberman took notice of what she believed was Lewinsky's 'inappropriate and immature behavior' and decided to move Lewinsky out of the White House. Lieberman allegedly nicknamed Lewinsky 'the stalker' because she was always hanging around the Oval Office."[1057]

This move proved to be catastrophic, for now Monica Lewinsky was in the clutches of a primary nemesis. "Clinton inadvertently set himself up for the real trouble with Monica Lewinsky; when the White House sent Monica to the Pentagon to keep her away from Clinton, they sent her right into Linda Tripp's path – the one person with incentive and determination to get the president. 'Linda Tripp was so devious; if there was anyone she could team up with to get Clinton, she'd do it,' [Kathleen] Willey explains. 'Of all the people in the world,' Willey chuckles, for the White House to 'put Monica in Tripp's vicinity – someone really messed up on that one. They could have put Monica anywhere, but they sent her to the Pentagon where Linda Tripp befriended her.'"[1058]

Was this relocation simply a mistake or oversight, or was it somehow done on purpose? Plus, Linda Tripp pops up yet again at just the right time. Coincidence, or was something more involved?

As we've already seen, it was Monica who *insisted* that Bill Clinton ejaculate on her Gap dress instead of pulling out, and it was Monica – seemingly without reason – who conveniently saved the semen-splotched garment instead of having it cleaned. How many women would *really* act in such a manner, especially in regard to something which is so apparently disgusting (i.e. a man ejaculating on her clothes)?

Even more crucial – especially when high risk affairs are supposed to be kept secret – Monica started gabbing to everyone within earshot; a detail that didn't escape the president. "Bill ... suspected that Monica blabbed, and in fact she had – revealing their affair to at least eleven people: her psychologist, her mother, her aunt, and a number of friends."[1059] To further anger her lover, Monica resorted to a form of quasi-blackmail. "She demanded presidential help to get a job in the private sector – feigning exposure of their relationship if he did not. Her declaration, made in a fit of anger, infuriated Bill; who warned her that a threat against the president was illegal."[1060]

Events were spiraling out of control – even becoming dangerous – and Monica knew it. "Monica seemed afraid that Clinton
was going to have her killed: 'for fear of my life, I would not cross
these people.'"[1061] Still, those who were in stark opposition to Clinton – and who would do anything to get him – held all the cards,
for "they knew where all the evidence was – the dress, the tapes,
the courier receipts, and the witnesses. All that was left now was
to get it all in the hands of Paula Jones's new lawyers – and the
reading public."[1062]

But yet again, all is not as it seems because as you'll read in
section three, the Clintons were actually *ecstatic* that Kenneth
Starr was selected to head the Monica Lewinsky investigation,
for this 'scandal' – in reality – saved (rather than destroyed) the
Clinton presidency. You'll soon find out why.

For the moment, one thing is clear. Bill Clinton's fling with
Monica Lewinsky was not simply a one-dimensional affair; but
instead it existed on many different levels in a *Spy vs. Spy* sort of
context. Was Bill Clinton ultimately a victim of his own carnal de-
sires, or was he set up by hidden forces above and beyond a mere
right-wing conspiracy?

THE CALIGULA FROM ARKANSAS

In his book *A Vast Conspiracy*, Jeffrey Toobin recalls the words
of journalist Michael Isikoff, "Clinton was far more psychologically disturbed than the public ever imagined."[1063] Toobin continued, "Clinton was a sex addict ... and virtually everything
that had gone wrong in his presidency – from Whitewater to
Paula Jones to the health care debacle – could be explained by the
crippling effects of Clinton's obsessive pursuit of sex."[1064] We all
saw the bedeviled president on TV at his very lowest when the
demons of Paula Jones and Monica Lewinsky were chasing him.
"He was evasive, lied, licked his lips, squirmed, and generally did
a tolerable imitation of someone who had been caught in *flagrante
delicto*."[1065]

He was (and still is) a sick man. "Like former President John F. Kennedy, Bill Clinton liked the chase more than the kill. Gennifer Flowers believed this about Bill when she wrote, 'I think Bill was addicted to the chase, not the sex act itself, but the actual conquering of all these women.'"[1066] Flowers continued, "Bill is the most sex-crazed man I've ever known. His tastes in sex are incredibly varied to the point of being kinky."[1067] Tragically, if a woman resisted, Clinton turned violent. Monica Lewinsky's attorney called Clinton a misogynist – a hater of women.

But don't be fooled; Clinton is well aware of his problem, for he once told aide Dick Morris in regard to Monica Lewinsky, "I've tried to shut myself down, sexually, I mean. But sometimes I slipped up, and with this girl, I just slipped up."[1068] In the same breath, Clinton relished in his voracious appetites and indulgences.

One day, while Clinton was preparing to go jogging, [trooper] Perry said, "Governor, you're gonna make Gary Hart look like a damned saint." Clinton laughed and said, "Yeah, I do, don't I?"[1069]

A cottage industry of sorts sprung up around Clinton's dalliances, complete with nicknames ("Slick Willie"), monikers ("Fornigate" and "Troopergate"), and comedy skits. The Little Rock Bar Association, "in its biennial spoof called *The Gridiron*, featured in 1988 two lawyers portraying Gary Hart and Bill Clinton, who sang, 'To All the Girls We've Loved Before.' (Bill and Hillary did not attend)."[1070]

All joking aside, Clinton's flagrant practices were no laughing matter, for they not only placed him in jeopardy, but the entire nation. Writer Peggy Noonan imagined a scenario where instead of Bill Clinton engaging in late-night phone sex, it was another president. "President Bush is informed that these calls – lengthy, graphic – are being listened to and presumably taped by foreign intelligence operatives. This opens the President, and the United States, to blackmail."[1071]

As we saw earlier in regard to Monica Lewinsky, there's a strong possibility that certain forces seized upon Bill Clinton's vulnerabilities and used them to manipulate him. As we'll point out in an upcoming chapter, the implications for national security become even more troublesome. Also, please don't get me wrong; Bill Clinton was by no means a 'victim' or an innocent party, for he's a rapist and sexual harasser of the worst sort. Additionally, "sexual predators often repeat patterns,"[1072] making them even more prone to exploitation. Bill Clinton – due to his selfish indulgences – placed our entire nation in jeopardy.

To perpetuate his sordid behavior, Clinton surrounded himself with those who would facilitate and enable him. The Arkansas state troopers were one example, while fetishist Dick Morris was another. "Mr. Morris served for a long spell as Bill Clinton's pimp. He and Mr. Clinton shared some pretty foul evenings together, bloating and satiating themselves at public expense while consigning the poor and defenseless to more misery. The kinds of grossness and greed in which they indulged are perfectly cognate with one another – selfish and fleshy and hypocritical and exploitative. 'The Monster,' Morris called Clinton when in private congress with his whore. 'The creep,' she called Morris when she could get away and have a decent bath."[1073]

Bill Clinton and his twisted associates were akin to Nero, Caligula, and the debaucherous Roman satyrs of old who brought empires to ruin. Rather than being a virtuous, upstanding man; Clinton fiddled with his prostitutes, groupies, and sycophants. Christopher Hitchens writes in *No One Left to Lie To*: "The Oval Office may have presented itself to him as a potentially therapeutic location, but once he arrived there he half realized that he had no big plans, no grand thoughts, no noble dreams. He also realized that he might have to give up one of the few things that did bring him release from his demons."[1074]

The only problem is, Clinton never did forego his lust and libido, and the entire country suffered as a result. Like Richard

Nixon before he resigned, Bill Clinton was only inches away from being removed from office; and losing its 'leader' cannot be beneficial to any country. But Bill Clinton didn't give a damn about us, his nation, daughter, wife, or cabinet. He was consumed by juvenile phone sex, masturbation, and toying with chubby interns half his age. Renowned author Gore Vidal summed it up best. "Clinton doesn't much care for warm mature relationships with warm caring women. Hence an addiction to the impersonal [oral sex]."[1075]

When caught and possibly held accountable for his actions – when his world started crumbling around him – Clinton resorted to a tactic used by other maniacal, psychologically disturbed leaders – destruction. "Not once but three times ... Bill Clinton ordered the use of cruise missiles against remote and unpopular countries. On each occasion, the dispatch of the missiles coincided with bad moments in the calendar of his long and unsuccessful struggles to avoid impeachment."[1076] Moreover, "On August 20, 1998, the night of Monica Lewinsky's return to the grand jury and just three days after his dismal and self-pitying non-apology had 'bombed' on prime-time TV, Clinton personally ordered missile strikes against the El Shifa Pharmaceutical Industrial Company on the outskirts of Sudan's capital city."[1077]

How secure does it make you feel knowing that missile strikes (i.e. tactics to divert the public's attention, also known as *wagging the dog*) were used by the Clintons depending on how much hot water Bill's adulterous ways had gotten him into? It's reminiscent of Samson in the Old Testament – a man who, if he had to die, would have also caused the death of thousands of others who had gathered to see him be humiliated. In other words, Samson said: if I'm going, I'm taking all of you with me.

We're talking about a madman; an individual so unhinged that – if cornered – is capable of anything. "Some thought it all undeniably pathological. 'What has emerged,' Geordie Greig of the London *Sunday Times* wrote, 'is a man with what would appear to be an almost psychotic inability to control his zipper.'"[1078]

Bill Clinton was so uncouth about his practices that it likened him to a sort of *Chester the Molester* character out of a porn magazine. Former *Arkansas Gazette* reporter Carol Griffee described him in these words. "He made no attempt to hide his womanizing. His leering at pretty women around the Capitol was disgusting. It was just so obvious it made me sick."[1079] Pathetically, Clinton didn't even have the decency to be honest about himself.

> **"Did you ever think you were a sex addict?" Dolly [Kyle Browning] asked.**
>
> **There was a pause. Clinton nodded. "I know I am – and I've tried to overcome it," he said. "But it's so hard. Women are everywhere, and for some reason they seem to want me."[1080]**

But as we've seen, Bill Clinton was the pursuer, initiator, and attacker. *He* was the one who dispatched his trooper-pimps to procure women, not the other way around. The smug arrogance of transferring blame onto these women is indicative of a man satiated with sickness. Clearly, "Clinton was trouble, a man whose sexual compulsions were far greater than anybody suspected."[1081] However, the thrill – the rebellion against those he felt (rightly so) had *entrapped* him into a loveless political marriage – was so immense that he couldn't let go. "James Carville had asked Clinton about his tendency to live dangerously. 'Well, they haven't caught me yet,' he replied."[1082]

A few pages earlier I described Bill Clinton's Caligula-like hedonism as a form of rebellion against those forces which he felt entrapped him. I didn't use this term as an excuse or form of apology for Clinton; instead, he was thrust into a situation beyond his understanding due to one essential variable: an occult-like, mesmerizing charisma. Sure, the word charisma is bandied about quite a bit these days; but Bill Clinton's gift, or power, is so extraordinary that it's almost supernatural. Secondly, this talent wasn't something that he solely developed with practice or hard work. No, his was a transcendent, genetic ability that certainly did not originate with his supposed father, the lowly William Blythe. Bill Clinton is an *adept*; a magician whose powers have lifted him into the uppermost echelon of political power.

I once had a neighbor, very conservative and ultra-opposed to Bill Clinton and his policies, who went to see him speak. I could even go so far as to say this man was an unabashed Clinton hater. But afterward, he told me that Clinton had cast such a spell over the audience that even *he* was almost ready to go out and vote for him!

This power fed into Clinton's insatiable appetite for danger, especially when he felt excessively imprisoned by his pre-arranged handler, Hillary Rodham. Privately, Bill Clinton *despises* his controllers; yet likewise he knows that since they had designs on him (i.e. long-range plans), that he would ultimately be protected. Thus, he sees just how much he can get away with – all the while laughing while Hillary and the hidden elite squirm in their seats. "There was always the sneaking suspicion that Clinton was a bit bored, that he needed the thrill of a crisis – and that if the world didn't present him with a challenge, he'd create one himself."[1083]

Over time, due to his protected status, Bill Clinton became the consummate liar and deceiver, as can be seen from his testimony after being deposed as a defendant in the Paula Jones case. "Mr. Bennett, in my lifetime, I've never sexually harassed a woman, and I've never done what she [Paula Jones] accused me of doing. I didn't do it then, because I never have, and I wouldn't."[1084] Now, the truth: "He is a sexual predator and exploiter of women, his behavior may be more egregious than that which destroyed the political careers and reputations of Gary Hart, John Tower and, most recently, Bob Packwood."[1085]

Over the years, even supporters have had to reevaluate their stance on this man, especially when allegations arose from a very credible source (and former Clinton supporter) Kathleen Willey.

"Feminists seemed torn and divided about how to respond to Willey. Patricia Ireland, then president of NOW, said of Willey's story, 'If it's true, it's sexual assault,' not just sexual harassment. Now we're talking about, really, sexual predators and people who in positions of power use that power to take advantage of women."[1086]

Even more direct was "the president of a renegade state chapter of NOW [that] broke ranks with the national organization over Clinton's behavior and warned White House staffers to be careful: 'Mr. Clinton is an abuser of women ... is there anyone there to protect them? Can they report an assault safely, or will they and their families be threatened?'"[1087]

Lastly, some may wonder: why is this subject still relevant? The answer is obvious. Do you want this man back in the White House? Do we need to have this type of sickness directly affect our lives yet again; for, as a psychologist notes, "It is important to discuss Clinton's sexual liaisons because they exceed normal behavior and do affect his presidential abilities. This sexual behavior most adequately can be described as pathological."[1088]

What we have is a dangerous combination of not only an extremist personality, but one that is mentally unbalanced and immoral to the highest degree. To compound matters, Clinton is "a glutton rather than a gourmet [who] had to have a woman almost daily. His appetite was so voracious that any girl would do, provided she was willing and they could find a private place."[1089]

Bill Clinton is a pig; and if that's not reprehensible enough, when his wife Hillary is added to the mix – a woman so extreme in her obsession with power that she did everything humanly possible to cover up her husband's deplorable behavior – we face an authentic danger as a nation if we return them to the White House.

THE ADULTERER'S ENABLER

Prior to touching upon Hillary's own brand of marital infidelity, let's first deconstruct the myth that she was simply a naïve little wife that lived in a cave and knew absolutely nothing about her husband's scurrilous ways. The truth of the matter is: Hillary is a control freak, an information junkie, and the primary reason she was paired with Bill as his fixer in a pre-arranged marriage was to (a) keep an eagle's eye on him, and (b) bail him out of all the hot water that he'd inevitably get himself into due to his teen-like libido and mobster ways.

Let's look at it this way. "After Gennifer Flowers, Paula Jones, Elizabeth Ward Gracen, Dolly Kyle Browning, Kathleen Willey, Sally Perdue, the testimony of state troopers L.D. Brown and Danny Ferguson, Betsey Wright's warning about the women problems that would emerge if Bill ran for president in 1988, and dozens of others, *is Hillary seriously asking us to believe that she gave Bill the benefit of the doubt?* And when it came out that Bill had spoken to Monica more than one-hundred times in person or on the phone – including late night calls – didn't Hillary think twice about Bill's limited admission that he had 'talked to her a few times?'"[1090]

When Hillary Clinton puts on a pretense of simply being a 1950s June Cleaver wife that was kept in the dark about her husband's philandering, she is a liar. Let's call a spade a spade. This woman is equally as dishonest and disingenuous as the rat-fink man she's married to, and it's time to expose her deceitful ways.

Going back over three decades, Hillary was already establishing a spy network that would monitor Bill's actions, initially using her own family to do so. "Her father's role as private detective in Bill's 1974 congressional campaign [was] to keep track of the young law professor's intense affair with an undergraduate campaign volunteer, and numerous flings with other girls in towns around the district. That Hugh Rodham would undertake such a mission suggests the family's pliancy before their bossy daughter."[1091] During this time, Hillary's family actually relocated to Arkansas. "The

Rodham men's real reason for being in Arkansas had nothing to do with helping out in the campaign. They were there to spy on Bill, and what they learned disturbed Hillary's father."[1092] Hugh Rodham and others soon discovered that "Bill was having affairs with, by one count, thirty young women – one for each of the twenty-one counties – plus some spares."[1093]

Her father wasn't the only Rodham placed on Bill's trail. "Hillary pushed her brother to take out one of the women Bill was dating, but the ploy didn't work. While Bill was out on the campaign trail, Hillary rifled through his desk and tore up girlfriends' telephone numbers."[1094] Hillary's brother didn't take his hatchet man responsibilities lightly. "Hughie Rodham went after that girl with both barrels. Hillary sent him to do her bidding for her, to get her ass gone. He was putting a rush on that girl something hard."[1095] Ironically, in *Spy vs. Spy* fashion, Bill had his own counter cover-up network operating in opposition to Hillary's. "Unbeknownst to Hillary, one of Mary Lee [Fray's] jobs in the campaign was to hide Bill's other girlfriends from Hillary."[1096]

For thirty-plus years, Hillary has been hounding, harassing, spying upon, and bailing out her husband when he had engaged in – by his own admission – thousands of illicit affairs. So, "it is hard to imagine Mrs. Clinton had literally never heard of Monica Lewinsky ... In fact, one White House source claimed that it was Hillary's aide, Roberta Green, not the President, who was the first to brief her on the breaking story."[1097] Therefore, *all* that she wrote in her autobiography was a lie, and all the stories she floated to the media were likewise lies.

Hillary knew, and she's always known. How are we to tolerate and accept her history of deception? "In early 1982, she [Hillary] contacted a private investigator named Ivan Duda to compile a list of the women Bill had allegedly been seeing."[1098] Does this account sound like innocence and naivete? How many wives hire Mickey Spillane to trail their husbands? To show how extensive her secret police network was, "Hillary learned about private investigators in her work on behalf of the Black Panthers and the Communist apol-

ogists Robert Treuhaft and Jessica Mitford. Now Hillary was constantly checking up on Bill, not just to learn the extent of his betrayals, but to assess the danger he posed to their joint political
career."[1099] Don't you get it: it was Hillary's *job* to spy on her husband ... that was part of the contract she signed!

After Bill became governor, Hillary knew about another longtime mistress. "Gennifer Flowers claims that she and Bill discussed whether Hillary knew about their affair, and both assumed
she did ... Gennifer also claimed that one evening, shortly after
Bill hung up the telephone after having a conversation with her,
Hillary walked into the room and asked Bill, 'How's Gennifer?'"[1100]
Hillary was so aware of Bill's infidelities, and pushed so far with
frustration that "according to Clinton biographer David Maraniss,
one time after Hillary discussed one of Bill's affairs, she told him
she intended to sleep around just to get back at him."[1101]

If we're to believe Hillary, though, she's had the wool pulled
over her eyes all these years. If their marriage is a sham, why
doesn't Hillary simply stand up and admit it instead of clinging to
this unconvincing charade? "As first lady of Arkansas, Hillary used
the governor's chief of staff, Betsey Wright, to fish him out of countless bedrooms all over the state."[1102] The same Betsey Wright "said
that he was having a serious affair with another woman, and was
not even being discreet about it. Everyone knew, she said. She
knew, the troopers knew, *Hillary knew*."[1103]

To rub her face in his filth even further, Joyce Milton writes, "At
times, he flirted outrageously with women in front of Hillary, and
even in front of the women's husbands."[1104] On another occasion,
"Bill had chatted at length with an attractive woman. After he returned to a fuming Hillary's side, she was heard to rasp, 'Come on,
Bill, put up your [penis]. You can't f*** her here.'"[1105]

To combat these obvious *threats* to her political career (as opposed to a mere secondary concern – her marriage), Hillary assumed an unmitigated combative stance. One adviser described
their behind-the-scenes strategy. "She was never to play the poor
little wife. They would be prepared to strike back at any woman

accusers – 'taking on the bitches' as one former staff member put it."[1106] After the Gennifer Flowers story broke during the 1992 Democratic primaries in New Hampshire, "The Clinton campaign made a strategic decision that Hillary would take the lead in deflecting the womanizing stories, just as she had deflected rumors in Arkansas by invoking the 'zone of privacy.'"[1107]

In what became a sickening portrayal of a woman who called herself a feminist, yet tried to destroy women her husband had pursued and sexually harassed, Hillary would use any tactic necessary to protect herself (at the women's expense). A prime example is Paula Jones and what "Clinton advisor Dick Morris would later describe as a standard Clinton 'secret police' smear campaign. Jones was portrayed as a promiscuous practitioner of oral sex, white trash, a cheap slut, and a dupe of radical-right Republicans."[1108]

It's hard to imagine a phonier person on the planet than Hillary Clinton. Years earlier, when rock & roll groupie Connie Hamzy went public with her recollection of how she and Bill almost made it in a hotel laundry room, Hillary was not entertained. "We have to destroy her story, she said."[1109] Hillary wasn't a sweet little wife to be patted on the head and kept out of the loop; she was the snarling dog let off its leash!

When Monica Lewinsky came onto the scene, Hillary had another plan of attack. "Her main watchdog was Deputy Chief of Staff Evelyn Lieberman, a short, overweight, gray-haired woman ... Hillary assigned her loyal friend the task of monitoring the sexual activity of Bill Clinton – a role that helped earn Evelyn the nickname 'Mother Superior.'"[1110] After all, as Edward Klein tells us, "Nobody was surprised about Monica. The Secret Security knew all about her. Everyone I talked to knew she was obsessed with the President. And when I say everyone, I mean everyone – including *Hillary*."[1111] As a result:

If Monica had any doubt about who was behind her transfer [to the Pentagon], her

confusion was cleared up during a twenty-minute telephone conversation with the President on April 12, 1996. During that call, Bill Clinton revealed that Evelyn Lieberman, a.k.a. Mother Superior, had spearheaded Monica's removal from the White House because he had been paying too much attention to her. Monica didn't have to be told that Evelyn was Hillary's chief spear-carrier.[1112]

Needless to say, Hillary has been behind the attacks on Bill's women since day one. "Months before Betsey Wright ever inserted herself into the campaign [1992], Hillary was in command of the damage control required by those first and potentially most damaging bimbo eruptions."[1113] But she didn't stop at simple surveillance. "Hillary hired private detectives to identify the women her husband was sleeping with, and to intimidate these women so they would not go public with their stories."[1114] Then, after Bill was elected president: "upon her arrival in the White House in January, 1993, Hillary put together a team of aides whose primary job was to keep an eye on her faithless husband."[1115]

To Hillary and her henchmen, this was a full-scale assault. When Gennifer Flowers finally spoke publicly, "Dee Dee Myers called Clinton media man Frank Greer, who said, 'our smoking bimbo has emerged.' After Flowers held her press conference, Clinton advisor James Carville declared, 'we're going to have to go to war,' and appeared on the *Today* show the next morning to attack Flowers' credibility."[1116]

To prove how aware and in control of this situation Hillary was, she even determined which of Bill's affairs were *acceptable*. "Hillary was selective about how she used the club of infidelity to beat her husband. For instance, she allowed him to keep a virtual harem under the roof of the White House."[1117] Even Evelyn Lieberman (aka Mother Superior) was given her marching orders. "She adopted a hands-off attitude when Bill Clinton indulged in affairs with women who were labeled 'safe' by the First Lady. As a result, several of Bill Clinton's former girlfriends, who were known as 'the graduates,' were given cushy jobs in the White House."[1118]

Before moving on, just so there is no mistake, by 1998:

> • **Hillary knew that Linda Tripp had taped Monica describing her affair explicitly.**
>
> • **Hillary knew that Lewinsky had visited the White House more than three dozen times since leaving her job.**
>
> • **Hillary knew that her friend Evelyn Lieberman, Clinton's deputy chief of staff, had transferred Monica from the White House to the Pentagon because she was around Bill too much.**
>
> • **Hillary knew that Clinton had lied to her about his relationship with Gennifer Flowers.**
>
> • **Hillary knew that Betty Currie, Clinton's loyal secretary, was often listed as the cover for Monica's meetings with him.**
>
> • **Hillary knew that Monica Lewinsky had told Vernon Jordan that "she had had sex with Clinton and that she planned to lie to the court."**
>
> • **Hillary knew that Bill had given Monica a copy of Walt Whitman's *Leaves of Grass*, the same book he'd given Hillary "after our second date."**
>
> • **Hillary knew that Starr had asked for a blood sample from the president, and press leaks linked it to Monica's blue dress.**[1119]

The Clinton marriage is an absolute farce: a sneaky, vicious, political arrangement that is more toxic than a nuclear waste site. To keep this lie alive before the public, Hillary "couldn't admit to knowing that Bill and Monica were an item ... because that would make it impossible for her to stand by her man in public."[1120]

Despite her outward face, privately Hillary was enraged by her role as the humiliated doormat wife. Monica Lewinsky was the last straw. "Behind closed doors, the Clintons' union – the pact they had made years earlier – was all but shattered by the scandal. Hillary yelled and cursed and threw things, and on at least one occasion smacked Bill in the face."[1121]

Hillary, ever the violent domestic partner who could give any wife-beater a run for his money, erupted over the Barbara Streisand incident too. "Tales of a bloody confrontation between the Clintons prompted by Streisand's visit circulated wildly. Paul Fray put it succinctly: 'Hillary left Little Rock like a rocket, went back, and caught the son of a bitch. You know who got hit in the chops, and who got smacked around.'"[1122]

How many times has Hillary stood on her soapbox and championed the subject of spousal abuse in public, but after she catches Bill in another one of his dalliances, she does precisely what she speaks out against. After nailing Bill yet again, Christopher Andersen describes what ensued. "This time, she screamed obscenities at Bill at the top of her lungs. 'What do you mean?' she yelled as Bill turned vermilion. 'What are you saying? Why did you lie to me? You stupid, stupid, stupid bastard!' Hillary leaped up and slapped Bill hard across the face."[1123] It's like reading about two mental patients.

Yet, there were more lies ... and lies and lies and lies. "Bill Clinton lies like a man detached from conscience, or perhaps born without one."[1124] Worse, Hillary lies to cover for her husband's lies. As a well-noted writer stated, "Most self-respecting women would have left. Hillary chose to stay."[1125] Why? Because she signed a deal with the devil – a prearranged marriage pact that now – due to her own excessive criminality and the threat of imprisonment – has her trapped. Bill's escape was to cheat on her. "Bill and Hillary often slept in separate bedrooms, so he had no fear on those occasions of disturbing his wife when he was sneaking out of the mansion."[1126] Without recourse, Hillary simply growled that her husband "had gone off to be in the arms of 'another one of your sluts,' as she referred to them."[1127] [It is troublesome how many derogatory terms for women the Clintons use, especially since they are such self-proclaimed proponents of the feminist cause.]

Here's how sick their contractual partnership really is. "Many close to the first family maintain that Hillary and Bill came to an arrangement to have an 'open marriage,' whereby he would continue to play around – and she would be free to engage in extramarital activity whenever she so desired."[1128]

We're going to delve into the subject of Hillary's sordid sex life in a few pages, but for the moment let's ponder what one of Bill's mistresses – Gennifer Flowers – had to say. "Hillary's reasons for putting up with Bill's adultery baffled me at the time. Maybe she was into women, as Bill's 'she's [performed] more [oral sex on women] than I ever will' remark conveyed. Or maybe Hillary really was having an affair with Vince Foster or some other man. In retrospect, the best guess is that Bill and Hillary's marriage was – and still is – essentially a business arrangement."[1129]

One of the consequences, quite obviously, was the danger involved in such a 'partnership'. "The growing list of Bill's partners was a wake-up call for Hillary. In light of Bill's long-standing aversion to wearing a condom, Hillary was now worried that he was putting her health at risk in this age of AIDS and other sexually transmitted diseases. She demanded that he be tested for HIV."[1130]

Theirs was truly a marriage made in hell, and the only compensation was for the ever-opportunistic Hillary to get all she could for herself. "Bill Clinton might get a lot of 'pussy' – to use one of his favorite words – but every time Hillary came to his defense, he fell deeper and deeper into her debt. How many times had aides heard Hillary say, 'Bill owes me?'"[1131]

Considering the adultery, humiliation, violence, abuse, and mockery, Mrs. Clinton cared only about one thing: her political survival and advancement. "Hillary had long ago washed her hands of him, not because of his womanizing, but because of his getting caught womanizing. For years the word has been that the two sleep in separate bedrooms, putting on a united front for the public and media, but disappearing into their own separate worlds in private ... Bill and Hillary's marriage was dead and buried a long, long time ago. Had it not been for public office, they undoubtedly would have gotten divorced."[1132]

If these two weren't so vicious and self-serving, their situation would almost evoke some sympathy. But as it is, they seemed fated for joint misery. As for their 'marriage,' it certainly didn't deteriorate overnight; in fact, it was doomed before it ever began. "Bill had been unfaithful to Hillary even during their engagement, and moving to Little Rock as an attorney general had only broadened his opportunities with other women."[1133]

To further alienate his wife and inspire hatred in her for him, Clinton continued to belittle and degrade her to his girlfriends. "One of Bill's alleged mistresses claims that he told her that Hillary did not enjoy sex with him, that she was not playful in bed and insisted they make love only in the missionary position."[1134] His mean streak seems particularly aimed at inflicting cruelty upon Hillary, as can be seen from her response after learning about a specific incident with Monica Lewinsky. "When it was revealed that Bill had given Monica a number of gifts, including a copy of Walt Whitman's *Leaves of Grass*, Hillary became noticeably upset. 'He gave me the same book,' she told an aide, 'on our second date.'"[1135]

How does Hillary survive such humiliations? Answer: either by distancing herself from the subject, or further burrowing in a secluded shell. For example, when state troopers came forward with stories about Bill Clinton while he was governor of Arkansas, "Mrs. Clinton barred Troopergate questions from Christmas interviews."[1136]

Another tactic was to create an illusion so far-removed from reality that it was hard to imagine anyone falling for it. What follows is a monstrous spin she put on the Monica Lewinsky affair. "Mrs. Clinton took [Sidney] Blumenthal aside and explained her view of what had happened – that is, what the president had told her about

Monica Lewinsky that morning. Monica was a troubled young woman, Mrs. Clinton said, and her husband had 'ministered' to her. 'He ministers to troubled people all the time,' she said. 'He's done it dozens if not hundreds of times. He does it out of religious conviction and personal temperament.'"[1137]

So, let's get this straight. When Bill Clinton performed a quasi-form of cunnilingus on Monica Lewinsky with a cigar, then put it in his mouth and commented on how good it tasted, he was really *ministering* to her? And when he received sexual gratification in Chelsea's elementary school parking lot, that too was a form of spiritual *ministering?* When he took quickies with Gennifer Flowers in a bathroom, groped and terrorized Kathleen Willey, or engaged in a ménage a trois with Little Rock prostitutes; was that *ministering* too? In fact, maybe the word 'adultery' should be changed to *ministering* because Bill Clinton sure seems to be good at it! He could even give Jimmy Swaggart a run for his money in that department when Jimmy was *ministering* to cheap hookers in a sleazy hotel room.

Let's face it: this woman is a fake feminist in the same exact way that she has a fake marriage, for "Hillary Rodham Clinton is a feminist who averts her eye from the foulest treatment of women."[1138] By enabling her husband's vile, boorish behavior, the message she sends to every female across the world is as such: "Accept your victimhood. You're trapped. Whatever your accomplishments in life, you're bound to the man who brought you to the dance. Never mind shattered trust, broken vows, serial cheating, a lifetime of explanations and denial."[1139]

Denial is a key, as is blame, such as on *other* women. In a 1999 *Talk* magazine interview, Hillary "hinted that her husband's life-long compulsive philandering was related to being 'scarred by abuse' as a four-year-old. Apparently his mother and grandmother had quarreled and vied for his affection."[1140] Of course this explanation was widely ridiculed and received with a chorus of boos, even from Hillary's most loyal supporters. "Nobody surpassed Hillary in the role of enabler. Every addict or alcoholic needs one.

The enabler is usually an intimate of the addicted person who allows him to persist in self-destructive behavior by making excuses
or helping him avoid the consequences of his actions."[1141]

Still, Hillary wants us to keep thinking she's merely in a state
of denial, when – if the truth is told – she's been Bill's primary pit
bull for decades. Her tactics are an authentic sign of sickness. "She
was well aware that her husband cheated, but reflexively sided
with him, displacing her anger at Bill's betrayal of her onto the
women. How satisfying to vent her rage at women who romped
with Bill by demonizing them as lying tramps. [Joyce] Milton also
reports that 'campaign aides who happened to overhear her and
Bill discussing the 'bitches' who were making his life miserable
were shocked by the level of vitriol. Hillary had almost worked
herself around to believing that Bill was the sexual harassment victim, beset by predatory females."[1142]

Bill, ever the slimy conman, fed right into Hillary's self-decep-
tive ploy. Try this one on for size. "He [Clinton] told her that Kathleen Willey's sexual harassment allegations were ludicrous because
'he would never be interested in small-breasted women.'"[1143] What
a hoot! Bill didn't care if they were big-breasted, small-breasted,
triple-breasted, Kentucky Fried Chicken breasted, or sideshow car-
nival freak-breasted; just so they said yes.

Surrounded by so much deception, skullduggery, and betrayal,
the end result is that Hillary skulks further and further into an isolated world of paranoia and distrust. Of course she's frequently
surrounded by staff, aides, and glad-handers; but her world is ultimately lonely and quiet. "After the humiliating disclosure that her
husband had left behind what was politely termed 'DNA material'
on Monica's blue dress, Hillary retreated into what commentators
called a 'dignified silence.'"[1144]

The word *dignity* in this context is a misnomer, for there is nothing whatsoever dignified about her prearranged marriage. She is
a woman alone. One campaign donor said sadly, "I'm not sure
how many people are close to Hillary at all."[1145] Or, as Edward
Klein observed,

> **She never confided in anyone. "She is so
> shrewd," Jan Piercy told the *New Yorker* writer
> Connie Bruck. "She has known all along that
> people around [the Clintons] would be placed
> in a position of being interviewed by the press
> – and, while she as a public figure has been
> very schooled in how to protect your privacy,
> she realized that her friends wouldn't have
> that sophistication. So she has kept her own
> counsel. She has not availed herself of what
> the rest of us do – crying on someone's shoul-
> der. She has extraordinary self-possession and
> discipline."[1146]**

LESBIANISM + THE AFFAIR WITH VINCE FOSTER

In advance of our examination of Hillary Clinton's extramarital
relationship with Vince Foster, we need to first re-explore the
rumors of Hillary's lesbianism. Ironically, one of the primary
contributors to this smorgasbord of information is Bill Clinton
himself. "Gennifer Flowers contributed a naughty one-liner in her
book, saying Bill had told her Hillary had 'eaten more pussy' than
he had."[1147]

Another Clinton aide publicly hinted in the same direction.
"One-time Clinton advisor Dick Morris made a series of vaguer
comments on a Los Angeles radio talk show in 1988. 'Let's assume
some of the allegations that Hillary is sometimes not into regular
sex with men might be true.'"[1148]

Such talk wasn't simply limited to her husband and Dick Morris. "There were other, more generalized rumors about Hillary that
circulated around Arkansas, and later, Washington, as well – that
Hillary was a lesbian, or at least bisexual; and this was what explained their odd marriage."[1149] Another woman, "Mandy Merck,
Bill's radical feminist (and lesbian) friend from Oxford, heard them
when she visited America in the spring of 1999. 'When I was in

New York and Washington, tons of people said Hillary was gay. I heard 'lover' in New York, I heard 'lover' in L.A.'"[1150]

The origin of these stories can be traced to several sources. "When Hillary came to Arkansas, drinking cronies of the Stephens brothers spread the rumor that Hillary was a lesbian."[1151]

[Note: It is widely agreed that the Stephens family is one of the most influential power brokers in the state of Arkansas and, as you'll see, intimately linked to the Clinton crime network.]

Shortly thereafter, "Hillary had the company of Nancy 'Peach' Pietrafesa, an outspoken feminist. Pietrafesa and Danner [her husband] had come to Arkansas a few months before the election to work as volunteers on Clinton's campaign. They stayed with Bill and Hillary to save money, a situation that quickly gave rise to rumors that Pietrafesa was Hillary's lesbian lover, imported from out of state.

After the election, Clinton appointed Pietrafesa liaison officer to the Ozarks Regional Committee, making her the highest-ranking woman in his administration."[1152] The link between them extends back several decades. "This same Nancy 'Peach' Pietrafesa had been Hillary's best friend during her senior year at Wellesley, and who, after moving to Little Rock, was rumored to be Hillary's lesbian lover."[1153]

Another piece of the puzzle emerged after the Clintons relocated to our nation's capital.

"One particularly peculiar tale circulated among the Washington cognoscenti around the time of Clinton's impeachment trial – that a well-known Washington veterinarian, visiting the White House to treat Socks the cat, had opened the wrong door and discovered Hillary locked in a passionate embrace with another woman.

The oddest thing about this tale was who was telling it: it had been passed on by a stalwart Clinton loyalist, a man who repeatedly demonstrated his willingness to fall on his sword in defense of the president."[1154]

Still, the most damning source of information derives from

someone who would know better than anyone about Hillary's sexuality: her husband. In an interview with Larry Nichols late in Clinton's second term, Gennifer Flowers had the following to say:

> **Nichols: What is one of the most juicy things that Bill told you about Hillary ...?**
> **Flowers: The things that Bill told me about Hillary, I think a lot of this has already been out there. You know, he called her 'Hilla the Hun.' And he told me that she was bisexual. But everybody knows that.**[1155]

Then, when questioned by Alan Colmes, the liberal half of Fox's *Hannity & Colmes*, Flowers revealed even more.

> **Colmes: Did Bill confide anything to you about Hillary that you think the public should know?**
> **Flowers: Let me see if I can figure out what you're really asking here. No, what Bill told me about Hillary he never planned for the public to know. Clearly he knew that she was bisexual. That didn't matter to him.**
> **Colmes: Clearly he knew that?**
> **Flowers: He knew that. He told me that. That's been knowledge in Arkansas for a number of years. I'm very surprised that that hasn't come to light in a more definitive manner.**[1156]

Hillary's husband made an even further admission to Gennifer Flowers. "Bill had always led me to believe that he and Hillary didn't have much of a sex life, and even confirmed a rumor I'd heard that she was having an affair with a woman."[1157]

Despite Hillary's attempts to guard her sexual orientation, even the gay community itself has outed her.

"During a huge, gay activist March on Washington in the spring of 1993, a lesbian leader stood on the main platform before an audience of untold thousands of other lesbians and homosexuals and joyfully divulged this repulsive bit of information: 'I'm going to tell you a secret,' she said, 'Hillary Clinton has had a lesbian affair. At last we have a First Lady in the White House we can f***.'"[1158]

The question arises: was this self-professed lesbian speaker lying about Mrs. Clinton? One writer comments, "Even though the entire city of Washington DC was abuzz with people talking about it, *Hillary Clinton has never issued a flat denial.* If this was a lie, Hillary should have been outraged. She could have immediately called a press conference and adamantly stated, 'I am *not* a lesbian. That would be wrong.' But she did not."[1159]

Further, Jack Wheeler, publisher of the *Strategic Investment* newsletter, states, "My sources indicate that Hillary Clinton is bisexual and fools around more than her husband. The stories you hear from the Secret Service, detailed to guard her, are mind-boggling ... It is Hillary that is pushing the White House's homosexual agenda."[1160]

Since Hillary remains mum on the subject, speculation still arises as to precisely what her sexuality is. From my perspective, if Hillary is bisexual, why doesn't she simply come out and stand by her convictions and decisions? Why hide in shame? Plus, if everyone remembers correctly, what was the first scandal (prior to all the *other* skirmishes) that marked the Clinton presidency? Answer: gays in the military. Was their insistence on pushing this issue merely a coincidence, or something much more personal?

Like so many other aspects of Hillary's life, her sexuality is clouded in secrecy. But when it comes to attorney Vince Foster, once her closet doors begin opening, quite a number of skeletons are revealed. As we'll see, those troopers closest to Bill Clinton revealed "that the First Lady had been having an affair with a recently deceased White House counsel whose suicide was that of the highest-ranking government official since James Forrestal."[1161]

This *suicide*, though, was actually a murder; but we'll cover that aspect of the story in a later chapter.

For the time being, when author R. Emmett Tyrrell investigated this matter, he showed it to Kenneth Lynn, a noted history professor from John Hopkins University, who thought, "The active love affair between the First Lady and the White House lawyer, now dead, was ... the stuff of headlines."[1162]

Yet, as an extension of the entire Vince Foster cover-up, "Even a year-and-a-half later when the Senate Whitewater Committee was probing Foster's death, no one mentioned the famous couple's affair."[1163]

Why was this subject being avoided, especially when various reports stated that "the two were exceedingly close and even had a 'love nest' which they utilized whenever they could find time on their schedules?"[1164] More specifically, "'Within the small circle of politically clued-in people in Little Rock, it was accepted as fact that Hillary and Vince were sleeping with each other,' said Michael Galster, a medical worker whose wife, Vali, was a good friend of Hillary's and worked closely with her on children's educational issues. 'Hillary and Vince's love affair was an open secret.'"[1165]

Even the media started uncovering details that pointed in the direction of an affair. "During Bill's first presidential run, a number of researchers for the television shows came to town [Little Rock] to investigate the tales about Bill's infidelities – and all they kept coming up with were rumors about Vince and Hillary."[1166] Prior to delving into the troopers' revelations, we should initially take a glance at how Vince and Hillary's paths converged. The couple "had met years before while working with the Legal Services Corporation. In Little Rock, they spent endless hours together, establishing an intimate bond, and consoled each other about their unhappy marriages."[1167]

Their attraction was centered on a shared misery. "What drew her and Vince together was that they were two unhappy people who had freely chosen lives that made them unhappy."[1168] Does this description sound like anything that would result from a contractual, prearranged marriage?

Clearly, the Clinton's loveless bond did not only affect Bill; for both of them lived lives of despair and longing for something authentic.

Moving on, during their Little Rock years, Foster became Hillary's "longtime partner at Arkansas's now defunct Rose Law Firm, [then] accompanied her to Washington as deputy White House counsel."[1169] More importantly, it was Vince who "handled all of her private affairs in the White House, and who guarded her secrets."[1170] In fact, "The Clintons would install the First Lady's confidant in one of the nation's most sensitive positions as deputy counsel to the president, where he would handle controversial matters stemming from their Arkansas past as well as highly classified presidential matters."[1171]

Over the years, one observation became noticeable to many. "Hillary and Vince spent entirely too much time together, [and] he had a mysterious way of appearing at her doorstep whenever the governor was out of town."[1172] Driving them even closer was Mrs. Clinton's disgust with her husband's womanizing. "During this period of disaffection from Bill, Hillary was clearly growing closer to law partner Vince Foster."[1173]

The coterie (or clique) that became aware of their extended fling eventually grew larger. "There would be several sources – including a former U.S. attorney, sometime aides, a number of lawyers, social friends, and many of the same troopers who testified about the governor's illicit acts – who described the First Lady's affair, dating to the mid-1980s, with Rose partner Vince Foster. A relationship evident in the semiprivate kisses and furtive squeezes at parties and dinners described by the security guards."[1174]

Speaking of which, our story now becomes even more interesting. "Several Arkansas State Troopers charged that Vince and Hillary had been lovers, and that when Bill Clinton was out of town, Vince would spend the night with Hillary at the governor's mansion. There were also reports that Hillary and Vince stayed to-

gether overnight in a remote cabin in the woods."[1175] This cabin
was "kept by the Rose Firm in the nearby mountain resort of Heber
Springs, where the two spent significant amounts of time together."[1176]

L.D. Brown describes an especially frivolous night at Charlie
Trie's restaurant in Little Rock. "Vince and Hillary looked like they
were in the back seat of a '57 Chevy at a drive-in. Hillary was kissing Vince like I've never seen her kiss Bill, and the same sort of
thing was going on with Bill and the wife of a third couple. Vince,
good looking, tall and suave obviously knew what he was doing,
but Hillary looked awkward and unbalanced."[1177]

Who was the other woman involved in this kinky little arrangement? "Hillary and Bill's unorthodox marriage was so open, it
verged on partner swapping. The 'significant other' for Bill Clinton
was Beth Coulson ... described as a 'Kewpie doll with brains,' being
diminutive with sky-blue eyes while an intellectual lawyer as well.
Beth was always there for Bill and was indeed his soul mate, writes
[L.D.] Brown.

The Clinton bodyguard describes numerous Clinton rendezvous with Coulson, then a Little Rock attorney, including one
that took place in front of her husband, Mike – as well as Hillary.
They had all gathered at Little Rock's Fu Lin restaurant, owned by
Charlie Trie, who would eventually become infamous for his illegal
donations to the Clintons.

Vince Foster – who, according to numerous sources in Little
Rock, was involved with Hillary – along with his wife Lisa, was
also on hand. 'Hillary was kissing Vince like I've never seen her
kiss Bill,' Brown claimed. 'And the same sort of thing was going on
with Bill and Beth.'"[1178]

Another account picks up after they had finished dinner.
"Vince and Hillary became openly affectionate. Leaving the
restaurant, Lisa Foster and the judge's husband walked on ahead,
while the other two couples lagged behind. Hell, it was a twenty
minute walk – they are drunk, running tongues down each other's
throats. It was a diagonal swap."[1179] The same trooper continues,

saying that he "saw Foster groping Hillary's behind. He'd be kissing her – I mean real heavy, open-mouthed, tongue-down-the-
throat stuff. Then he winked at me. They didn't care who
knew."[1180]

Once, Hillary even spoke to L.D. Brown about her situation
with Vince Foster. "Hillary advised him that sometimes you have
to go outside your marriage to get what you need, telling him,
'L.D., sometimes you just have to make a leap of faith.'"[1181]

Troopers other than Brown also witnessed interaction between
Vince and Hillary that went above and beyond normal friendship.
"Patterson and Perry knew not only of the liaisons at the Heber
Springs hideaway, but also once even eyeballed Vince and Hillary
in a car stopped for a light on a Hot Springs street – and observed
them embracing and open-mouth kissing."[1182]

Roger Perry also "recounted how he heard Hillary scream at
Bill one night, 'I need to be f***ed more than twice a year!'"[1183] At
another point, Perry said, "Bill Clinton was infatuated with black
women. He loved black women."[1184]

L.D. Brown weighs in again. "Hillary and Vince were two people who were obviously *deeply* in love. I saw them locked in each
other's arms, necking, nuzzling ... Vince was a great, great guy, and
he was just totally devoted to Hillary in a way Bill never was."[1185]

He then surmised that if the troopers assisted Bill with his
cheating, then the same applied to his wife. "The troopers were
driving Hillary and Vince to the mountain resort of Heber Springs,
where their law firm owned a cabin. There the couple spent hours
alone while the troopers waited outside. 'I guess Hillary figured
that if we did this for her husband, then we damn well better keep
our mouths shut and do it for her.'"[1186]

Another partner at the Rose Law Firm made similar observations. "Hillary's former law partner, disgraced associate attorney
general Webb Hubbell makes it clear in his memoir, *Friends in High
Places*, that the relationship between Foster and Hillary was unusually close."[1187]

Even the mainstream media had its own particular take on this matter. "*Newsweek* reported that some Clintonites believed Foster had a 'crush' on her [Hillary]. In late 1995, a report in the *Washington Post* on the contents of a diary Foster had left behind also suggested that Foster and Hillary have had more than a professional relationship."[1188]

Instead of relying on anecdotal testimony, though, why don't we go straight to the horse's mouth – Hillary herself:

> **Barbara Walters would later ask Hillary point blank if she and Vince were lovers.**
> **"I miss him very much. And I just wish he could be left in peace, because he was a wonderful man to everyone who knew him."**

There's only one problem with Hillary's response: she didn't *deny* the allegation, or directly answer the question. "The artful dodge was a truly Clinton trademark; as in other instances it spoke volumes."[1189]

On another occasion, WGR-AM's Tom Bauerle dropped a bombshell on Hillary. "'Mrs. Clinton, you're going to hate me,' Bauerle began. 'You were on television last night talking about your relationship with the president, Bill Clinton. Have you ever been sexually unfaithful to him, and specifically, the stories about Vince Foster – any truth in them?'"[1190]

Hillary's response was classic. "'Well, you know, Tom, I do hate you for that. Because, you know, those questions – I think – are really out of bounds. And everybody who knows me knows the answers to those questions. You know, I just ...' Bauerle pressed ahead. 'Is the answer no?' 'Well, yes. Of course it's no,' Clinton shot back."[1191] [Note: "Less than twenty-four hours after his encounter with America's most celebrated Senate candidate, the radio host vanished from his perch on WGR's *Breakfast with Bauerle* broadcast.[1192]]

Although Hillary finally spurted a 'no' to the radio show host's question, it wasn't an immediate response.

Instead, she had to be prodded ... to have her feet held to the fire and be backed into a corner before denying the affair and responding in the negative. Wouldn't someone who absolutely never cheated on her spouse, especially with a specific individual, adamantly deny the charges without hesitation?

Hillary yet again tried to dance around the question like she did with Barbara Walters. Also, remember one of the initial premises of this book: the Clintons lie ... and lie and lie and lie. They lie to each other, their marriage is a lie, and they have no compunction whatsoever about lying to us.

Amazingly, when *Hillary's* infidelity was brought to Bill's attention, he wasn't quite so smug and self-possessed.:

"Regardless of his own infidelities, these trysts, assignations or whatever you want to call them, infuriated Bill Clinton following his reading of a private investigators' report who he had assigned to report on Hillary's activities. Allegations of Hillary and Vince Foster's *affaire d'amour* had persisted from the Little Rock days and into the White House itself. Hillary, not surprisingly, had done the same thing with Bill and discovered that one of his 'conquests' was an employee at her law firm."[1193]

Indeed, "Bill was extremely suspicious of Hillary's relationship with Vince. When confronted, she simply denied it was a romance and claimed they were just good friends ... 'Bill confronted her with the information and they had several explosive arguments – screaming, shouting, red-faced blow-outs,' [private investigator Ivan] Duda said. 'Hillary is not meek, and while she never confessed to cheating, she aggressively reminded Bill of his numerous affairs and how he not only humiliated her but nearly wrecked their own political careers with his behavior.'"[1194]

In the end, an attorney friend of Vince Foster who knew all the parties involved, said wryly of Vince and Hillary's affair, "Bill knew, of course he knew. But what the hell was *he* supposed to say to anybody about being faithful?"[1195]

So, the final question in regard to this fling: did Vince Foster commit suicide because he was afraid that news of his *true* relationship with Hillary would leak out to the public?

From my perspective, the notion is preposterous because, first of all, Vince Foster didn't take his own life. He was murdered. Still, some insist "he committed suicide because he feared the coming revelations about Clintons' business practices and their tax evasions or because relations had become painful."[1196]

FBI agent Gary Aldrich adds another element to the equation during this conversation with one of Hillary's hired henchmen, Craig Livingstone:

> **"Gary, I assure you, none of that stuff had anything to do with his death. He had bigger problems on his mind. He was worried that rumors about his affair with Hillary were resurfacing ... Vince thought if it surfaced it would ruin his life, his reputation, and his marriage, and he thought it would impact *big time* on Hillary and the presidency. He was worried sick about it."**
>
> **"What? An affair with Hillary?"**
>
> **Livingstone looked genuinely surprised. "You don't know? You're kidding me, right?"**
>
> **Craig went on, "There are some people down in Little Rock who are talking. About this and other stuff. We thought it was all put to bed, but it's resurfacing."[1197]**

As you'll see in a subsequent volume, Vince Foster (a) did not kill himself, and (b) he was murdered due to matters much more damning than an on-again off-again affair with Hillary Clinton. Nonetheless, their relationship simply added another variable to a marriage that was undoubtedly made in hell.

Democratic presidential candidate and U.S. Sen. Hillary Rodham Clinton (D-NY), hugs husband and former President Bill Clinton as they appear at her 60th birthday party at Beacon Theater October 25, 2007 in New York City. The party and concert included celebrities Elvis Costello and Billy Crystal.

(Photo by Mario Tama/Getty Images)

CHAPTER SIX

What Kind of People They Really Are

THE PHONY PLASTIC COUPLE

"Sometimes the devil's in that woman."
— The Clinton's cook at their Arkansas Mansion[1198]

A s part one of this trilogy draws to a close, I hope that you've noticed that it differs from many other works about the Clintons in one significant respect. Many of the others spend the vast majority of their time focusing on the Clinton policies (both pro and con), or they become wrapped up in historical data (names, dates, places, etc). Worse, some of these books are so tepid in their stance that they're either a complete whitewash, or they exist on the periphery and never get beyond analysis of the weakest, most superficial variety. In the end, the major problem we find is that the reader never gets to know who the Clintons are as *people*. Sure, they're informed about health care, NAFTA, and the larger meaning of democracy in relation to the Soviet Union. But the Clintons' true essence remains cloaked in mystery.

On the contrary, my primary objective – especially with what you've read so far – is to let you see who the Clintons *really* are. One thing should be perfectly clear at this point – the Clintons you see on TV are nothing but a phony, plastic couple. Behind the scenes, or in their limousine, they could be screaming, snarling psychopathic lunatics that are throwing punches and ready to kill each other; but once the camera is turned on they're all smiles and waves and pleasantries. A fitting illustration of this phenomenon can be found after Bill was caught fooling around with Monica Lewinsky. The First Couple was to attend a White House Endowment Fund dinner, and they were at logger-heads with each other. But once they entered the ballroom, Dick Morris said their demeanor immediately transformed. It was "like someone had just plugged them into a wall socket. I watched them all night, and they were totally, I mean totally, charming – just so up and *on* all the time."[1199]

This radiant image, however, is nothing more than illusion, for the Clintons are nasty, spiteful, paranoid, deceitful people so far removed from their public personas that it's mind-boggling. The Clintons are also inveterate liars. Take Hillary for example. She's one of the most foul-mouthed harpies alive; yet on the campaign trail she tries to make us think she's sugary sweet and polite as can be. Her husband, on the other hand, is a piggish sexual predator who uses huge doses of chicanery to fool us into thinking he's just a simple bubba from Arkansas.

But now you've seen differently because this book oozes and drips with Bill and Hillary Clinton — the real people, not political *creations* who dupe us every electoral cycle. What you've now encountered is authenticity, not fakery. If Hillary is bisexual, admit it. Tell us why you beat your husband, how you had an affair with Vince Foster, and the details of your prearranged marriage. Likewise, Bill Clinton should confess to not only his rampant adultery, but also how he raped Juanita Broaddrick and terrorized other hapless females. Regrettably, truth doesn't exist in the Clintons' world, for they have created such a huge lie-machine to cover their tracks that I'm not sure – at least publicly – if they're able to be honest. Privately, that's another story because these two have carefully invented their personas, just like the craftiest of stage magicians. And, similar to the most adept of illusionists, they never let their audience see the real *trick* that is taking place.

Even more damning is the fact that the first third of this trilogy is only the tip of a proverbial iceberg. After this chapter is concluded, you'll discover that the Clintons are full-fledged criminals and murderers of the worst sort. Don't take this statement lightly, for they're not merely politicians on the take like thousands of others across our great nation. No, these people are mobsters that belong to a vast political syndicate which runs drugs, launders money, deals arms, and kills anyone that attempts to expose their network.

ELITIST SNOBS

• It seems the Clintons are above performing such mundane tasks as buying their own groceries or toting their own luggage, as secret service agents in Washington, DC found out. "Unlike the [Arkansas] state troopers who had done his bidding for years, the agents were not willing to participate with Clinton in rating women, much less approach them on his behalf. Nor were they willing to caddy, go on shopping errands, or carry baggage – tasks that might prevent them from concentrating on their principal job: to protect the President. When an agent explained this to Hillary (code name: "Evergreen") after their plane touched down in Arkansas, she looked him over carefully. 'If you want to remain on this detail,' she said, 'get your f***ing ass over here and grab those bags.'"[1200]

• It appears the 'commoners' can't even exist in the same space as Mrs. Clinton. Hillary "told her Secret Service Protective Detail agents in public to 'stay the f*** back, stay the f*** away from me! Don't come within ten yards of me or else!' The agents tried to explain to the first lady that they cannot effectively guard her if they must remain so far away. Her reply was, 'Just f***ing do as I say, okay?'"[1201]

• Hillary wrote that it takes a village to raise children, but here is how they reared their own offspring. "Two Secret Service agents heard Hillary's daughter Chelsea refer to them as 'personal trained pigs' to some of her friends. When the friends had gone, the senior agent on the detail tried to scold Chelsea for such disrespect. He told her that he was willing to put his life on the line to save hers, and he believed that her father, the president, would be shocked if he heard what she had just said to her friends. Chelsea's response? 'I don't think so. That's what my parents call you.'"[1202]

- The apple doesn't fall far from the tree. According to Trooper L.D. Brown, Hillary treated his colleagues the same way. "'Those idiot guards,' [was what] she would call my buddies. She would often tell me she didn't want that 'f***ing idiot' or such to ever drive her again ... she would tell the troopers this to their faces as well ... Trooper Mark Allen was prone to crying spells after incurring Hillary's wrath over the most miniscule miscue. Many troopers would stay only one day at their new assignment at the Governor's Mansion after a run-in with Hillary. They preferred to return to highway patrol rather than suffer the humiliation at the hands of Hillary."[1203]

- Their arrogance gets worse ... much worse. What follows is what one White House employee told another. "When 'Queen Hillary' walks down the hall, you're not supposed to look at her. You're actually supposed to go into an office if there is one nearby. She doesn't want staff 'seeing' her."[1204]

- Hillary's sense of entitlement borders on royalty. "Hillary would insist that her Manhattan offices one block from the Waldorf-Astoria not only be more than twice as large as her fellow New York Senator's – 7,900 square feet to Chuck Schumer's 3,900 square feet – but that they cost the taxpayer more than twice as much. While Schumer paid $209,532 a year for his offices, the rent on Hillary's suite was $514,148 annually – far and away the most spent by any U.S. senator on office space."[1205]

- Hillary took particular delight in abusing the state troopers. "She called them 'shit-kickers,' 'rednecks,' 'hicks,' 'white trash,' and ridiculed them for being overweight ... At times, a simple 'Good morning, Mrs. Clinton' could provoke an attack. 'F*** off!' she would bark. 'It's enough that I have to see you shit-kickers every day. I'm not going to talk to you, too. Just do your g**damn job and keep your mouth shut.' She went so far as to instruct Trooper

Patterson not to utter a word when they went out in public. 'You sound,' she explained contemptuously, 'like a hick.'"[1206]

• As you've probably noticed, Hillary's private demeanor is far different than the way she addresses the public in her soothingly saccharin voice. "Hillary could cuss like a sailor and the levels of her attacks knew no bounds. Characteristic of the way she would run roughshod over people was the abuse she meted out to the troopers at the Mansion."[1207]

• It wasn't only the troopers to whom the Clintons felt superior. Officer Larry Gentry told Meredith Oakley in 1993: "They always held themselves to be quite a bit above the average Arkansan. They went on and on, talking about how stupid the people of Arkansas were for electing Frank White. God, they were mad."[1208]

• The following was what Hillary uttered "to her bodyguard, L.D. Brown, after meeting some of the colorful people at a county fair in northern Arkansas in the early 1980s. 'god damn L.D., did you see that family right out of *Deliverance*? Get me the hell out of here!'"[1209]

• There's more. "Officers Larry Gentry and Roger Perry would remember the temper tantrums both Clintons threw, sometimes in the back seat of the official limousine, throwing any object at hand at each other or their bodyguards. A 'bitchy' Hillary was openly hostile, given to calling them 'pigs.' She loathed them, the officers recalled, and it was part of their condescending attitude toward employees in general and Arkansans in general. Deep down, said another officer, 'That woman really hated this state, the people in it, and almost everything else except being top dog.'"[1210]

• A former Clinton employee explained, "Hillary totally, totally hated the people of Arkansas. She hated being in Arkansas. She hated being around the 'hicks' here. She hated having to be friendly to people that she was intellectually above. She hated being nice to people, including Bill."[1211]

• In their privileged world, "The Clintons never believed that normal standards applied to them. As Bill Clinton said, 'you

know, you can make too much of normalcy. A lot of normal people are assholes.' The Clintons, whatever else can be said of
them, were not normal."[1212]

• Bill Clinton's reaction at the funeral of a slain police officer:
"'Bill, do you want to go in the ballroom and shake hands with
some of the troopers?' Bill incredulously shot back, 'F*** those
ignorant sons-of-bitches. I don't want to go in there!'"[1213]

• "'What's all the fuss about; it was just a G**damn mother-
f***ing pig.' Governor Bill Clinton's reaction upon seeing all the
people at a funeral for a black state trooper killed in the line of
duty, as retold by former bodyguard Larry Patterson."[1214]

• Hillary's comments on the wife of former Vice President Al
Gore. "Tipper is an un-intellectual, nice lady who doesn't have a
brain in her head."[1215]

• Does Mrs. Clinton *really* feel our pain? "When Hillary left
the White House to read to sick children at the Georgetown University Medical Center, the excursion produced photographs of
the First Lady with a group of suspiciously healthy-looking kids
in street clothes. Hillary's aides insisted that the First Lady did
not wish to have her picture taken with children who had shaved
heads or unsightly breathing tubes. To the disappointment of
young patients, the children of staff were substituted."[1216]

• Is Hillary, supposedly so affectionate toward children, actually only using them as props in a series of photo ops? "On another occasion, preschoolers from the HIPPY program were on
the mansion lawn posing for a photograph. Hillary was overheard on the intercom saying, 'I want to get this shit over with
and get these damn people out of here.'"[1217] [Note: HIPPY stands
for 'Home Instruction for Parents of Preschool Youngsters' which
was begun at Israel's Hebrew University.]

• Maybe the lowest of all Hillary's lows: "There was, for example, a time when a female Clinton supporter proudly presented
Hillary with a pair of handcrafted earrings in the shape of a razorback hog, the University of Arkansas mascot. Hillary refused
to try them on and, barely waiting until the woman was out of

earshot, commented, 'This is the kind of shit I have to put up with.'"[1218]

Whenever you see Bill and/or Hillary on the nightly news and they try to make it appear as if they're simply 'one of us,' think long and hard before believing them because these people would rather spit on you than welcome you into their graces and consider you an equal. They want you for one thing, and one thing only: votes. Beyond that, you're not of their caliber, at least in their eyes.

VIOLENCE, RAGE, AND INTIMIDATION

For years there has been an enigmatic phrase in existence that has been used in some corners to describe what happens when somebody crosses Bill and Hillary. It's called the Clinton Body Count. This subject will be discussed at length in book three of this trilogy. But for the moment, to set the stage I'm going to show how the Clintons are well known for their notorious tempers and violent rages. Then, as if ascending toward more extreme examples of their violent natures, you will read how the Clintons have used intimidation and threats in an attempt to silence those individuals who could potentially expose them. Finally, two specific cases will be examined: Bill Clinton's attack of consultant Dick Morris, and the repugnant assault of attorney Gary Johnson. These case histories ultimately serve as a foundation so that one thing is abundantly clear: Bill and Hillary Clinton *are* capable of having their perceived enemies permanently silenced.

For beginners, as we've pointed out numerous times already, Hillary Clinton is prone to vulgar outbursts that are so pronounced that she appears to be insane. During her reign of terror in Arkansas, one state trooper noted, "Hillary had pulled out from the mansion in her blue Oldsmobile, only to return moments later, tires squealing. The guards ran out to her thinking something was terribly wrong ... 'Where's the G**damn f***ing flag?

I want the G**damn flag up every f***ing morning at f***ing sunrise,' she screamed maniacally."[1219]

Was this outburst Hillary's version of patriotism, supposedly coming from a normal, mature woman that we could rely on in times of emergency or danger? "'She is angry. Not all the time. But most of the time,' wrote a usually sympathetic Gail Sheehy in her Clinton biography."[1220]

Hillary's tantrums are so exaggerated that it makes everyone in close proximity tremble. "Temper is a trait she and Bill Clinton share, but while his is said to erupt with the force of a sudden squall and then be spent – leaving him, more often than not, eager to make amends – hers has inspired ongoing fear in some of those who have worked with her over the years. Grown men describe her as being, at such times, scary."[1221] Even men in the armed forces who survived combat had to walk on eggshells around her. As Lieutenant Colonel Buzz Patterson observed, "The other military aides had warned me, 'Whatever you do, don't piss off the first lady.' The first couple had notorious tempers, but hers was the worst. She was the one who could rip your heart out."[1222] Her whirlwind flightiness was so well known that "a presidential aide said, 'she's the only person around here people are afraid of.'"[1223]

Although it occurred rarely, people did fight back when Hillary spun into a rage. One individual at a White House meeting, "who was really humiliated and very angry, got up from her chair, looked Hillary in the eye and said, 'Mrs. Clinton, my sister warned me about you when she set up this meeting for me. She told me that I would be sorry that I ever asked her to set this up, because she said you are a real bitch. She was wrong! You're a f***ing bitch!'"[1224]

The atmosphere was even worse when she and Bill locked horns. "His [Bill's] most memorable eruptions came in arguments with Rodham, who seemed not the least bit timid about snapping back when he erupted. 'They'd have the biggest damn fights, shouting and swearing,' [Ronnie Paul] Addington recalled.

'They had two or three battle royals ... They started shouting at each other. I was driving. Bill was in the front seat, Hillary in the back. He was hitting the dashboard. She was hitting the seat. They were really going at it. We drove up a street near the headquarters, and stopped at a light. Hillary said, 'I'm getting out!' She got out and slammed the door. And Bill said, 'Go on.'"[1225]

As can be seen, Bill Clinton was no slouch either when it came to outbursts. "The real significance of Clinton's temper was what it said about his deeper nature. There was a self indulgence in Clinton's tantrums, an immaturity, a part of him that never grew up."[1226] According to one staffer, "the rages were pretty amazing. He'd scream [and] pound his fist on his desk. One of his favorite ploys was to walk up to an underling, glare at him with nostrils flaring, and then stick his forefinger within inches of the person's face. 'Never,' Clinton would say, '*never* do that to me again. Do you understand me?' The tantrums might have been comical – I mean, with all the ranting and raving it was like something a horribly spoiled child would do. But when the child is six-foot-two and weighs 220 pounds, it isn't funny – it's terrifying."[1227]

New York Times columnist Maureen Dowd once compared the couple. "Though Hillary was often depicted as a 'screamer,' it was Bill who had an ugly, abusive streak, which he often vented at underlings like George Stephanopoulos. (In Arkansas, Clinton had once slapped Betsey Wright and came to blows with Dick Morris, who later named Clinton 'The Monster' because of his explosive temper)."[1228]

One trooper observed, "I've seen times he'd get so mad at things fire would fly from his eyes,"[1229] while author Joe Klein wrote, "The President did bellow and thrash – his temper was shocking to those who didn't know him well."[1230] Even more frenzied was what Bob Woodward of Watergate fame saw. "During the [1992] presidential campaign, Woodward claims Clinton was so infuriated over a flunky's actions at a Little Rock function and flew off the handle by supposedly screaming, 'I want him dead! I want him killed! Get him horsewhipped!'"[1231]

Continuing this thought, "Bob Woodward in his book, *The Agenda*, describes how his [Clinton's] demeanor can suddenly turn from tenderness and sensitivity to extreme rage. The rage is not exhibited before the cameras."[1232] Woodward himself writes of these spasmodic incidents. "Others called them 'purple fits' or 'earthquakes.' Stephanopoulos simply called it 'the wave,' an overpowering, prolonged rage that would shock an outsider, and often way out of proportion to what caused it."[1233] Even one of Clinton's chief aides – a longtime D.C. insider – was shocked by his behavior. "[David] Gergen, watching the outburst, was stunned. He had never quite seen an adult, let alone a president, in such a rage."[1234]

Psychologist Paul Fick has studied Bill Clinton's mental disequilibrium. "He overreacts to situations by lashing out with anger in ways that far exceed any rational response to a present situation."[1235] In the fashion of a true sociopath, Clinton possessed two personas: one public, and the other private. In a chapter on White House Press Secretary Dee Dee Myers [*Madhouse* by Jeffrey Birnbaum], the president's *Dr. Jekyll and Mr. Hyde* mood swings were often apparent. "In public, Clinton showed only his huggable side. But people who knew him well, especially his staff, were also well acquainted with – and were often the brunt of – his considerable wrath. They called it Clinton's purple rage."[1236]

Veteran Democratic fundraiser and strategist Bert German Dickey III takes it a step further. "Clinton's got a violent temper. I mean, short fuse. It's either his way or no way, and if you crossed him, it was not good. I mean, he'd just go off in a heartbeat."[1237] Continuing, "Dickey described the president's physical response when his anger would get out of control. '[His] face would just turn beet red. You could see the muscles and veins in his neck. You could see it coming, and he would just go off.'"[1238] Oddly enough, three of Bill Clinton's victims of sexual harassment all described the same phenomenon of his face turning beet red: Juanita Broaddrick, Paula Jones, and Kathleen Willey.

In this sense, whether it's excessive anger or passionate (violent) arousal, Bill Clinton's face is his barometer – and beet red means extreme danger.

It's easy to determine that with such volatile tempers, the Clintons are apt to retaliate when they feel someone has exposed them, or if their sordid acts are brought to light. A good place to start is with Sally Perdue, who was categorized as one of Bill Clinton's "bimbo problems." Again, notice how the Clintons refer to women, especially ones that Bill seeks out and 'conquers.' When the Gennifer Flowers flap was reaching its crescendo, "Sally Perdue would later tell of being approached by a Democratic functionary in Illinois and none too subtly warned that she might have her knees broken or worse if she continued to speak publicly about her relationship with Clinton."[1239] Perdue further elaborated that the Clintons "were anxious about me and they wanted me to know that keeping my mouth shut would be worthwhile. If I was a good little girl, and I didn't kill the messenger, I'd be set for life: a federal job."[1240] Her account is reminiscent of the 'graduates' described by Linda Tripp as women who were rewarded with White House positions in return for keeping Bill's secrets private.

Perdue continued, "But if I didn't take the offer, then they knew that I went jogging by myself and [they] couldn't guarantee what would happen to my pretty little legs. Things just wouldn't be so much fun for me anymore. Life would get hard."[1241] Purdue ultimately didn't accept Clinton's offer, and that's when "things began to happen. She lost her job at the admissions office of Lindenwood College, Missouri, where she was also studying. A Missouri lawyer, Paul Ground, said that a college official had admitted to him that she had been fired because of outside pressure."[1242] The thug tactics got worse. "Soon after the firing, Perdue began receiving threatening mail and calls. She produced one of the letters: 'I'll pray you have a head-on collision and end up in a coma. Marilyn Monroe got snuffed.' Perdue found an unspent shotgun cartridge on the driver's seat of her Jeep. Later the back window of her vehicle was shattered, possibly by gun-fire."[1243]

This Mob-like mentality is what makes the Clinton dirty tricks machine operate. If you remember correctly, Kathleen Willey's "tires were punctured with nails and her cat was stolen," [1244] while "former Miss America Elizabeth Ward Gracen says she was offered acting jobs through the Hollywood connected Clinton operative Mickey Kantor."[1245]

Gennifer Flowers has written about being harassed by the Clintons as well. "My apartment had been illegally entered on three separate occasions, and my life was threatened. Worse still, they tried to intimidate my mother. Some man called her and without identifying himself said in gruff, muffled tones, 'You should be real proud of your daughter. She'd be better off dead.'"[1246] Then, to insure that everyone knew precisely who she thought was behind these cowardly acts, Flowers hones in with laser-like accuracy. "Over the years, I've seen what has happened to people who try to cross Bill Clinton. As in the case with Mafia dons, it is never the number-one man who directly makes threats, much less commits acts of violence. I envision these things going down very much like Mario Puzo described them in *The Godfather*."[1247] These words are very wise indeed, and ones that you should try to recall as we get deeper into subsequent books because Gennifer Flowers, a Mob-moll herself, knows first-hand how these men operate, and Bill Clinton is certainly one of them.

The Clintons didn't only target women; they were equal opportunity intimidators. Larry Nichols was the man primarily responsible for breaking the Gennifer Flowers story because of a lawsuit he filed in the early 1990s. He describes himself as having been "a secret personal assistant to then-Governor Bill Clinton, alleging that he transferred state funds into special accounts used by Clinton to entertain his mistresses. He also investigated opponents and fixed things behind the scenes."[1248] Events took a turn for the worse and Nichols was fired from his state job. After taking legal action against Clinton and airing his dirty laundry publicly, Nichols began being followed. "They'd been doing it pretty intensely for about a month. The way they rotate off like that, it makes me think its Arkansas State Police."[1249] Using members of his law enforcement squad was undoubtedly part of Bill Clinton's m.o., and Nichols knew full well what the Clintons were capable of as he commented on March 13, 1994. "It's getting real dangerous right now, and I don't want to end up another one of those mysterious suicides."[1250]

Despite his caution, adversity still befell Nichols. "Larry has been beaten twice recently. The second time his already-broken ribs were painfully re-injured by two Little Rock policemen. A few weeks later he was arrested on fallacious charges. After a public outcry, the charges were dismissed. The purpose of the arrest became clear when an informant told us that a bounty had been placed on Larry: $1,000 was offered to the prisoner who could beat or kill Larry while he was incarcerated."[1251]

Even Bill Clinton's former business partner, Jim McDougal, who was ensnared in the whole Whitewater fiasco, was earnestly scared of the Clintons. "I saw that article in the *Post* where some guy just accepted the Clintons' $68,000 loss. I could sink it (the estimate) quicker than they could lie about it if I could get in a position that I wouldn't have my head beaten off, and Bill knows that."[1252]

Nor are members of the media immune from this sort of bullying. In 1998, freelance writer Suzi Parker was working on a story about the infamous Arkansas tainted blood scandal. "Throughout the 1980s and early 1990s (while Clinton was governor) the prison system permitted prisoners to sell their plasma for seven dollars a pint. The plasma was then sold to Canada. The catch: the prisoners' plasma was so poorly screened that over 42,000 Canadians were infected with Hepatitis C, and thousands more with the HIV virus."[1253]

This story has always been a problem for the Clintons, so when Parker's article was published, she "began receiving mysterious, threatening phone calls in the middle of the night."[1254] Later, at a press conference where a group of individuals who were tainted by the blood threatened a lawsuit against the Clintons, "Parker says she knew she was being watched and followed, perhaps by government agents."[1255]

By May, 1999, "the plasma scandal whistleblower's clinic in Pine Bluff, Arkansas was firebombed; on the same night, the hemophiliac group's office in Canada was burglarized."[1256] As for the journalist in question, author Candice Jackson stated, "It's not in a reporter's nature to quit a story, but by 1999 Parker had been in Arkansas long enough to see how Clinton operated and to feel genuinely frightened for her safety. While we may never know who actually set the fires and burglarized the offices, Parker tells me she is convinced that Clinton and his associates were behind the intimidation tactics."[1257]

Similarly, in a *New York Times* article dated March 15, 1998, Linda Tripp, who had been working on a book entitled *Behind Closed Doors: What I Saw at the Clinton White House*, was also being terrorized. "Since the [Monica Lewinsky] scandal became public, Mrs. Tripp has told friends she has received a torrent of death threats and hate mail and had to go underground."[1258]

The Clintons didn't even stop at harassing the actual perceived threat themselves; they even resorted to going after acquaintances. "Loren Kirk had merely once shared an apartment with Gennifer Flowers, but that was enough for her to be chased down. San Francisco private eye Jack Palladino – referred to as a 'knee buster' by one Republican personally familiar with his 1992 work – paid Kirk a visit that summer. And according to the *American Spectator* in April 1994, Palladino posed a chilling question to her. 'Is Gennifer Flowers the sort of person who would commit suicide' the enforcer wanted to know?"[1259]

Similarly, when Bill and Hillary's state troopers went public with revelations of what transpired at the governor's mansion in Arkansas, the retaliation was swift and direct. The head of Bill Clinton's security detail, Buddy Young, who was awarded a lucrative FEMA position, once threatened Officer Larry Patterson, "If you know what's good for you, you'll keep your mouth shut."[1260] Similarly, Young warned Roger Perry about blowing the whistle. "If you and whoever do that, your reputation will be destroyed."[1261] Even criminally convicted Governor Jim Guy Tucker – Bill Clinton's successor – got in on the action, telling Trooper Perry that if he exposed the Clintons, "Roger, you will not survive this."[1262]

Perry and Ferguson were even offered bribes for federal jobs, which they turned down. The end result was one obviously intended by their attackers. "Roger Perry said at a press conference, 'I'm scared to death. Larry Patterson is scared to death. I've never felt so alone in all my life.'"[1263]

To further illustrate the Clintons' rage, there is the strange case of Dick Morris, a veteran campaign strategist, pollster, and aide. Yet regardless of their years together, Morris too became a victim of Bill Clinton's purple fits of rage. "Once again Hillary watched as Bill lashed out at his subordinates and advisors for failing him. In May of 1990 he accused Dick Morris of talking him into running and then abandoning him. 'You're screwing me!' he bellowed at Morris, who replied with, 'Go f*** yourself' before storming out of the room. Hillary, realizing how valuable Morris could be in a presidential race, pleaded with Bill to calm down. Instead, he lunged at Morris and pulled him to the floor. Then, Morris recalled of the incident, Clinton 'cocked his fist back to punch me.'"[1264]

An expanded version of this story is as follows. "'You got me into this race,' Dick Morris recalls Bill Clinton screaming at him in his book *Behind the Oval Office*, 'so you could make some money off me. That was the only reason. And now you give me no attention, no attention at all.' ... Morris responded, 'Go f*** yourself. I'm quitting your G**damn campaign, and now I'm a free agent.' Clinton apparently charged at him, wrapped his arms around Morris's torso, and they fell to the ground."[1265]

A third version has Morris remembering, "As I marched

through the kitchen to leave the Mansion, I heard hoof beats. Bill came up at a run, threw me to the ground, and drew back his fist to punch me. Hillary was on him in a flash, grabbing his arms and screaming at him: 'Bill! Stop! Think! Get control! What are you doing? Bill!'"[1266]

As I said earlier, these people are like wild animals, or adolescents who never learned how to control themselves. The scene continued as Hillary – ever the operative and controller – attempted to do some damage control. "As Morris got up and tried to make his escape, Hillary chased after him. 'He didn't mean it,' she pleaded. 'He's very sorry. He's over-tired. He hasn't slept well in days.' Then she put her arm around the shaken adviser and together they walked the grounds of the Governor's Mansion. 'He only does that,' she told Morris, 'to people he loves.'"[1267]

Alas, yet again we see another strange version of Clinton *love* – both Bill's exhibition of it, and Hillary's attempt to soft-soap his violent tendencies. When Clinton raped Juanita Broaddrick, was that also *love*? How about the time he morphed into sexual predator mode and abused Kathleen Willey – she was supposedly his friend, so was that *love* too?

With friends like the Clintons that *love* them so much, who needs enemies? Plus, just so there's no mistaking how sleazy these people are, Hillary had to include one last touch of deceit into the mix. "Morris also volunteers that when the story threatened to surface again during the 1992 presidential campaign, Hillary told him to 'say it never happened.'"[1268] Never forget: the Clintons lie!

A fitting way to close this section – one that shows a fraction of what the Clinton hit squad is capable of – concerns the near fatal assault of Gary Johnson. An introduction to this brutal case is provided by Gennifer Flowers, who was directly involved in the circumstances surrounding this matter.

An attorney named Gary Johnson lived next door to me in Quapaw Towers – the

high-rise in Little Rock where I lived in the late 1980s during the last stage of my affair with Bill. I didn't really know Gary Johnson other than to say hello when we met in the hall. For reasons that still aren't clear to me, Gary placed a video camera in the hall in such a way that it produced a clear view of my apartment door.

When rumors began circulating that Bill and I were having an affair, Gary let it be known that he was in possession of a video-tape of Bill coming to my apartment. Shortly thereafter, a couple of thugs forced their way into his place, beat Gary senseless and left him for dead. According to Gary, they kept asking him where 'the tape' was."[1269]

Another account gives a similar rendition. "When someone discovered that Johnson's camera had, on many occasions, actually taped Bill Clinton entering Flowers' apartment, thugs were sent to do some damage control: two men entered Gary's apartment and demanded the videotapes, which he quickly gave them. Then they brutally beat him – leaving him for dead. Yet the press showed no interest in investigating the attack, nor the reason it occurred."[1270] The attack was so extreme that "Johnson suffered massive head wounds. His nose and face were crushed; both elbows were dislocated; both collar bones broken; his bladder was perforated and his spleen so badly damaged that doctors had to remove it."[1271]

As the viciousness of this assault settles in your mind, ask: who had the motive and means to attack Gary Johnson and "beat the poor guy to a pulp,"[1272] especially when "Bill Clinton was shown entering and exiting Flowers' apartment with his own key?"[1273] Further, who had the *means* necessary to not only inflict such violence upon Gary Johnson, but then cover it up? After

years of lying, now there was physical proof that the presidential
candidate was involved with Flowers. "Clinton had denied everything, so Johnson and Larry [Nichols] realized the videotapes
would provide the proof they needed. If they could just prove
one major lie, the public might start to believe there were many
lies."[1274]

Consider: "Johnson's mistake was telling people about the
tapes following the Bill and Hillary lie-a-thon on *60 Minutes*.
Shortly thereafter some very large individuals, undoubtedly
Arkansas State Troopers who were noted for doing Bill Clinton's
bidding at the risk of losing their cushy jobs, showed up at Johnson's condo insisting that he give them the tapes. He surrendered
them without an argument. They then proceeded to break both
of Johnson's elbows [and] rupture his bladder and spleen. They
left him for dead on the floor of his condo."[1275] Here's the kicker:
"After that, nobody ever heard another word about incriminating
videotapes."[1276]

What we have here is a scene straight out of George Orwell's
Animal Farm where Bill and Hillary Clinton – the pigs in control
– get their vicious attack dogs (Arkansas state policemen) to do
their bidding by ripping any exposer to shreds. If such a scenario
doesn't appall and disgust you, then I extend my pity because
you seem to have no more heart than the monsters involved in
these attacks. What's worse, Bill and Hillary have been using
these Mob techniques for decades. Their Dixie Mafia thugs operate under the same criminal principles as does the La Cosa
Nostra or a renegade terrorist unit. They attack and kill with im-
punity, then use privilege and power to conceal their sinister
deeds.

Most despicable is the fact that when you see Bill and Hillary
on television, they're always wearing a mask; smiling and waving
to the crowds, telling them how great the Clinton dream is. But
these people are abject phonies of the lowest order, for "psy-
chopaths project an outward appearance of perfect normalcy,
and often even project tenderness and compassion, but will mur-

der anyone without a shred of conscience if it furthers or protects their interests."[1277]

What you'll see in volume three is that – despite their lies and distraction techniques – the Clinton Body Count is a very scary reality.

THIEVES FLEECE THE WHITE HOUSE

Some readers may feign being offended by the above title, but since we're not candy-coating anything else in this book, why start now? What the Clintons did during their final days in office was nothing less than unmitigated theft, for they were unscrupulous thieves who pulled a massive five-finger discount before leaving the White House.

As the last lame-duck weeks of Bill Clinton's presidency came coughing and sputtering to a halt, behind the scenes there was still quite a bit of furtive activity taking place. Although they tried to keep their affairs under wraps (like most everything else they do), Bill and Hillary "stripped the White House of hundreds of thousands of dollars' worth of furniture."[1278]

How did the first couple embark upon such an undertaking? Quite simply, "A twenty-six-foot-long moving van was backed up to the White House and loaded with valuable furnishings – two sofas, an iron-and-glass coffee table, an ottoman, a painted TV armoire, a custom wood gaming table, and a wicker center table with a wood top. Much of the furniture had been acquired by Hillary's interior decorator, Kaki Hockersmith, for the 1993 redecoration project, and therefore legally belonged to the government, not the Clintons. When the media blew the whistle on the Clintons, they reluctantly agreed to return some of the items to the White House."[1279]

This description is just the tip of the iceberg in regard to their thievery. "As Hillary prepared to leave Washington for Chappaqua [her newly acquired New York carpetbagger residence], she and the former president took with them an additional

$360,000 worth of gifts given to the White House itself, including $173,000 in art objects and books, $69,000 in furniture, $26,000 in golf items, and $24,000 in clothing. The *Washington Post* reports that the gifts even included 137 five-piece china settings, representing five patterns and costing $38,000."[1280]

How could such blatant pilfering take place, especially from the most visible residence in our entire political system? Aide Dick Morris summarized what author Barbara Olson uncovered. "Olson explains how the Clintons got away with their legal burglary: while still in office, Bill and Hillary shipped seventy museum pieces, donated to the White House by prominent American artists, to the Clinton Presidential Library in Little Rock. The items were part of a White House American Craft Collection ... White House curator Betty Monkman said the decision to move them was made by Mrs. Clinton herself. Once these items were in the possession of the library, the compliant board of directors, appointed by Clinton, could do with them as they wished."[1281]

Hillary, it appears, doesn't like to let go of her royalty-like lifestyle once she gets her hands on it, especially the many official presents she received as first lady. "This gifting orgy points up the raging materialism Hillary must have been holding in check throughout most of her husband's governorship and presidency. Once the Clintons were facing the loss of the opulent lifestyle they'd led since their days in the Arkansas Governor's Mansion, Hillary seems to have gone into a panic, anxious to hold onto as many of the luxurious trappings as she could."[1282]

Quite embarrassingly, the Clintons got caught once again trying to pull a fast one. Eventually, "the Clintons returned a truckload of couches, lamps and other furnishings taken from the White House. Unfortunately, no one knows for sure how much the Clintons got away with. That information has been withheld despite numerous attempts for disclosure."[1283] The same applied to all the presents that they scurried away with. "So extensive was the negative publicity about the avalanche of gifts that the

Clintons agreed to pay back $86,000, about half their value. As [Barbara] Olson notes, 'No one explained exactly how that compromise was arrived at.'"[1284]

Naturally, Hillary couldn't admit any wrongdoing on her or Bill's behalf. "And yet, once again, Hillary found a way to rewrite this bit of unflattering history. What caused the gift scandal? A 'clerical error,' according to *Living History*."[1285] But, as Dick Morris notes on the media backlash, "Those news stories weren't generated by any 'clerical error.' They were the direct result of the Clintons' decision to back a moving truck up to the White House and take tens of thousands of dollars' worth of furniture and other objects that belonged not to them, but to the American people. It was greed, not a bookkeeping mistake."[1286] Coincidentally, following Hillary Clinton's 2006 senatorial campaign, it was discovered that a significant amount of money was illegally funneled to one of her longtime aides. Mrs. Clinton's explanation: once again it was a 'clerical error.' Isn't it funny how they keep using the same excuses time after time after time?

True to their nature, the White House wasn't the only place the Clintons trashed and looted. When Bill Clinton's second term was completed and they were leaving Washington, DC, their departure was facilitated by Air Force One. "When the plane that had been loaned to them was returned to its hangar at Andrews [Air Force Base] later that day, the maintenance crew was shocked to see that the interior had been stripped bare. The silverware and china bearing the presidential seal, the glassware, condiments, blankets, pillows, candies – even toiletries like toothpaste and mouthwash – were gone. 'Thank God,' said one dumfounded crew member, 'the seats were bolted down.'"[1287]

Washington Times reporter John McCaslin confirmed these reports. "What astonished the military steward was that even a cache of Colgate toothpaste, not stamped with the presidential seal, was snatched from a compartment beneath the presidential plane's sink."[1288] Literally, the Clintons took everything they could lay their hands on. "Missing items reportedly included the entire collection of Air Force One porcelain china, silverware, salt and pepper shakers, blankets and pillowcases – most of which bore the presidential seal."[1289]

Amazingly, the Clinton entourage even took their thieving ways overseas. A member of their security force recounts:

> **During the May 1997 presidential visit to Holland, our Dutch hosts rolled out the red carpet. Each Royal Palace room was stocked with food and a complete liquor bar for every staff member. A very thoughtful gesture, I thought, since we were getting in so late – a snack and a drink sounded great. The next morning, as we were leaving for Air Force One and our next country, the Dutch military aide pulled me aside to complain. "Your people took all of the liquor," he said under his breath, obviously embarrassed for me. "And they stole crystal and china, too," he added. He was completely floored by the audacity of the Americans from the White House. I apologized for the White House staff. But I'd seen it before. This presidency was all about *them*.[1290]**

The above account certainly doesn't apply to low-level staffers, aides, or interns as being the guilty parties; they obviously wouldn't be staying in the Royal Palace. Rather, the culprits were high-ranking members of the Clinton cabinet, including the Clintons themselves, for they were flying on Air Force One. Their behavior is reminiscent of immature high school students on a field trip that steal everything from a Motel 6. But the Clintons aren't teenagers. At the time they were grown adults in their fifties – still pilfering, looting, and acting like juvenile delinquents – a very poor reflection upon our country.

But why should their behavior change abroad when they carried themselves the exact same way in America, especially after Bill Clinton had concluded his second term in office and was getting ready to vacate the White House? Sadly, do you know who was the *most* immature, deviant, and childish of all? Hillary Clinton!

> **"Wouldn't it be hysterical if someone just happened to remove all the *W*s from the computer keyboards?"** The outgoing First Lady ponders this thought out loud on their final evening in the White House. Even though Democrats claimed there was no actual damage to the White House, a General Accounting Office investigation revealed that Clinton staffers caused $19,000 in various damages to the White House.[1291]

Following the first lady's lead and "taking Hillary at her word, outgoing staffers dashed from office to office plucking the offending *w* keys from scores of keyboards. Others went much further, pouring coffee into file cabinets, overturning desks, leaving x-rated messages on voice-mail machines, soiling carpets, tinkering with computers, and drawing obscene pictures on office walls. (Unlike Hillary, Tipper Gore would later apologize for the vandalism of government property and the disrespect shown toward the incoming president and his family.)"[1292]

Hillary Clinton, as a person in a respected position of power, was supposed to set an example for those around her. Considering that we're discussing the most esteemed structure in our land – the White House – what kind of tone did she set? Answer: one of adolescent capriciousness, degeneracy, maliciousness, and childish immaturity. Needless to say, these aren't qualities that befit a first lady, or a woman who intends to run for the presidency of this nation. Hillary Clinton had absolutely no respect whatsoever for the esteemed office that she vandalized, the same as her husband who was being fellated by a chubby, immature intern while talking on the phone with congressmen or other world dignitaries. These two not only disgraced the office of the presidency during their eight-year tenure, they spat upon the very concept of what a leader should be. They stole from the Oval Office and incited a destructive rampage through other wings of the White House. It's inconceivable that these *children* could ever be let back into the White House again. To do so would be disgraceful beyond words.

BOOED OFF THE STAGE

The Clintons have suffered their fair share of political embarrassments over the years which have caused them to exert even tighter control over their public appearances and interaction with those individuals whom they can't control. One such event – 2001's Concert for New York City – was such a calamity for Mrs. Clinton that it likely still traumatizes her to this day.

Before delving into that public relations disaster, I'd first like to provide a few other examples of how Hillary had to learn her lessons the hard way. One of the first *faux pas* she committed was a direct result of her unabashed enmity for the people of Arkansas when her husband began his political career.

As anyone in that region of the country knows, college football is a major event every fall. Hillary, of course, didn't give a damn about what was taking place on the gridiron, but since Bill had to glad-hand with the crowd, she was expected to be there. But Ms. Rodham couldn't even *feign* interest in the game, for she "once outraged Arkansans by sitting next to her husband at a Razorback game – engrossed in a book."[1293] The fallout was immediate. "People in small towns across Arkansas fumed that Hillary used her maiden name, dressed in 'unfeminine clothes,' and was seen reading a book at an Arkansas Razorback's football game. It all went to prove, said his political enemies, that Bill Clinton could not even control his wife – a grave sin in a macho southern state."[1294]

Many years later, to show voters that she wasn't an Eastern establishment elitist (due to her derogatory statements about Tammy Wynette and being a little wife who stayed home to make tea and cookies), "During the 1992 campaign, Hillary and Barbara Bush took part in a cookie-baking contest, with Hillary prevailing."[1295] There was only one problem. Hillary's deceptiveness was yet again exposed. "It was later discovered that a friend actually baked Hillary's cookies."[1296]

I suppose this is Hillary's version of mom, apple pie, and the American flag.

Hillary's dark macabre side emerged when she ran for the senate in 2000 against a man known as America's mayor – Rudy Giuliani. Events took a peculiar turn, though, when similar to the numerous scandals which plagued her husband, Giuliani too was caught in an adulterous brouhaha. But instead of showing empathy for his situation, Hillary's true colors shone through. "Over the spring, Hillary crept up in the polls as Giuliani found himself caught up in his own extramarital scandal.

While she would later claim to have sympathized with the mayor's plight, at the time Hillary was, said a campaign volunteer, 'thrilled about the whole sordid mess. I watched her reading a story about Giuliani's affair in the *Daily News*, and at one point she just *howled* with laughter.'"[1297]

When it came to her own husband's philandering, however, Hillary wasn't quite so amused. Instead, she spat venom, attacked the women whom Bill had preyed upon, and blamed the accusations on a vast paranoid conspiracy, not the man who brought all these charges upon himself.

The above embarrassments aren't really as much of a concern to the Clintons as are those occasions when the public directly turns on them by showing their disgust. Such an event turned ugly during Mrs. Clinton's ill-fated health care campaign when things spun wildly out of control.

> **Hillary launched an invasion of her own in July, barnstorming the country from coast to coast aboard a bus christened the "Health Security Express." The tour was aimed at whipping up enough grassroots support to convince Congress to reconsider her health care package. "When these guys see the people out there demanding reform," she said, "then they'll get off their asses and do something about it."**
>
> **Unfortunately, Hillary wildly misjudged the mood of the American people – and how they felt about her. Thousands of demonstrators showed up at every stop to scream obscenities at the First Lady. In Seattle, angry protesters swarmed her motorcade, rocking her limousine and pounding their fists on the windows. Fearing for her life, Hillary agreed for the first time to wear a bulletproof vest."[1298]**

It appeared Queen Hillary grossly overestimated the voting public's reaction – rather than bowing to her majesty's royal wishes, they instead smelled a rat and let her know they weren't buying what she was selling (a grossly overpriced pipedream). Likewise, Bill Clinton was also faced with those who wouldn't tolerate his phoniness. Specifically, "When Clinton was president, Marine guards failed to execute a right face to stand facing his back as he walked away."[1299] Up until that point with other presidents, no one in the military seemed to have this same problem. A similar incident occurred once when Bill Clinton met with a group that was expected to win over his detractors. "He boldly delivered his Memorial Day address at the very same memorial whose war he had evaded, the Vietnam Memorial. Boasting that he was the first president to so honor the Vietnam Vets, he arrived at the podium only to discover that the vets were neither charmed nor honored. Repeatedly his speech was interrupted with shouts of 'Draft dodger,' 'Liar,' 'Shut up, coward,'"[1300]

An even more humiliating event took place at what was supposed to have been Bill Clinton's big day in the spotlight and first taste of national exposure when he delivered Michael Dukakis' nominating speech at the 1988 Democratic National Convention. But due to miscues with the houselights and delegates, as well as the length of his speech, Clinton's debut quickly turned disastrous. "For thirty-three unbearable minutes, Bill prattled on as the crowd booed, hissed, and hollered for him to get off the stage."[1301] As Clinton continued, his presentation "was greeted with boos and catcalls. Beads of perspiration rolled down the angry speaker's face. Unbeknownst to him, after the speech extended beyond the time the TV networks scheduled for it, NBC and ABC had cut to other coverage of the convention. 'I am afraid,' commented John Chancellor, 'that one of the most attractive governors just put a blot on his record.'"[1302]

After what seemed like an eternity, "There was thunderous applause for only one line in Bill Clinton's speech: 'And now in conclusion ...'"[1303]

As he walked offstage, Bill Clinton erupted at what he perceived Michael Dukakis had done to him. "'That motherf***in' Greek son-of-a-bitch ... bastard!' Someone tried to shush him but Clinton wouldn't hear it. 'I'll destroy that c***sucker!' he ranted. 'He tried to ruin me politically by f***in' up my speech. I'll kick his dirty f***in' Greek ass in, if I can only get my hands on that [expletive deleted]-faced a**hole.'"[1304]

The initial fallout was devastating for this rising star. "The pride of Hope and Hot Springs had become the butt of jokes. 'What a windbag,' Johnny Carson remarked to his audience of millions."[1305] For the first time in his career, due admittedly to circumstances beyond his control, Bill Clinton's oratorical skills failed him. "It was clear to television viewers that Clinton was confused and frightened."[1306] As a result, the downward spiral continued. "Bill Clinton returned to Little Rock a national joke, the stuff of late-night monologue humor and cocktail party chatter. Ridicule can be deadly to a politician, and the jokes heaped on Bill Clinton were killing his career."[1307]

Luckily for him, Clinton's movie star friends came to his rescue. "A group of Hollywood Razorbacks [Harry Thomason, Linda Bloodworth-Thomason, Gil Gerard, and Mary Steenburgen] – transplanted Arkansans who had found wealth and fame on the West Coast – rallied to save his national reputation"[1308] by booking him on *The Tonight Show* with Johnny Carson where he played saxophone with Doc Severinsen.

Privately, the Clintons were still irate, especially Hillary who "saw the hand of conspiracy in every misfortune."[1309] Others agreed that Bill had been set-up. "[State auditor Julia Hughes] Jones believed that Dukakis considered Bill Clinton a political threat and did not want to be pressured into choosing Clinton as his running mate. 'There were other people in line to be a running mate, but Clinton and Dukakis went back a long way, so I believe that Dukakis wanted to eliminate Clinton as a potential running mate,' she said."[1310]

Whether Dukakis sabotaged Clinton or not with the long-winded speech is water under the bridge, for Bill Clinton escaped possible doom yet again due to a last minute rescue by the media, very reminiscent of how CBS and *60 Minutes* pulled him out of the fire after Gennifer Flowers dropped her bombshell in 1992.

The worst public embarrassment of all for the Clintons was one that has actually gotten airbrushed out of the historical record. Yes, straight out of George Orwell's *1984* and the Memory Hole, a disastrous appearance by Hillary Clinton following the 9-11 terrorist attacks was censored from all rebroadcasts.

What follows is an overview of what may quite possibly be the most overtly censored moment in recent television history.

On October 20, 2001, during Paul McCartney's nationally televised Madison Square

Garden concert honoring the 343 firefighters and 87 police officers killed on 9/11, [a] five-hour concert featuring such performers as Mick Jagger, David Bowie, Elton John, Billy Joel, and James Taylor, raised more than thirty million dollars for the victims' families.

The crowd cheered when Rudy Giuliani stepped onto the stage, and offered a warm welcome for the Democrats' leader in the Senate, Tom Daschle. But when Hillary walked to the microphone to introduce a short clip by comedian Jerry Seinfeld, the throng erupted in a chorus of boos. "Get off the stage!" yelled one firefighter in the front row. "We don't want you here!" Stunned, Hillary tried to be heard over the jeers by shouting into the mike. After a few minutes she was forced to beat a hasty retreat."[1311]

Another account tells the same story.

When Senator Clinton took the stage at an October 21 appearance at the Concert for New York City, Matt Drudge reported that "VH1 cameras captured firemen and police wildly booing" her and that "anti-Clinton slurs spread and intensified throughout the Garden, with many standing near the stage lobbying profanities, "Get off the stage! We don't want you here!" shouted one cop a few feet from the podium.

Author Richard Poe of *Hillary's Secret War* watched the live broadcast and recounted the real-time Internet coverage of the program in his book. "As Hillary approached the

> **podium," Poe wrote, "the audience erupted in boos, jeers, and catcalls, so clearly audible on our television that my wife and I turned in amazement ... the jeers and catcalls came through loud and clear."[1312]**

"One eyewitness to the scene reported to the website FreeRepublic.com that Clinton was booed so loudly, she had to yell into the mike to be heard; [while] another estimated that ninety percent of the crowd jeered the former first lady."[1313]

The most obvious question is: why would New York's finest police officers and firefighters have such a vociferously negative reaction to Hillary's appearance? Naturally, the Clintons' aversion to the military and law enforcement is legendary, as has been pointed out numerous times in a variety of books, including this one. But another event took place a year before the Paul McCartney concert that solidified in the police officers' minds how much they loathed Mrs. Clinton. "New York cops have never forgotten what happened when Hillary was nominated for the U.S. Senate in May 2000. The setting was the New York State Democratic Convention in Albany. As the Albany Police honor guard marched past a crowd of Hillary supporters, delegates spat on them, calling them Nazis and mocking them as lackeys of 'Giuliani's Third Reich.'"[1314]

Such disrespect was not soon forgotten. Following 9-11 when a congregation of politicians gathered at Ground Zero to meet with the rescue workers and firefighters, the crowd was drawn to President George Bush. One witness said later, "They couldn't wait to shake his hand. And they did the same with Giuliani and Pataki – even Schumer, too. But when her [Hillary's] turn came the guys just folded their arms and wouldn't shake her hand. I'm no fan of Hillary, but even I felt bad for her."[1315]

Such a disgrace cannot be easily stomached; but let's return to the 9-11 memorial concert. After being heckled and jeered, "Hillary fled the stage after just less than twenty seconds, making hers the shortest presentation of the evening."[1316] Once offstage, "the boos from New York City cops and firemen gathered at Madison Square Garden just thirty-nine days after the September 11 attacks reportedly reduced Senator Clinton to tears behind the scenes."[1317]

As Hillary bawled, her husband, "Ex-President Bill Clinton pitched a fit backstage after his wife was roundly booed by the audience."[1318] To prevent this real-life catastrophe from becoming an even bigger embarrassment, drastic actions had to be taken. "The efforts to expunge the record of Mrs. Clinton's McCartney concert humiliation took on a particularly extreme form, though it's not clear whether she, her husband, or some unknown third party instigated the cover-up. The concert had been telecast live on VH1, and millions of people nationwide saw firefighters and cops boo her off the stage. But when the cable channel rebroadcast the McCartney concert, the booing and jeers for Mrs. Clinton had vanished. 'The boos were replaced with general crowd noise,' reported the late New York gossip maven Neal Travis."[1319]

You read correctly. "Although millions watching the live broadcast of VH1 witnessed Hillary being booed off the stage, the tape was doctored so that during subsequent airings the jeers were disguised by general crowd noise."[1320]

Indeed, the concert was historic for "those sixteen million people were quite possibly the largest audience ever permitted to see an uncensored broadcast of Hillary being heckled."[1321] But the heavy hand of Big Brother soon took over and clamped down. When VH1 re-aired the New York City event on Christmas Day, 2001, "The jeers and catcalls were gone. In their place, applause and cheers greeted Hillary as she walked onstage. Across America, every video and DVD on sale featured the same doctored version of the concert. Thanks to the magic of digital editing, Hillary's public-relations disaster was recast as a triumph."[1322]

To show the magnitude of how high this censorship reaches into the upper echelons of Big Media, consider that VH1 is "a subsidiary of MTV, which is owned by Viacom, which, in turn, owns

CBS."[1323]   In other words, some very big people had a vested interest in never again allowing anyone to see Hillary Clinton being booed offstage in Madison Square Garden. This act, I'm sorry to say, is a 100% Big Brother conspiracy of the worst sort, and one that should scare the hell out of everyone; for if the Clinton power-brokers are able to wield such *1984*-like control over the media when Hillary isn't even president, think what they could do if she is 'selected.'

Despite being *saved* by the media elite yet again, the McCartney concert did have an everlasting effect on Hillary; for after 9-11, "she never appeared at any of the victims' funerals."[1324] Why? Because "Hillary was afraid that she might be booed again, and instructed her staff not to schedule any appearances in front of large groups of firefighters or police officers."[1325]

That's correct: "Hillary avoided the funerals of 9/11 victims because she feared being booed by mourners."[1326] 9-11 ... the single worst terrorist attack in our nation's history: over 3,000 innocent deceased; with countless funerals, especially in the state of New York, where she was the junior senator. Yet "Hillary attended not a single one. While Schumer showed up at a dozen funerals and Giuliani and Pataki paid their respects literally hundreds of times, Hillary avoided the possibility of being heckled by hunkering down in Washington."[1327]

Hillary might be able to spin most events with her vast public relations team; but in New York City directly after 9-11 – that was real life, and it was the real people speaking. Get out! We don't want you here!

THEIR "JEWISH PROBLEM"

"'You Jew bastard ... You Jew motherf***er.' [These were] common insults that both Hillary and Bill Clinton used with each other and towards others who angered them, according to former bodyguard Larry Patterson."[1328]

The battles, outbursts, and rage exhibited by Bill and Hillary crossed every boundary and every line, even deteriorating into the cesspool of ethnic slurs and racial epithets. In 1999, Trooper Patterson commented again on this subject. "'It was fairly common for both Clintons to tell ethnic jokes and use ethnic slurs.' When asked for the exact words, the trooper responded, 'Jew Motherf***er, Jew Bastard.'"[1329] Lastly, "in Hillary's case, Patterson said he had heard her make anti-Semitic slurs at least twenty times in the heat of anger."[1330]

Hillary, it seems, was prone to use such language against others, too. During Bill's first unsuccessful political race against Senator John Paul Hammerschmidt, Hillary flew off into a rage after realizing a narrow defeat was imminent. "The now legendary confrontation with Clinton campaign manager Paul Fray took place in 1974 on election night ... By three a.m. it was all over. Clinton lost by a mere 6000 votes. He, Hillary and Fray went back to Fayetteville in their cars ... The minute Paul walked into the back room at Fayetteville headquarters, she was angrier than Paul had ever seen her. 'You f***ing Jew bastard!' she screamed."[1331]

Naturally, Hillary denied everything. "'It did not happen,' Hillary responded to Paul Fray's allegations. 'I have never said anything like that. Ever. Ever.'"[1332] Hillary's denial is hard to believe, as an acquaintance who knew her well declared. "Hillary always knows what buttons to push. There aren't many things in life she does that aren't calculated. Everything is thought out. She looks at the enemy and decides which kinds of weapons to use."[1333] Also, much to her dismay, Hillary wasn't alone when she called Fray a "f***ing Jew bastard." "The accusations would have been enough to deflect if it had been Hillary's word against Fray's. But this time there were at least two other witnesses who heard the outburst and two more from the Clintons' past who remember similar outbursts."[1334] With Fray's allegations now out in the open, "In the ensuing days, three more witnesses to the ethnic slur – or other incidents like it – came forward with damning accounts."[1335]

To further cover her tracks, Mrs. Clinton resorted to her ultimate ace-in-the-hole: smear tactics. "Hillary instructed an aide to
send a memo to Clinton's 'Jewish Advisory Committee' outlining
ways in which to cast doubt on the credibility of these three people who allegedly went on record as hearing Hillary make the
anti-Semitic slur: Fray, his wife Mary, and 1974 Clinton for Congress campaign worker Neil McDonald. The same memo urged
Hillary's Jewish backers to come forward and claim they had
never heard her make an anti-Semitic remark, but not to mention
that they had been asked to defend her."[1336]

Not wanting to become a victim of Hillary's hate campaign,
Fray took matters into his own hands. "Regarding her alleged
racial obscenity to Paul Fray, the *New York Post* arranged to have
Paul Fray take a polygraph test to verify he was telling the truth
about this incident. According to a state-licensed Arkansas poly-
grapher, 'There's no doubt in my mind that Mr. Fray is truth-
ful.'"[1337]

HILLARY: ANTI-SEMITE, RACIST, LIAR

B
ut please don't think this damning account is an isolated
event. "On one of Hillary's first trips to Arkansas, she and
Bill stopped by the home of one of his friends who had a
menorah (a Jewish symbol) on his door. When Hillary
saw this, she refused to get out of the car, causing Bill to tell his
friend, 'I'm sorry, but Hillary's really tight with the people in the
PLO in New York. They're friends of hers, and she just doesn't
feel right about the menorah. Hillary really backs the PLO and
doesn't like what Israel is up to.'"[1338]

Hillary's none-too-subtle racism was also evident in an exchange with strategist Dick Morris. During a meeting with Bill
and Hillary, Morris "quoted a fee that made Bill's hackles rise."[1339]
After some further conversation where Bill made an off-color reference; Hillary directed her venom at Morris, who is Jewish.

> **Hillary chimed in with an ethnic remark**
> **of her own: "That's all you people care about**
> **is money!" Stiffening at the implied slur,**
> **[Morris] gave her an escape hatch: "Hillary, I**
> **assume by 'you people' that you mean polit-**
> **ical consultants?" "Yeah, yeah," she said with**
> **apparent relief. "That's what I mean, politi-**
> **cal consultants."**[1340]

Morris later commented "that Hillary's anti-Semitic outburst came as she exploded with anger over his request"[1341] for a pay raise.

Yet when confronted with these accusations, what do the Clintons invariably do? They lie. When the Dick Morris charges about Hillary were brought to Bill Clinton's attention, he declared, "In twenty-nine years my wife has never, ever, uttered an ethnic or racial slur against anybody ever. She's so straight on this she squeaks. She can't tell an ethnic joke. It's not in her."[1342]

Is that so? How about Hillary's crack about one of India's most revered citizens? "You all remember Mahatma Ghandi. He ran a gas station down in St. Louis. (Hillary during a speech at a Democratic fundraiser. Senator Clinton was later forced to apologize, saying it was a lame attempt at humor.)"[1343]

Bill's feeble attempt to cover up for his wife is understandable because, in his own right, he's guilty of the same offenses. "[Trooper Larry] Patterson claims Bill Clinton would occasionally use the word 'nigger' when angry with black opponents. He cites its particular use in reference to Arkansas activist, Say McIntosh, a Clinton critic [who accused him of fathering a black love child]. Patterson contends Clinton referred to Jesse Jackson as a 'nigger' as late as 1992 and routinely tolerated racial slurs by others."[1344] If you question the accuracy of this account because Bill Clinton would never badmouth a fellow Democrat, think again for he was caught live on tape doing so. "'That was in October of 1991,' recalled Trooper Roger Perry, who was on the scene in the governor's mansion during the meeting. 'I'll never forget what Clinton turned and said to me after [Jesse] Jackson left the room. He snapped: that Jesse's a smart dude – but I can no more stand that motherf***er than I can Mario Cuomo.' Clinton's rage at the Phoenix TV station about Jackson's seeming favoritism toward Tom Harkin became volcanic when, to his mortification, he learned that the CBS camera and microphones had recorded the entire diatribe."[1345]

Even more embarrassing to Bill Clinton were his conversations with White House mistress Monica Lewinsky.

> **According to one excerpt of a phone call between Lewinsky and Tripp, Lewinsky recounts how she told Clinton a joke her father had been telling.**
>
> **"Why do Jewish men like to watch porno films backwards?" Lewinsky asked Tripp.**
>
> **"So they can watch the prostitute give back the money," Lewinsky answered.**
>
> **Lewinsky told Tripp that when she told Clinton the joke, he laughed and quickly responded with his own joke. Clinton's joke was apparently so obscene it was redacted by censors.[1346]**

Yes, Bill and Hillary, the sensitive liberals; the politically correct couple; the duo that advocates tolerance, compassion and sensitivity toward minorities and the oppressed. Sure! Just like everything else in their lives, this characterization is simply just another myth ... a fabrication that in reality is completely untrue.

Another very interesting aspect to this subject is Bill Clinton's very tight relationship with a man who many have called his mentor, Senator J. William Fulbright. After all, Clinton not only worked for Fulbright, but the Arkansas senator also recommended Clinton for the Rhodes scholarship program, and was also instrumental in getting Clinton out of the Vietnam draft. But Fulbright's views certainly don't fall in line with those of the Jewish Lobby.

> **Appearing on CBS television's *Face the Nation* in 1973, Fulbright declared that the Senate was 'subservient' to Israeli policies which were inimical to American interests. He said the United States bears "a very great share of the responsibility" for the continuation of Middle East violence. "It's quite obvious that without the all-out support by the United States in money and weapons and so on, the Israelis couldn't do what they've been doing."**
>
> **Fulbright said the United States failed to pressure Israel for a negotiated settlement because, "the great majority of the Senate of the United States – somewhere around eighty percent – are completely in support of Israel, anything Israel wants. This has been demonstrated time and time again, and this has made it difficult for our government."[1347]**

The real embarrassment in regard to this subject came when Hillary Clinton was yet again heckled by an audience. "'There was a spontaneous uprising of anger and boos from the crowd,' Jewish Action Alliance spokeswoman Beth Gilinsky told WOR Radio's Bob Grant. 'And we sustained the boos for quite a while to the point where she [Hillary] finally just walked off the stage. New York City Council member Noach Dear told WABC Radio's Sean Hannity that 'it was unbelievable: she gets up there and she starts to speak and they don't let her speak. She's trying to say something but they don't let her. The Senate candidate who was counting on up to 70 percent of New York's Jewish vote had just been booed off the stage at a rally in support of the Jewish state."[1348]

That wasn't the only time Hillary came under the wrath of the pro-Israelis. During her first senatorial campaign, "Hillary was 'thrown into a panic' when crowds booed her as she marched up Fifth Avenue in New York's annual Israel Day Parade. Later, at a 'Solidarity for Israel' rally in front of the Israeli consulate, in Manhattan, she was booed off the stage."[1349]

What caused such a strong reaction in these crowds? One reason could be that "In May 2000, Hillary attended a controversial off-the-record fundraiser hosted by Hani Masri, a Yasser Arafat crony."[1350] After collecting $50,000, it was disclosed that Hillary wanted this event to be kept so hush-hush that "it wasn't even listed on the Senate candidate's daily public schedule."[1351]

Even more incendiary to the Jews was an event Hillary attended in the Middle East during her 2000 campaign (while still First Lady). It was during a certain speech that fireworks began to erupt. "At one point, she [Hillary] nodded in approval as Suha Arafat, wife of PLO leader Yasser Arafat, accused Israel of, among other things, using poison gas on Palestinians. Then Hillary marched to the podium, embraced Mrs. Arafat warmly – and kissed her."[1352]

Another version of the story has Arafat citing "intensive daily use of gas by the Israeli forces in the past years which has led to an increase of cancer cases among Palestinian women and children."[1353]

A third account states, "Hillary is in trouble again for sitting idly by during a West Bank address by Mrs. Yasser Arafat, who accused the Israelis of gassing Palestinian women and children on a regular basis. Journalists are 'shocked, shocked' at Hillary's stone-faced reaction and failure to condemn Arafat's remarks even after she left the scene ... Mrs. Clinton's meeting with Mrs. Arafat ended the way it began, with a warm embrace and a kiss on the cheek."[1354]

The blowback was harsh. "From the beginning of the campaign, Harold Ickes and Susan Thomases wrestled with a perplexing problem. A must-win demographic group – observant Jews – did not like their candidate. In fact, they despised her."[1355] At another point during her campaign, Hillary met with Liz Moynihan, wife of Senator Daniel P. Moynihan, who told her, "The reason you're not doing well in New York is because Jews don't like you."[1356]

Also, remember that Liz Moynihan had the following words to say about Mrs. Clinton. "She's duplicitous. She would say or do anything that would forward her ambitions. She can look you straight in the eye and lie, and sort of not know she's lying. Lying isn't a sufficient word; it's distortion – distorting the truth to fit the case."[1357]

These words are quite poignant and prophetic because – as her "Jewish problem" grew increasingly worse – Hillary once again reverted to this duplicity to which Liz Moynihan referred. So, here's what she did. "When Hillary realized that she had gotten herself in a jam with Jewish voters, she suddenly turned up a long-lost Jewish stepfather – an announcement that was dismissed by many cynical New York voters as an example of pandering."[1358]

Hillary was aware of this Jewish relative since childhood – for fifty-plus years – but she kept him in mothballs until it was expedient to serve her own political ambitions. Then all of a sudden she trots him out like she's been worshipping at the Temple for ages. It's amazing the lengths to which this woman will go to save her skin.

But not everyone was buying her *schtick*. Jewish comedian Joan Rivers cracked, "The reason Hillary had recently shown up as a surprise speaker at a Mount Sinai Medical Center fundraising luncheon was because she figured – 'Jews! I can make up for Arafat, kissing Arafat's wife. If you don't see what a phony she is ... she's so anti-Jewish!'"[1359]

Paul Fray, Bill Clinton's first campaign manager who Hillary slammed with the "Jew bastard" comment, took things one step

further. "To some people, particularly those in Zionist organizations, Hillary became an enemy long before she entered the campaign for the Senate – when she spoke out favorably about the
possibility of a Palestinian state."[1360] He continued, "'the boys
across the water,' as Paul calls the Mossad, Israel's intelligence
unit, 'are aware of Hillary's anti-Semitic comments.' This may
ring of conspiracy theory to some, but in fact, Israel intelligence
has always made it their business to know everything they can
about political leaders and their relationship to Jews."[1361]

Before anyone jumps to conclusions and thinks this section is
too one-sided, please don't overlook the fact that the Clintons are
masters at playing both ends against the middle, while at the
same time recognizing the importance of key political factions.
In other words, the Clintons are much too politically adept to
alienate such an influential force as the Jewish Lobby. After all,
"the only real 'ethnics' with any real power in the Clinton administration were Jewish. In [Bob Woodward's] *The Agenda*, Jews
play a prominent role. Three of them – Robert Reich, Robert
Rubin, and Alan Greenspan – are essential. In Clinton's second
term, people of Jewish origin would head the Departments of
State, Defense, Treasury, Commerce (briefly), and serve as national security advisor and director of central intelligence."[1362]

So, as I've explained earlier, look beyond the rhetoric to see
what reality actually is. The Clintons realize how powerful and
important the Jews are, as can be evidenced by a move they
made in 1980. After serving one-term as governor of Arkansas,
Bill Clinton suffered a humiliating and traumatic loss in the 1980
election. Following this devastating blow, "In 1980, Bill and
Hillary Clinton went on a religious pilgrimage to Israel ... the trip
reinforced Clinton's support for the people of Israel. 'Bill and
Hillary understood the profound effect that Israel has on American Jews and around the world,' said Sarah Ehrman, their friend
from the McGovern campaign, 'and share a feeling for the security and stability of the State of Israel.'"[1363]

Some may want you to believe that the Clintons are rabid anti-

Semites, but that's simply not the case. Would a Jew-hater make the following statement?

> **"I have believed in supporting Israel as long as I have known anything about the issue," Clinton later said. "It may have something to do with my religious upbringing, for the last several years until he died, I was very much under the influence of my pastor. He was a close friend of Israel and began visiting even before the State of Israel was created. And when he was on his deathbed he said to me that he hoped someday I would have a chance to run for President, but that if I ever let Israel down, God would never forgive me. I will never let Israel down."[1364]**

Simple political posturing and pandering, or have the Clintons thrown their support to the State of Israel? If Bill Clinton's statement on August 2, 2002 at a Jewish fundraiser is any indication, the answer is clear: "If Iraq came across the Jordan River, I would grab a rifle and get in the trench and fight and die."[1365] Amazing? Let me get this straight. Bill Clinton refused to fight for his *own* country in Vietnam and did everything in his power to dodge the draft, but if a foreign country invaded Israel, he'd strap on a rifle and fight to the death for *them*? What kind of traitorous nonsense is that?

Hillary has also worked closely with Jewish organizations, for she was "instrumental in the establishment of a preschool program in Arkansas which encouraged parents to teach their own children. Aimed at four and five year olds, the program is called the Home Instruction Program for Preschool Youngsters, or HIPPY."[1366] Where did this program originate? It was "developed in Israel by the National Council of Jewish Women."[1367]

In addition, although we don't have the space to explore this subject in depth, the Clintons have received enormous amounts of money over the years from a multitude of Jewish groups, as "AIPAC (the American-Israeli Public Affairs Committee) contributed at least $400,000 to the Democratic party and to Mr. Clinton's election campaigns between 1991 and 1996."[1368]

So, as you can see, this issue is quite complex, and becomes even more complicated when another twist is added to the equation. The Clintons seemed to have been straddling a very delicate line between bashing the Jews, while also catering to them. But here's where matters become even more intriguing. In a book entitled *Gideon's Spies*, author "Gordon Thomas claims that the Israeli spy agency Mossad secretly taped thirty hours of Clinton-Lewinsky phone sex, then blackmailed the president to shut down an FBI investigation into a Mossad mole."[1369]

If you think such a notion is too far-fetched, consider that "the *Wall Street Journal* revealed on its editorial page on February 12 [1999], the day the Clinton trial closed, [that] U.S. intelligence agencies taped White House phone calls central to the Lewinsky investigation."[1370]

The president himself was even aware that his actions were being monitored. "On March 27 [1997], Clinton once more invited Lewinsky to the Oval Office and revealed he believed a foreign embassy was taping their conversations. He did not give her any more details, but shortly afterwards the affair ended."[1371]

A deeper insight into this situation can be found in the following passage. "The featureless corridors of Mossad's headquarters building in Tel Aviv had echoed with the scandalized whispers of how Sara Netanyahu had demanded to see psychological profiles of world leaders she and her husband would be entertaining or visiting. She had especially asked for details about President Bill Clinton's sexual activities."[1372]

It should be clear to everyone that when the Monica Lewinsky scandal broke and Clinton apologists objected, "why does everyone care so much about what Bill Clinton does in his personal life," there was certainly more to the picture, especially when we get to the section on Bill Clinton's highly controversial pardons during his final days in office. Slick Willie's irresponsible behavior *did* matter because he placed not only himself and the office of presidency in grave danger, but the entire nation. With such damning information held over one's head, a person becomes completely vulnerable to blackmail in any number of ways, such as selling military secrets to the Chinese, pardoning criminals, or passing legislation which does not benefit the American people. Bill Clinton's sexual predatory practices *did* matter, and he had complete disregard for our nation while engaging in such sordid practices (with Hillary covering his tracks every step of the way).

Anyway, returning to the surveillance of Bill Clinton's x-rated phone sex, according to Gordon Thomas, Israeli intelligence knew "that the White House was totally protected by electronic counter-measures."[1373] So, what they did instead was "focus on Lewinsky's apartment. They began to intercept explicit phone calls from the president to Lewinsky. The recordings were [then] couriered by diplomatic bag to Tel Aviv."[1374] Once there, "In Tel Aviv, Mossad strategists pondered how to use the highly embarrassing taped conversations; they were the stuff of blackmail."[1375]

As Clinton became more flamboyant in his perverse, self-centered ways, so too was there a proportional increase in the network of individuals who knew what he was doing. "There was common consensus that the FBI must also be aware of the conversations between Clinton and Lewinsky."[1376] By "September 1998 the Starr report was published and ... the report contained a short reference to Clinton warning Lewinsky back in March 1997 that his phone was being bugged by a foreign embassy."[1377]

Lastly, "six months later, March 5th 1999, the *New York Post* published in a cover story the revelations in the original edition of this book [*Gideon's Spies*]. The *Post* story began: 'Israel blackmailed President Clinton with phone-tapped tapes of his steamy sex talks with Monica Lewinsky, a blockbuster new book charges.'"[1378]

Bill Clinton's romps with Monica Lewinsky and others were

more than just *sex*. His egotism and libido – not to mention his enabler wife – seriously jeopardized the security of this nation, and that's not something to take lightly.

CULTURE OF DEATH

I realize that at the outset of this book we promised we would not be discussing policy issues, but we need to make one exception to that rule in regard to the matter of life and death. More specifically, we'd like to briefly use two examples to illustrate how Bill and Hillary Clinton have absolutely no respect for the sanctity of life, and instead are participants in the macabre culture of death which is permeating our society.

The first example we would like to use is partial-birth abortion; or as some prefer to call it: partial-birth murder. Of course we could debate back and forth along the entire spectrum of abortion, *Roe v. Wade*, and the morality of this practice. But rather than go down that road – one which we could argue for years – we would rather focus on what is undoubtedly the most gruesome form of murder in our society: partial-birth abortion. The practice is so barbaric that it equals those medieval forms of torture found in the Dark Ages. It is "a procedure [former Senator Daniel Patrick] Moynihan (D) once deemed 'infanticide.'"[1379]

To those unfamiliar with what we're discussing (and also those who need a reminder), below is a step-by-step overview of what people like Bill and Hillary Clinton are in *full* support of: the sickening murder of fully-formed, birthed babies.

Anatomy of a D & X Killing
(Partial-birth abortion)

Step One – while the child is still inside the mother's womb, "the abortionist grasps one of the baby's legs with forceps."

Step Two – "The [baby's] leg is pulled into the birth canal.

Step Three – "Using his hands, the abortionist delivers the

baby's body. The [baby's] head remains inside [the mother's womb]." What we now have at this point is a fully-born child with its *entire* body outside the mother's womb except for a few centimeters of its head. For all intents and purposes, the child has been delivered.

Step Four – "The abortionist forces scissors into the back of the baby's skull. He then opens the scissors to enlarge the hole."

Step Five – "A suction catheter is inserted into the wound, and the baby's brains are sucked out. The child is then removed."[1380]

What I have just outlined is the most repellent medical procedure in our society today; a murderous act that reeks with sickness and evil in what is supposed to be our advanced, progressive, 21st century civilized world. But what we have is something far removed from civilized: the mother's womb has been turned into a butcher's shop where a legalized killer pulls a fully-formed child – with a beating heart, blinking eyes, two arms and two legs with ten fingers and ten toes – from its mother's birth canal. This is a baby that is BORN – its entire body has been delivered except for the head. The baby would otherwise live like any other *born* child. It can feel pain. It can eat, drink, cry and breathe. The child is alive.

But instead of allowing this child to live – again, a child that is fully capable of feeling pain – the abortionist takes a pair of scissors and jams them through the baby's skull. After opening the scissors (or forceps) to make the bleeding gash even larger, the murderer "inserts a suction catheter into the baby's skull and sucks out the brain, which he describes as 'evacuating the skull's contents.'"[1381]

In simplest terms, a mini vacuum sweeper is inserted into the baby's head, which then in turn sucks its brains out. Almost immediately, with no brain matter remaining, the baby's skull collapses upon itself and it dies. Only seconds earlier this child was delivered into the world. Now it is dead. At that point, the abortionist removes the rest of the baby's body from the mother's womb (i.e. its collapsed skull) and disposes of it like yesterday's garbage.

This procedure is so sadistically extreme and inhumane that it doesn't even register on the bell curve. In fact, it is so appalling that the vast majority of pro-choice advocates refuse to support it, and want it outlawed. But not Hillary Clinton. "On March 12, 2003, Senator Clinton took to the Senate floor to oppose a bill that would outlaw partial-birth abortion, a procedure in which a late-term fetus is partly delivered and then aborted."[1382]

Virtually nobody in this country wants partial-birth abortions to be legal. It's murder, it's an embarrassment to us as a people, and it's a total violation of the life-force. In addition, it has always been my understanding that 'liberals' and 'progressives' and 'feminists' (such as what Hillary Clinton claims to be) stood for the protection of those members of society who were most innocent, weak, and helpless. Yet Hillary adamantly *supports* the brutal, outright murder of children that are only centimeters away from being fully born. Fellow Democrats in her own political party have even taken a stand against this form of infant-slaughter. "Sixty-four members of the Senate, including Democratic minority leader Tom Daschle and other liberal stalwarts like Joseph Biden and Ernest Hollings, found the practice repugnant enough to vote against it."[1383]

But not Bill and Hillary. They still, to this day, fully support partial-birth abortion and want it to be 100% legal.

Below is an excerpt which provides an idea of how devilish this couple truly is.

The following is an account as told to *Washington Week* by Lurleen Stackhouse, who approached President and Mrs. Clinton at the pre-inaugural prayer service held at the AMEC church in Washington, DC, on Inauguration Day [1993].

"When the service concluded we were asked to stay seated until the President and Mrs. Clinton departed for the White House.

> **However, as they walked down the aisle I stood and reached out for Mr. Clinton. 'Mr. Clinton, America must stop killing babies.' He looked at me with a blank stare on his face. I repeated this statement to him.**
>
> **"Hillary (not hearing my comment) then came to give me a hug and I said (in a voice only audible to her), 'Hillary, it's against God's law to kill babies.' She stepped back, shaking and trembling, and then grabbed my arm. Her countenance transformed from a pleasant demeanor to the appearance of being possessed. Her eyes were enraged as she replied, *"It is God's law to kill babies."*[1384]**

Considering Hillary's acceptance and promotion of partial-birth abortion, it is not surprising that she'd hold such a view, especially on Inauguration Day when she and Bill got into such a venomous battle with each other over his philandering and supposedly cheating her out of Al Gore's office.

Bill Clinton's lack of respect for the sanctity of life isn't any less troublesome, for he also holds a membership in the culture of death. A perfect example of his callousness and submission to what is politically expedient can be found in an incident which took place during the early stages of his 1992 presidential campaign.

Rickey Rector killed three men in cold blood during the spring of 1981. After these cowardly slayings, Rector turned the gun on himself and put a bullet into his own head. "He survived the shooting, but the bullet wound and subsequent surgery resulted in a prefrontal lobotomy."[1385]

Rector was eventually found guilty of murder and sentenced to death, but due to his lobotomy and quite possibly severe brain damage, Rector "stretched and yawned after the judge sentenced him to die."[1386] In the ensuing years, "Rector seemed to be unaware of his surroundings and ... sometimes howled and barked like a dog."[1387]

Still, in January 1992, Rector was on death row sentenced to die. "Two journalists, Jimmy Breslin of *Newsday* and Derrick Jackson of the *Boston Globe*, wrote scathing columns about the execution. 'The killing of human vegetables' is 'an exercise for brutes,' Jackson wrote."[1388]

Bill Clinton, to appear tough on crime and not fall into the same trap as wishy-washy Michael Dukakis, refused to stay the execution, even thou when "Rector was served his last meal of fried steak, baked chicken, beans, pecan pie and cherry Kool-Aid, one press report said he did not eat all the pie; he was saving it for later."[1389]

Rickey Ray Rector was so out of sorts that he was saving some of his last meal for *after* he was executed; yet Bill Clinton still let this mentally deficient man die. Rickey Rector wasn't a good man; he was a killer, and I don't feel the least bit of compassion for anyone that takes the life of three innocent human beings. But when put to death, "It took medical technicians fifty minutes to find a vein in which to inject the lethal drugs"[1390] which would ultimately kill him.

I have presented the previous information not to debate the pros and cons of abortion or the death penalty; but rather to show how little regard Bill and Hillary Clinton have for the sanctity of life. They'll allow fully-formed babies to have their skulls penetrated by a pair of scissors, then have their brains sucked out. Likewise, to augment their political advancement, they'll lethally inject a man who was, essentially, mentally retarded and didn't understand the concept that he couldn't eat part of his final meal *after* his execution.

That's what kind of people Bill and Hillary Clinton are.

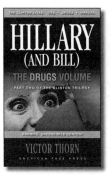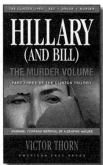

UPCOMING VOLUMES IN THE
HILLARY (And BILL)
TRILOGY

HILLARY (And Bill)
The Drugs Volume
PART 2 of the Clinton Trilogy

AND

HILLARY (And Bill)
The Murder Volume
PART 3 of the Clinton Trilogy

Coming from Victor Thorn &
***American Free Press* in 2008!**

About the Author

VICTOR THORN FOUNDED SISYPHUS PRESS in the fall of 2000, and is the author of eight books, as well as ten other chapbooks. He has published the works of numerous writers in the alternative media, and has also produced four CD-ROMs and DVDs, one of which is a five-disc collection which covers the John F. Kennedy Assassination (*Evidence of Revision*). Thorn is also the editor of four anthologies, and his political articles have appeared in various newspapers and magazines around the country.

One of his books, *The New World Order Exposed*, was translated and published in Japan in 2006, while *9-11 on Trial* has been republished by Progressive Press (Joshua Tree, Ca.), and was released in France coinciding with the fifth anniversary of 9-11.

He was also co-host of *The Victor Thorn Show* on the Reality Radio Network from 2002-2003.

In February, 2004 he and Lisa Guliani began WING TV (World Independent News Group), which was a daily Internet television and radio talk show which was viewed in over 100 countries worldwide.

Thorn has also made hundreds of different radio and television appearances (including *Coast-to-Coast AM*, *The Lionel Show* on WOR 710, and Frank Whalen's *Frankly Speaking* on RBN), and did a weekly one-hour news update on Alex Merklinger's *Mysteries of the Mind*, while also appearing weekly on Vyzygoth's *From the Grassy Knoll* radio show.

Lastly, Thorn has been an avid political activist who spoke at the OKC Bombing 10th anniversary, as well as before the America First Party. He has also protested in six different states, not to mention in New York City on several occasions, and in front of the White House in Washington, DC.

The WING TV website can be found at:
www.wingtv.net

Endnotes

Preface:
The Rape of Juanita Broaddrick

1. Christopher Andersen, *American Evita* (New York: William Morrow, 2004), p. 65
2. Ibid., p. 65
3. Carl Limbacher, *Hillary's Scheme* (New York: Crown Forum, 2003), p. 171
4. Andersen, p. 65
5. Christopher Ruddy & Carl Limbacher, *Bitter Legacy* (West Palm Beach, NewsMax, 2001), p. 50
6. Christopher Andersen, *Bill and Hillary* (New York: William Morrow, 1999), p. 163
7. Ruddy & Limbacher, p. 50
8. Limbacher, p. 171
9. Andersen, *American Evita*, p. 65
10. Ruddy, Limbacher, p. 50
11. Limbacher, p. 171
12. Ruddy, Limbacher, p. 58
13. Limbacher, p. 167
14. Ruddy, Limbacher, pp. 42-3
15. Limbacher, p. 171
16. John Austin, *Rkansides* (Bloomington, 1st Books, 2000), p. 92
17. Candice Jackson, *Their Lives* (Los Angeles: World Ahead Publishing, 2005), p. 227
18. Ruddy, Limbacher, p. 43
19. Jackson, p. 226
20. Ibid.
21. Ibid., p. 240
22. Ibid.
23. Ibid., p. 247
24. Ibid., p. 235
25. Andersen, *Bill and Hillary*, p. 178
26. Jackson, p. 246
27. Sam Smith, *Arkansas Connections*, p. 6
28. Roger Morris, *Partners in Power* (Washington: Regnery Publishing, 1996), p. 238
29. Andersen, *American Evita*, p. 67
30. Ibid.
31. Emmett Tyrrell & Mark Davis, *Madame Hillary* (Washington: Regnery Publishing, 2004), p. 92
32. Limbacher, p. 174
33. Andersen, *American Evita*, pp. 67-8
34. Limbacher, p. 174
35. Ibid.
36. Tyrrell, Davis, p. 93
37. Andersen, *American Evita*, p. 68
38. Ibid.
39. Edward Klein, *The Truth About Hillary* (New York: Sentinel, 2005), p. 89
40. Limbacher, p. 174
41. Andersen, *American Evita*, p. 68
42. Ibid.
43. Ibid.
44. Limbacher, p. 175
45. Andersen, *American Evita*, p. 66
46. Barbara Olson, *Hell to Pay* (Washington: Regnery Publishing, 1999), p. 308
47. Jackson, p. 241
48. Klein, p. 137
49. Austin, p. 90
50. Limbacher, p. 176
51. Ibid., p. 204
52. Ibid., p. 205
53. Ibid.
54. Ibid.
55. Ibid.
56. Ibid.
57. Limbacher, p. 169
58. Jackson, pp. 227-8
59. Jeffrey Toobin, *A Vast Conspiracy* (New York: Touchstone Books, 1999), p. 270

Introduction:
The Clinton Lie Machine

60. George Carpozi, *Clinton Confidential* (Columbia: CLS Publishing, 1995), p. 368
61. James B. Stewart, *Blood Sport* (New York: Touchstone Books, 1996), pp. 213-4
62. R. Emmett Tyrrell, *Boy Clinton* (Washington: Regnery Publishing, 1996), p. 255
63. Alexander Cockburn & Ken Silverstein, *Washington Babylon* (London: Verso, 1996), p. 408
64. Edward Klein, *The Truth About Hillary* (New York: Sentinel, 2005), p. 169
65. Ibid., p. 165
66. Dick Morris, *Rewriting History* (New York: Regan Books, 2004), p. 146

67. Joyce Milton, *The First Partner* (New York: Perennial, 1999), p. 415

68. Ibid.

69. Morris, p. 12

70. Thomas D. Kuiper, *I've Always Been a Yankees Fan* (Los Angeles: World Ahead Publishing, 2006), p. 139

71. Morris, p. 12

72. Kuiper, p. 139

73. Christopher Andersen, *American Evita* (New York: William Morrow, 2004), p. 189

74. Morris, p. 246

75. Andersen, p. 189

76. Morris, p. 246

77. Andersen, p. 189

78. Peggy Noonan, *The Case Against Hillary* (New York: Harper Collins, 2000), p. xx

79. Morris, p. 11

80. Ibid.

81. Emmett Tyrrell & Mark Davis, *Madame Hillary* (Washington: Regnery Publishing, 2004), p. 79

82. Barbara Olson, *Hell to Pay* (Washington: Regnery Publishing, 1999), p. 277

83. Morris, p. 126

84. Tyrrell, Davis, p. 69

85. Andersen, p. 145

86. Ibid., p. 144

87. Olson, p. 313

88. Hillary Rodham Clinton, *Living History* (New York: Scribner, 2003), p. 258

89. Tyrrell, p. 223

90. Kuiper, p. 77

91. Roger Morris, *Partners in Power* (Washington: Regnery Publishing, 1996), p. 315

92. Charles F. Allen & Jonathan Portis, *The Comeback Kid* (New York: Birch Lane Press, 1992), p. 216

93. Dick Morris, p. 224

94. Andersen, p. 225

95. Olson, p. 18

96. Noonan, p. 96

97. Olson, p. 136

98. Noonan, p. 96

99. Paul Fick, *The Dysfunctional President* (New York: Citadel Press, 1998), pp. 3-4

100. Richard Poe, *Hillary's Secret War* (Nashville: WND Books, 2004), p. 57

101. Barbara Olson, *The Final Days* (Washington: Regnery Publishing, 2001), p. 199

102. Ibid., p. 200

103. Ibid., p. 98

104. Fick, p. 11

105. Kuiper, p. 153

106. Gennifer Flowers, *Sleeping with the President* (New York: Anonymous Press, 1996), p. 19

107. Carpozi, p. 388

108. Patrick Matrisciana, *The Clinton Chronicles Book*, (Hemet: Jeremiah Books, 1994), p. 40

109. Ibid., p. 41

110. Ibid., p. 17

111. Kuiper, p. 155

112. Ibid., p. 153

113. Paul Roer, *The Rants, Raves & Thoughts of Bill Clinton* (Brooklyn: On Your Own Publications, 2002), p. 150

114. Ibid., p. 143

115. Paul Fick, *The Dysfunctional President* (New York: Citadel Press, 1995), p. 145

116. Allen, Portis, p. 156

117. Tyrrell, p. 260

118. Gary Aldrich, *Unlimited Access*, (Washington: Regnery Publishing, 1998), p. 219

119. Christopher Andersen, *Bill and Hillary* (New York: William Morrow, 1999), p. 2

120. John Austin, *Rkansides* (Bloomington: 1st Books, 2000), p. 168

121. Ibid.

122. Ibid., p. 171

123. Ibid., p. 177

124. Michael Isikoff, *Uncovering Clinton* (New York: Crown Publishers, 1999), p. 168

125. Ibid., p. 29

126. Tyrrell, p. 159

127. Ibid., p. 155

128. Christopher Ruddy & Carl Limbacher, *Bitter Legacy* (NewsMax: West Palm Beach, 2001), p. 50

129. Kevin H. Watson, *The Clinton Record* (Bellevue: Merril Press, 1996), p. 91

130. R. W. Bradford, *It Came From Arkansas* (Port Townsend: Liberty Publishing, 1993), p. 10

131. Flowers, p. 11

132. D. Morris, p. 220

133. Austin, p. 40

134. Rich Lowry, *Legacy* (Washington: Regnery Publishing, 2003), p. 125

135. Christopher Hitchens, *No One Left to Lie To* (London: Verso, 1999), p. 24

136. Joe Klein, *The Natural* (New York: Sen-

tinel, 2005), p. 1

137. Olson, p. 99

138. Ibid., p. 101

139. George Stephanopoulos, *All Too Human* (Boston: Little Brown & Company, 1999), p. 436

140. Tyrrell, p. 257

141. Olson, p. 56

142. Ibid., p. 59

143. Michael Kellett, *Phantoms of the World Stage* (Columbia, MD: Evidence First Publishing, 2006), p. 224

144. Lt. Colonel Robert Patterson, *Dereliction of Duty* (Washington: Regnery Publishing, 2003), p. 51

145. Kellett, p. 229

146. Meredith Oakley, *On the Make* (Washington: Regnery Publishing, 1994), p. 419

147. Ibid., p. 441

148. Tyrrell, p. 285

149. Noonan, p. 50

150. Ibid., p. 14

151. Kuiper, p. 158

152. Ibid.

153. Ibid.

154. Jeffrey Toobin, *A Vast Conspiracy* (New York: Touchstone Books, 1999), p. 379

155. Karen Tumulty, *Hollywood Scuffle* (New York: Time magazine, March 5, 2007), p. 46

Chapter One:
Who Was Bill Clinton's Real Father?

156. R. Emmett Tyrrell, *Boy Clinton* (Washington: Regnery Publishing, 1996), p. 156

157. Ibid.

158. Jack Cashill, *Ron Brown's Body* (Nashville: WND Books, 2004), p. 98

159. Christopher Andersen, *American Evita* (New York: William Morrow, 2004), p. 41

160. Meredith Oakley, *On the Make* (Washington: Regnery Publishing, 1994), p. 21

161. Jerry Oppenheimer, *State of a Union* (New York: Harper Collins, 2000), p. 97

162. Virginia Clinton Kelly, *Leading With My Heart* (New York: Pocket Star Books, 1994), p. 43

163. Oppenheimer, p. 99

164. David Maraniss, *First in His Class* (New York: Touchstone Books, 1995), p. 28

165. Ibid.

166. Oakley, p. 18

167. Maraniss, p. 28

168. Ibid.

169. Ibid.

170. Gail Sheehy, *Hillary's Choice* (New York: Random House, 1999), p. 95

171. Ibid.

172. Maraniss, p. 28

173. Tyrrell, p. 148

174. Barbara Olson, *Hell to Pay* (Washington: Regnery Publishing, 1999), p. 72

175. Joyce Milton, *The First Partner* (New York: Perennial, 1999), p. 71

176. Tyrrell, p. 145

177. Tyrrell, p. 147

178. Christopher Andersen, *Bill and Hillary* (New York: William Morrow, 1999), p. 48

179. Paul Fick, *The Dysfunctional President* (New York: Citadel Press, 1995), p. 220

180. Edward P. Moser, *Willy Nilly* (Nashville, Caliban Books, 1994), p. 66

181. Milton, p. 231

182. Ibid.

183. Ibid., p. 253

184. Ibid., p. 231

185. Oakley, p. 18

186. Maraniss, p. 28

187. Kelly, p. 52

188. George Carpozi, *Clinton Confidential* (Columbia: CLS Publishing, 1995), p. 10

189. Ibid.

190. Maraniss, p. 29

191. Oakley, p. 18

192. Charles Allen & Jonathan Portis, *The Comeback Kid* (New York: Birch Lane Press, 1992), p. 5

193. Christopher Andersen, *American Evita* (New York: William Morrow, 2004), p. 41

194. Maraniss, p. 29

195. Kelly, p. 52

196. Ibid.

197. Ibid., pp. 52-3

198. Maraniss, p. 29

199. Ibid., p. 18

200. Joe Klein, *The Natural* (New York: Sentinel, 2005), p. 23

201. Michael Isikoff, *Uncovering Clinton* (New York: Crown Publishers, 1999), p. 9

202. Roger Morris, *Partners in Power* (Washington: Regnery Publishing, 1996), p. xviii

203. Ibid. p. 37

204. Kelly, p. 65
205. Morris, p. 38
206. Patrick Matrisciana, *The Clinton Chronicles Book*, (Hemet: Jeremiah Books, 1994), p. 28
207. Ibid.
208. Morris, p. 38
209. Sam Smith, *Arkansas Connections*, p. 3
210. Ibid.
211. Kelly, p. 65
212. Morris, p. 58
213. Robert E. Levin, *Bill Clinton: The Inside Story* (New York: S.P.I. Books, 1992), p. 103
214. Jim Marrs, *Rule by Secrecy* (New York: Perennial, 2000), pp. 50-1
215. Kelly, p. 65
216. Morris, p. xviii
217. Kelly, p. 66
218. Ibid., p. 40
219. Ibid., p. 31
220. Morris, p. 39
221. Ibid., p. 40
222. Smith, p. 5
223. Morris, p. xx
224. David Brock, *The Seduction of Hillary Rodham* (New York: Free Press Paperbacks, 1996), p. 46
225. Morris, p. xx
226. Ibid., p. xxv
227. Ibid., p. 41
228. Ibid.
229. Bill Clinton, *My Life* (New York: Alfred P. Knopf, 2004), p. 33
230. Smith, p. 5
231. Ibid., p. 4
232. Ambrose Evans-Pritchard, *The Secret Life of Bill Clinton* (Washington: Regnery Publishing, 1997), p. 275
233. Milton, p. 75
234. Tyrrell, p. 115
235. Clinton, p. 61
236. Allen, Portis, p. 11
237. Morris, p. 55
238. Ibid.
239. Ibid., p. 57
240. Maraniss, pp. 19-20

Chapter Two: Sister Frigidaire - Future Mob Queen

241. American Conservative Union, *Hillary Rodham Clinton* (Ottawa: Green Hill Publishers, 2005), p. 10
242. Meredith Oakley, *On the Make* (Washington: Regnery Publishing, 1994), p. 93
243. Ibid., p. 94
244. Hillary Clinton, *Living History* (New York: Scribner, 2003), p. 9
245. Roger Morris, *Partners in Power* (Washington: Regnery Publishing, 1996), p. xx
246. Ibid.
247. Jerry Oppenheimer, *State of a Union* (New York: Harper Collins, 2000), p. 102
248. Ibid., p. 19
249. Ibid.
250. Ibid., p. 21
251. Ibid., p. 22
252. Ibid., p. 23
253. Ibid.
254. Ibid., p. 24
255. Ibid., p. 25
256. Ibid.
257. Ibid., p. 48
258. Ibid.
259. Ibid., p. 60
260. Ibid.
261. Ibid.
262. Ibid.
263. Ibid., p. 61
264. Ibid.
265. Ibid.
266. Barbara Olson, *Hell to Pay* (Washington: Regnery Publishing, 1999), p. 28
267. Morris, p. 115
268. Judith Warner, *Hillary Clinton: The Inside Story* (New York: Signet, 1993), p. 24
269. Ibid.
270. Clinton, p. 25
271. Christopher Andersen, *American Evita* (New York: William Morrow, 2004), p. 25
272. Morris, p. 117
273. Ibid.
274. David Brock, *The Seduction of Hillary Rodham* (New York: Free Press Paperbacks, 1996), p. 4
275. Morris, p. 117
276. Edward Klein, *The Truth About Hillary* (New York: Sentinel, 2005), p. 50
277. R. Emmett Tyrrell, *Boy Clinton* (Washington: Regnery Publishing, 1996), p. 196

Chapter Three:
Operation Chaos – CIA Campus Co-eds

"The Speech"

278. Jack Cashill, *Ron Brown's Body* (Nashville: WND Books, 2004), p. 9

279. David Brock, *The Seduction of Hillary Rodham* (New York: Free Press Paperbacks, 1996), p. 21

280. Hillary Clinton, *Living History* (New York: Scribner, 2003), p. 38

281. Ibid.

282. Ibid.

283. Ibid.

284. Edward Klein, *The Truth About Hillary* (New York: Sentinel, 2005), p. 61

285. Ibid., p. 61

286. Barbara Olson, *Hell to Pay* (Washington: Regnery Publishing, 1999), p. 45

287. Judith Warner, *Hillary Clinton: The Inside Story* (New York: Signet, 1993), p. 38

288. Brock, p. 21

289. Martin L. Gross, *The Great Whitewater Fiasco* (New York: Ballantine Books, 1994), pp. 28-9

290. Ibid., p. 28

291. Ibid., p. 29

292. Christopher Andersen, *American Evita* (New York: William Morrow, 2004), p. 16

293. Roger Morris, *Partners in Power* (Washington: Regnery Publishing, 1996), p. 135

294. Ibid., p. 134

295. Ibid., p. 135

296. Ibid.

297. Ibid.

298. Ibid.

299. Andersen, p. 16

300. Brock, p. 23

301. Andersen, p. 16

302. Morris, p. 137

303. Brock, p. 23

304. Richard Poe, *Hillary's Secret War* (Nashville: WND Books, 2004), p. 61

Yale: Radicals versus the Establishment

305. Judith Warner, *Hillary Clinton: The Inside Story* (New York: Signet, 1993), p. 50

306. Andersen, p. 37

307. Brock, p. 36

308. Olson, p. 51

309. Ibid.

310. Klein, p. 107

311. Olson, p. 101

312. Ibid.

313. Brock, p. 30

314. Ibid., p. 36

315. Ibid., p. 26

316. Clinton, p. 35

317. Ibid., p. 36

318. Emmett Tyrrell & Mark Davis, *Madame Hillary* (Washington: Regnery Publishing, 2004), p. 4

319. Brock, p. 37

320. Gross, p. 33

321. Clinton, p. 47

322. Tyrrell, Davis, p. 106

323. Morris, p. 119

324. American Conservative Union, *Hillary Rodham Clinton* (Ottawa: Green Hill Publishers, 2005), p. 13

325. Brock, p. 17

326. Tyrrell, Davis, p. 101

327. Brock, p. 17

328. Olson, p. 50

329. Ibid., p. 49

330. Ibid., p. 183

331. Tyrrell, Davis, p. 107

332. Brock, p. 16

333. Tyrrell, Davis, p. 7

334. Ibid., p. 107

335. Olson, p. 57

336. Ibid.

337. Brock, p. 33

338. Ibid., p. 32

339. Ibid.

340. Warner, p. 16

341. Brock, pp. 33-4

342. Joyce Milton, *The First Partner* (New York: Perennial, 1999), p. 53

343. Ibid.

Georgetown-Oxford Connections

344. Daniel Brandt, *Clinton, Quigley, and Conspiracy* (Name Base News Line, 1993), p. 7

345. Jim Marrs, *Rule by Secrecy* (New York: Perennial, 2000), p. 96

346. Morris, p. 72

347. Ibid., p. 60

348. Marrs, p. 32

349. Des Griffin, *Fourth Reich of the Rich* (Clackamas: Emissary Publications, 1976), p. 111

350. James Perloff, *The Shadows of Power* (Appleton: Western Islands, 1988), p. 20

351. Brandt, p. 2

352. Morris, pp. 64-5

353. Meredith Oakley, *On the Make* (Washington: Regnery Publishing, 1994), p. 46

354. David Maraniss, *First in His Class* (New York: Touchstone Books, 1995), p. 61

355. Ibid., p. 93

356. Morris, p. 76

357. Ibid., p. 75

358. Brock, p. 37

359. Morris, p. 68

360. Brandt, pp. 7-8

361. Morris, p. 66

362. Oakley, p. 48

363. John Austin, *Rkansides* (Bloomington: 1st Books, 2000), p. xv

364. Paul Fick, *The Dysfunctional President* (New York: Citadel Press, 1998), p. 219

"The Meeting," Lesbianism, and a Prearranged Marriage

365. Oppenheimer, p. 8

366. Maraniss, p. 248

367. Brock, p. 39

368. Ibid., p. 38

369. Maraniss, p. 246

370. Oakley, p. 102

371. Oppenheimer, p. 6

372. Oakley, p. 102

373. Maraniss, p. 246

374. Ibid.

375. Oppenheimer, p. 7

376. Ibid.

377. Ibid., pp. 7-8

378. Klein, p. 24

379. Ibid., p. 25

380. L.D. Brown, *Crossfire* (San Diego: Black Forest Press, 1999), p. 85

381. Milton, pp. 69-70

382. Christopher Andersen, *Bill and Hillary* (New York: William Morrow, 1999), p. 133

383. Oppenheimer, p. 114

384. Ibid.

385. Ibid., p. 113

386. Andersen, *American Evita*, p. 53

387. Brock, p. 60

388. Ibid.

389. Ibid., p. 40

390. Klein, p. 25

391. Brock, p. 60

392. Oppenheimer, p. 115

393. Klein, p. 85

394. Olson, p. 82

395. Morris, p. 151

396. Ibid.

397. Oppenheimer, p. 116

398. Morris, p. 151

399. Klein, p. 62

400. David Southwell & Sean Twist, *Conspiracy Files* (New York: Gramercy Books, 2004), p. 108

401. Klein, p. 63

402. Ibid., p. 86

403. David Bresnahan, *Damage Control* (Salt Lake City: Camden Court Publishers, 1997), p. 46

404. Milton, p. 78

405. American Conservative Union, p. 20

406. Klein, p. 86

407. American Conservative Union, p. 20

408. Klein, pp. 64-5

409. Ibid., p. 64

410. Morris, p. 140

411. Klein, p. 72

412. Ibid.

413. Bresnahan, p. 45

414. Ibid.

415. Morris, p. 145

416. Ibid., p. 147

417. Klein, p. 73

418. James B. Stewart, *Blood Sport* (New York: Touchstone Books, 1996), p. 239

419. Ibid.

420. Oppenheimer, pp. 15-6

421. Thomas D. Kuiper, *I've Always Been a Yankees Fan* (Los Angeles: World Ahead Publishing, 2006), p. 7

422. Christopher Andersen, *Bill and Hillary*, p. 137

423. Ibid.

424. Kuiper, p. 7

425. Robert E. Levin, *Bill Clinton: The Inside Story* (New York: S.P.I. Books, 1992), pp. 114-5

426. Morris, p. 141

427. Kuiper, p. 63

428. Klein, p. 41

429. Ibid.
430. Morris, p. 141
431. Brock, p. 56
432. Oakley, p. 41
433. Ibid.
434. Klein, p. 70
435. Ibid., p. 71
436. Ibid.
437. Ibid., p. 87
438. Ibid.
439. Oppenheimer, p. 2
440. Ibid., p. 4
441. Ibid., p. 3
442. Ibid.
443. Ibid., p. 130
444. Klein, p. 87

Operation CHAOS

445. Mick Farren, *CIA: Secrets of the Company* (New York: Chrysalis Books Group, 2003), p. 100
446. Gross, p. 41
447. Levin, p. 76
448. Oakley, p. 75
449. Levin, p. 76
450. Ibid., pp. 76-7
451. Morris, p. 93
452. Oakley, p. 73
453. Ibid., p. 66
454. Oakley, p. 67
455. Ambrose Evans-Pritchard, *Student Bill Clinton Spied on Americans Abroad for CIA*, Sunday Telegraph, pp. 2-3
456. Robert Anton Wilson, *Cosmic Trigger* (Tempe: New Falcon Publications, 1977), pp. 171-2
457. Ibid., p. 156
458. Brandt, p. 9
459. Ibid., pp 9-10
460. Ibid., p. 1
461. Ibid.
462. Edward P. Moser, *Willy Nilly* (Nashville, Caliban Books, 1994), p. 22
463. Levin, p. 76
464. Oakley, pp. 65-6
465. Ibid., p. 75
466. Charles F. Allen & Jonathan Portis, *The Comeback Kid* (New York: Birch Lane Press, 1992), p. 28
467. Gary Aldrich, *Unlimited Access*, (Washington: Regnery Publishing, 1998), p. 220

468. Ibid., p. 221
469. Ibid.
470. Ibid.
471. Ibid.
472. Ibid.
473. Evans-Pritchard, p. 2
474. Oakley, p. 80
475. Morris, p. 102
476. Michael Collins Piper, *The Judas Goats* (Washington: American Free Press, 2006), p. 232
477. Mark Zepezauer, *The CIA's Greatest Hits* (Tucson: Odonian Press, 1994), pp. 46-7
478. Morris, p. 102
479. Ibid., p. 103-4
480. Ibid. p. 104
481. Piper, pp. 232-3
482. Ibid., p. 235
483. Ibid., p. 234
484. Morris, p. 104
485. Piper, p. 237
486. Ibid.
487. Morris, p. 20

Behind the Iron Curtain

488. Evans-Pritchard, p. 1
489. Ibid., p. 2
490. Ibid.
491. Sam Smith, *Arkansas Connections*, p. 4
492. Daniel Brandt, *Clinton's Long CIA Connection*, p. 1
493. Ibid., p. 2
494. Ibid., p. 3
495. Oakley, p. 82
496. Maraniss, p. 206
497. Oakley, p. 82
498. Aldrich, p. 222
499. George Carpozi, *Clinton Confidential* (Columbia: CLS Publishing, 1995), p. 63
500. Aldrich, p. 223
501. Oakley, p. 83
502. Carpozi, pp. 64-5
503. Floyd Brown, *Slick Willie* (Annapolis: Annapolis-Washington Book Publishers, 1993), p. 10
504. Ibid.
505. Maraniss, p. 207
506. Ibid.
507. Ibid.
508. Brown, p. 11
509. Carpozi, p. 58

510. Oakley, p. 83
511. Morris, p. 93
512. Ibid.
513. Carpozi, p. 64
514. Ibid.
515. Des Griffin, *Descent Into Slavery* (Clacka-mas: Emissary Publications, 1980), p. 295
516. Carpozi, p. 63
517. Oakley, p. 84
518. Ibid.
519. Morris, p. 104
520. Oakley, p. 84
521. Maraniss, p. 211
522. Ibid., p. 212
523. Ibid.
524. Piper, p. 235

Draft-Dodger

525. Brown, p. 1
526. Kevin H. Watson, *The Clinton Record* (Bellevue: Merril Press, 1996), p. 19
527. Morris, p. 97
528. Brown, p. 1
529. Watson, p. 23
530. Morris, p. 90
531. Ibid.
532. Ibid., p. 91
533. Ibid.
534. Ibid.
535. Ibid., pp. 95-6
536. Watson, p. 26
537. Ibid.
538. Brock, p. 259
539. Morris, p. 100
540. Brown, p. 6
541. Morris, p. 100
542. R. Emmett Tyrrell, *Boy Clinton* (Washing-ton: Regnery Publishing, 1996), p. 42
543. Ibid.
544. Ibid., p. 36
545. Patrick Matrisciana, *The Clinton Chronicles Book*, (Hemet: Jeremiah Books, 1994), p. 190
546. Paul Fick, *The Dysfunctional President* (New York: Citadel Press, 1995), p. 5
547. Milton, p. 76
548. Ibid.
549. Barbara Olson, *The Final Days* (Washing-ton: Regnery Publishing, 2001), p. 28
550. Ibid.

551. Maraniss, p. 118
552. Morris, p. 81
553. Maraniss, p. 118
554. Ibid., p. 119
555. Carpozi, p. 395
556. Brown, p. 2
557. Maraniss, p. 119
558. Brown, p. 3
559. Maraniss, p. 119
560. Carpozi, p. 394
561. Ibid.
562. Watson, p. 21
563. Brown, p. 2
564. Watson, p. 23
565. R. W. Bradford, *It Came From Arkansas* (Port Townsend: Liberty Publishing, 1993), p. 35
566. Moser, p. 25
567. Ibid.
568. Morris, p. 89
569. Maraniss, p. 173
570. Brown, pp. 3-4
571. Maraniss, p. 175
572. Ibid., pp. 175-6
573. Ibid., p. 147
574. Michael Isikoff, *Uncovering Clinton* (New York: Crown Publishers, 1999), p. 27
575. Maraniss, pp. 173-4
576. Ibid., p. 173

Hillary: "CIA Container"

577. Gross, p. 35
578. Ibid.
579. Ibid.
580. Ibid., pp. 35-6
581. Warner, pp. 51-2
582. Ambrose Evans-Pritchard, *Student Bill Clinton Spied on Americans Abroad for CIA*, (Lon-don: Sunday Telegraph: 1996), p. 2

Watergate

583. Piper, p. 235
584. Morris, p. 164
585. Ibid., p. 165
586. Ibid.
587. Poe, p. 63
588. Milton, p. 61
589. Warner, p. 67
590. Olson, p. 120

591. H. Clinton, p. 65
592. Ibid.
593. Milton, pp. 61-2
594. Laura Ingraham, *The Hillary Trap* (New York: Hyperion, 2000), p. 6
595. Olson, p. 121
596. Milton, p. 63
597. Warner, p. 71
598. Ibid.
599. Oakley, p. 123
600. Brock, p. 52
601. Clinton, p. 67
602. Morris, pp. 165-6
603. Klein, p. 81
604. Ibid.
605. Milton, p. 65
606. Ibid., p. 66
607. Ibid., p. 65
608. Ingraham, p. 7
609. Ibid.
610. Brock, p. 47
611. Ibid., p. 55
612. Ibid., pp. 52-3
613. Andersen, p. 55

Chapter Four:
Marriage Made in Hell

Battered and Bruised

614. Thomas D. Kuiper, *I've Always Been a Yankees Fan* (Los Angeles: World Ahead Publishing, 2006), p. 28
615. Ibid., p. 39
616. Ibid., p. 11
617. Ibid., p. 145
618. Joyce Milton, *The First Partner* (New York: Perennial, 1999), p. 94
619. Ibid.
620. Gennifer Flowers, *Sleeping with the President* (New York: Anonymous Press, 1996), p. 79
621. Edward Klein, *The Truth About Hillary* (New York: Sentinel, 2005), p. 11
622. David Brock, *The Seduction of Hillary Rodham* (New York: Free Press Paperbacks, 1996), p. 153
623. Ibid., p. 417
624. James B. Stewart, *Blood Sport* (New York: Touchstone Books, 1996), p. 121
625. Paul Fick, *The Dysfunctional President* (New York: Citadel Press, 1998), p. 7
626. David Maraniss, *First in His Class* (New York: Touchstone Books, 1995), p. 342
627. Stewart, p. 70
628. George Carpozi, *Clinton Confidential* (Columbia: CLS Publishing, 1995), p. 418
629. Brock, p. 321
630. Klein, p. 15
631. Ibid., p. 49
632. Edward P. Moser, *Willy Nilly* (Nashville, Caliban Books, 1994), pp. 86-7
633. R. Emmett Tyrrell, *Boy Clinton* (Washington: Regnery Publishing, 1996), p. 251
634. Brock, p. 65
635. Christopher Andersen, *American Evita* (New York: William Morrow, 2004), p. 57
636. Ibid., p. 120
637. Ibid., p. 125
638. Jerry Oppenheimer, *State of a Union* (New York: Harper Collins, 2000), p. 144
639. Stewart, p. 172
640. Andersen, p. 89
641. Stewart, pp. 247-8
642. Andersen, p. 89
643. Brock, p. 85
644. Kuiper, p. 11
645. Peggy Noonan, *The Case Against Hillary* (New York: Harper Collins, 2000), pp. 30-1
646. Klein, pp. 90-1
647. Ibid., p. 91
648. Tyrrell, p. 251
649. Barbara Olson, *Hell to Pay* (Washington: Regnery Publishing, 1999), p. 238
650. Brock, p. 383
651. Andersen, p. 124
652. Gary Aldrich, *Unlimited Access*, (Washington: Regnery Publishing, 1998), p. 94
653. Noonan, p. 31

Inauguration Day Melee

654. Milton, p. 260
655. Aldrich, p. 11
656. Kuiper, p. 18
657. Brock, p. 320
658. Kuiper, p. 19
659. Brock, pp. 320-1
660. Milton, p. 262
661. Olson, p. 66
662. Aldrich, p. 11

Political Marriage

663. Brock, p. 178
664. Milton, p. 93
665. Oppenheimer, p. 148
666. Gail Sheehy, *Hillary's Choice* (New York: Random House, 1999), p. 122
667. Oppenheimer, p. 198
668. Ibid., p. 145
669. Kuiper, p. 44
670. Olson, p. 178
671. Laura Ingraham, *The Hillary Trap* (New York: Hyperion, 2000), p. 3
672. Oppenheimer, p. 215
673. Ibid., p. 198
674. Emmett Tyrrell & Mark Davis, *Madame Hillary* (Wash.: Regnery Publishing, 2004), p. 81
675. Oppenheimer, p. 134
676. Brock, p. 417
677. Oppenheimer, p. 215
678. Barbara Olson, *The Final Days* (Washington: Regnery Publishing, 2001), p. 194
679. Flowers, p. 5
680. Ibid., p. 66
681. Milton, p. 194
682. Olson, *Hell to Pay*, p. 68
683. Flowers, p. 7
684. Dr. John Coleman, *The Road to Socialism* (Carson City: Joseph Publishing Company, 1994), p. 233
685. Tyrrell, Davis, p. 84
686. Ibid., p. 85
687. Amanda Carpenter, *The Vast Right-Wing Conspiracy* (Washington: Regnery Publishing, 2006), p. 88
688. Dick Morris, *Rewriting History* (New York: Regan Books, 2004), p. 197
689. Ibid.
690. Andersen, p. 80
691. Milton, p. 183
692. Andersen, p. 3
693. Klein, p. 6
694. Ibid.
695. Ibid.
696. Ibid., p. 115
697. Carl Limbacher, *Hillary's Scheme* (New York: Crown Forum, 2003), p. 179
698. Olson, *The Final Days*, p. 15
699. Flowers, p. 6
700. Andersen, pp. 170-1

701. Milton, p. 170
702. Ingraham, p. 139
703. Kuiper, p. 70
704. Tyrrell, Davis, p. 81
705. Ibid., p. 82
706. D. Morris, p. 190
707. Oppenheimer, p. 198
708. Ibid., p. 146
709. D. Morris, p. 190
710. Maraniss, p. 326
711. Ingraham, p. 2
712. Ibid., p. 3
713. Noonan, p. 103
714. Meredith Oakley, *On the Make* (Washington: Regnery Publishing, 1994), p. 90
715. Noonan, p. 104
716. Roger Morris, *Partners in Power* (Washington: Regnery Publishing, 1996), p. xxii
717. D. Morris, p. 196
718. Olson, *Hell to Pay*, pp. 10-11

Billary

719. Brock, p. 184
720. Ibid., p. 185
721. D. Morris, p. 2
722. Olson, *Hell to Pay*, p. 151
723. Lt. Colonel Robert Patterson, *Dereliction of Duty* (Washington: Regnery Publishing, 2003), p. 72
724. Oakley, p. 263
725. Brock, p. 290
726. Andersen, p. 13
727. Oppenheimer, p. 174
728. Milton, p. 398
729. Elizabeth Drew, *On the Edge* (New York: Simon & Schuster, 1994), p. 102
730. Ibid., pp. 103-4
731. Joe Klein, *The Natural* (New York: Sentinel, 2005), p. 130
732. Patterson, p. 68
733. Brock, pp. 82-3
734. Oppenheimer, p. 175
735. Ibid., p. 200
736. Ibid., p. 201
737. David Bresnahan, *Damage Control* (Salt Lake City: Camden Court Publishers, 1997), pp. 63-4
738. Patterson, p. 67
739. Ibid., p. 72
740. Olson, *The Final Days*, p. 48

Divorce?

741. Olson, *Hell to Pay*, p. 95
742. Maraniss, p. 450
743. Oakley, p. 258
744. Judith Warner, *Hillary Clinton: The Inside Story* (New York: Signet, 1993), p. 147
745. Oakley, p. 259
746. Milton, p. 169
747. Ibid.
748. D. Morris, p. 191
749. Oppenheimer, p. 225
750. Brock, p. 226
751. Milton, p. 406
752. Ibid.
753. Ibid.
754. Olson, *Hell to Pay*, p. 95
755. Ibid.
756. Milton, p. 193
757. Ibid.
758. Paul Fick, *The Dysfunctional President* (New York: Citadel Press, 1995), pp. 129-30
759. Milton, p. 396
760. Klein, p. 128
761. Milton, p. 397
762. Maraniss, p. 450
763. Jeffrey Toobin, *A Vast Conspiracy* (New York: Touchstone Books, 1999), p. 21
764. Ingraham, p. 142
765. Limbacher, p. 156
766. Warner, p. 147

Chapter Five:
Bill & Hillary's Sordid Sex Lives

Rapist and Repeat Offender

767. John Austin, *Rkansides* (Bloomington, 1st Books, 2000), p. 77
768. Sam Smith, *Arkansas Connections*, p. 8
769. Christopher Andersen, *American Evita* (New York: William Morrow, 2004), p. 100
770. Gail Sheehy, *Hillary's Choice* (New York: Random House, 1999), p. 185
771. Meredith Oakley, *On the Make* (Washington: Regnery Publishing, 1994), p. 260
772. George Carpozi, *Clinton Confidential* (Columbia: CLS Publishing, 1995), p. 222
773. Joyce Milton, *The First Partner* (New York: Perennial, 1999), p. 265
774. Ambrose Evans-Pritchard, *The Secret Life of Bill Clinton* (Washington: Regnery Publishing, 1997), p. 224
775. Milton, p. 265
776. Andersen, p. 122
777. Ibid.
778. Ibid.
779. Ibid., p. 118
780. Ibid., p. 184
781. Carpozi, pp. 154-5
782. Wesley Hagood, *Presidential Sex* (New York: Citadel Press, 1995), p. 205
783. Ibid.
784. Jeffrey Toobin, *A Vast Conspiracy* (New York: Touchstone Books, 1999), p. 211
785. Jim McDougal & Curtis Wilkie, *Arkansas Mischief* (New York: Henry Holt, 1998), p. 181
786. Ibid., p. 182
787. Toobin, P. 211
788. Christopher Andersen, *Bill and Hillary* (New York: William Morrow, 1999), p. 178
789. Ibid., p. 144
790. Toobin, p. 211
791. Ibid., p. 124
792. Carpozi, p. 224
793. Ibid.
794. Ibid., p. 82
795. Ibid., p. 236
796. Ibid.
797. Ibid., p. 237
798. Ibid., p. 235
799. Ibid.
800. Michael Isikoff, *Uncovering Clinton* (New York: Crown Publishers, 1999), p. 66
801. Carpozi, p. 183
802. Patrick Matrisciana, *The Clinton Chronicles Book*, (Hemet: Jeremiah Books, 1994), p. 163
803. Elizabeth Drew, *On the Edge* (New York: Simon & Schuster, 1994), p. 380
804. Ibid., p. 381
805. R. Emmett Tyrrell, *Boy Clinton* (Washington: Regnery Publishing, 1996), p. 273
806. Carpozi, p. 184
807. Tyrrell, p. 130
808. Roger Morris, *Partners in Power* (Washington: Regnery Publishing, 1996), p. 436
809. Ibid.
810. Ibid., p. 442
811. Milton, p. 259
812. David Brock, *The Seduction of Hillary Rod-*

ham (New York: Free Press Paperbacks, 1996), p. 84

813. Thomas D. Kuiper, *I've Always Been a Yankees Fan* (Los Angeles: World Ahead Publishing, 2006), p. 146

814. Tyrrell, p. 228

815. Kuiper, p. 147

816. Isikoff, p. 24

817. Ibid.

818. Tyrrell, p. 278

819. Ibid., pp. 188-9

820. Andersen, *American Evita*, p. 86

821. Candice Jackson, *Their Lives* (Los Angeles: World Ahead Publishing, 2005), p. 27

822. Carl Limbacher, *Hillary's Scheme* (New York: Crown Forum, 2003), p. 200

823. Ibid., p. 201

824. Ibid., p. 203

825. Christopher Ruddy & Carl Limbacher, *Bitter Legacy* (NewsMax: West Palm Beach, 2001), p. 59

826. Morris, p. 238

827. Limbacher, p. 166

828. Ibid., p. 173

829. Ibid.., p. 167

830. Barbara Olson, *Hell to Pay* (Washington: Regnery Publishing, 1999), p. 91

831. Lt. Colonel Robert Patterson, *Dereliction of Duty* (Washington: Regnery Publishing, 2003), pp. 86-7

Sex Galore!

832. Morris, p. 442

833. Matrisciana, p. 160

834. Evans-Pritchard, p. 359

835. Carpozi, pp. 181-2

836. Ibid., p. 182

837. Ibid.

838. Ibid.

839. Ibid.

840. Ibid., p. 225

841. Ibid., pp. 84-5

842. Ibid., p. 85

843. Ibid.

844. Ibid., p. 225

845. Andersen, *American Evita*, p. 101

846. Ibid., p. 85

847. Andersen, *Bill and Hillary*, p. 16

848. Milton, p. 401

849. Carpozi, p. 222

850. Ruddy, Limbacher, p. 50

851. Milton, p. 241

852. Ibid., p. 242

853. Hagood, p. 222

854. Carpozi, p. 186

855. Milton, p. 191

856. Andersen, *American Evita*, p. 60

857. Limbacher, pp. 160-1

858. Gennifer Flowers, *Sleeping with the President* (New York: Anonymous Press, 1996), p. 114

859. Gary Aldrich, *Unlimited Access*, (Washington: Regnery Publishing, 1998), p. 137

860. Ibid.

861. Ibid.

862. Ibid., p. 246

863. Ibid., p. 247

864. Ibid.

865. Olson, p. 212

866. Hagood, p. 226

867. James B. Stewart, *Blood Sport* (New York: Touchstone Books, 1996), p. 71

868. Dick Morris, *Rewriting History* (New York: Regan Books, 2004), p. 198

869. Oakley, pp. 504-5

870. Charles Allen & Jonathan Portis, *The Comeback Kid* (New York: Birch Lane Press, 1992), p. 164

871. Brock, p. 245

872. Andersen, *American Evita*, p. 105

873. Oakley, p. 505

874. Tyrrell, p. 273

Gennifer Flowers Aborts Clinton's Baby

875. Flowers, p. 91

876. Jackson, p. 69

877. Andersen, *Bill and Hillary*, p. 154

878. David Bresnahan, *Damage Control* (Salt Lake City: Camden Court Publishers, 1997), p. 85

879. Andersen, *American Evita*, p. 64

880. Ruddy, Limbacher, p. 112

881. Ibid., p. 113

882. Andersen, *American Evita*, p. 64

883. Paul Roer, *The Rants, Raves & Thoughts of Bill Clinton* (Brooklyn: On Your Own Publications, 2002), p. 157

884. Hagood, p. 209

885. Flowers, p. 82

886. Hagood, p. 210

887. Flowers, p. 84

888. Ibid., p. 85
889. Hagood, pp. 209-10
890. Ibid., p. 210
891. Carpozi, p. 328
892. Jerry Oppenheimer, *State of a Union* (New York: Harper Collins, 2000), p. 182
893. Edward Klein, *The Truth About Hillary* (New York: Sentinel, 2005), p. 35
894. Ibid.
895. Jackson, p. 89
896. Allen, Portis, p. 193
897. Carpozi, p. 336
898. Isikoff, p. 56
899. Allen, Portis, p. 193
900. Carpozi, p. 324
901. Ibid.
902. Ibid.
903. Ibid.
904. Ibid., p. 325
905. Ibid.
906. Ibid., p. 326
907. Ibid.
908. Andersen, *American Evita*, p. 64
909. Oppenheimer, p. 183
910. Carpozi, p. 234
911. Ibid.
912. Ibid.
913. Hagood, p. 208
914. Flowers, p. 68
915. Ibid., p. 70
916. Andersen, *American Evita*, p. 64
917. Flowers, p. 70
918. Ibid., pp. 71-2
919. Ibid., p. 72
920. Oppenheimer, p. 192
921. Andersen, *American Evita*, p. 64

Hookers' Row and a Black Love Child

922. Hagood, p. 225
923. Andersen, *American Evita*, p. 95
924. Ibid., p. 9
925. Ibid., p. 86
926. Ibid., p. 87
927. Olson, p. 179
928. Des Griffin, *Fourth Reich of the Rich* (Clackamas: Emissary Publications, 1976), p. 117
929. Olson, p. 179
930. Griffin, p. 117
931. Carpozi, p. 173

932. Ibid., p. 175
933. Ibid.
934. Ibid., p. 173
935. Ibid., p. 175
936. Ibid.
937. Ibid., p. 176
938. Ibid.
939. Ibid.
940. Ibid.
941. Ibid.
942. Ibid.
943. Milton, p. 215
944. Ibid.
945. Carpozi, p. 179
946. Ibid., p. 180
947. Ibid.
948. Andersen, *American Evita*, p. 88
949. Ibid., p. 87
950. Carpozi, p. 180
951. Andersen, *American Evita*, p. 87
952. Ibid., p. 88
953. Milton, p. 217
954. Ibid.
955. Ibid., p. 216
956. Ibid., p. 217
957. Ibid.
958. Andersen, *American Evita*, p. 88

Bill Clinton's Crooked Penis

959. Olson, p. 295
960. Andersen, *American Evita*, p. 166
961. Milton, p. 403
962. Andersen, *American Evita*, p. 166
963. Andersen, *Bill and Hillary*, p. 16
964. Andersen, *American Evita*, p. 140
965. Toobin, p. 10
966. Stewart, p. 386
967. Toobin, p. 10
968. Roer, pp. 56-7
969. Jackson, p. 129
970. Toobin, p. 10
971. Tyrrell, p. 279
972. Jackson, pp. 129-30
973. Ruddy, Limbacher, p. 61
974. Evans-Pritchard, p. 358
975. Jackson, p. 130
976. Isikoff, p. 89
977. Hagood, p. p. 236
978. Isikoff, p. 184

979. Ibid., p. 89
980. Toobin, p. 161
981. Ibid., pp. 137-8
982. David Bresnahan, *Damage Control* (Salt Lake City: Camden Court Publishers, 1997), pp. 95-6

The Groper Strikes Again

983. Toobin, p. 107
984. Hagood, p. 242
985. Ibid.
986. Jackson, p. 152
987. Ibid., p. 144
988. Toobin, p. 107
989. Ibid.
990. Jackson, p. 163
991. Ibid., p. 144
992. Toobin, p. 107
993. Jackson, p. 144
994. Ruddy, Limbacher, p. 57
995. Ibid.
996. Ibid.
997. Jackson, p. 152
998. Ibid., p. 142
999. Isikoff, p. 121
1000.   Jackson, pp. 144-5
1001.   Isikoff, p. 123
1002.   Jackson, p. 145
1003.   Isikoff, p. 120
1004.   Jackson, p. 153

Semen, Cigars, & the Big Creep

1005.   Klein, p. 130
1006.   Joe Klein, *The Natural* (New York: Sentinel, 2005), p. 2
1007.   Olson, p. 298
1008.   J. Klein, p. 173
1009.   Oppenheimer, p. 255
1010.   Isikoff, p. 352
1011.   Toobin, p. 103
1012.   Isikoff, p. 135
1013.   Jackson, p. 194-5
1014.   Toobin, p. 91
1015.   Andersen, *American Evita*, 167
1016.   Hagood, p. 245
1017.   Oppenheimer, p. 256
1018.   Olson, p. 300
1019.   Toobin, p. 90

1020.   Ibid.
1021.   Oppenheimer, p. 255
1022.   Hagood, p. 255
1023.   Toobin, p. 323
1024.   Ibid., p. 289
1025.   Ibid., p. 110
1026.   Ibid., p. 111
1027.   Ibid., p. 86
1028.   Ruddy, Limbacher, p. 54
1029.   Ibid., p. 55
1030.   Ibid., p. 61
1031.   Ibid., p. 62
1032.   Isikoff, p. 233
1033.   Ibid.
1034.   Ibid., p. 135
1035.   Jackson, p. 192
1036.   Toobin, p. 324
1037.   Oppenheimer, p. 255
1038.   Toobin, p. 307
1039.   Ibid., p. 149
1040.   Ibid., p. 307
1041.   E. Klein, p. 136
1042.   Sidney Blumenthal, *The Clinton Wars* (New York: Plume, 2003) p. 341
1043.   Isikoff, p. 250
1044.   Ibid.
1045.   Ibid., p. 252
1046.   Ibid., p. 303
1047.   Ibid., p. 246
1048.   Hagood, p. 250
1049.   Toobin, p. 196
1050.   Jackson, p. 202
1051.   Milton, p. 4
1052.   Brock, p. 219
1053.   Toobin, p. 87
1054.   Barbara Olson, *The Final Days* (Washington: Regnery Publishing, 2001), p. 109
1055.   Toobin, p. 85
1056.   Hagood, p. 247
1057.   Ibid.
1058.   Jackson, p. 149
1059.   Oppenheimer, p. 256
1060.   Ibid.
1061.   Toobin, p. 196
1062.   Ibid., p. 149

The Caligula from Arkansas

1063.   Toobin, p. 107
1064.   Ibid.

1065. Olson, *The Final Days*, p. 109
1066. Hagood, p. 220
1067. Flowers, p. 81
1068. Toobin, p. 243
1069. Stewart, p. 171
1070. John Brummett, *High Wire* (New York: Hyperion, 1994), p. 233
1071. Peggy Noonan, *The Case Against Hillary* (New York: Harper Collins, 2000), p. 33
1072. Ibid.
1073. Christopher Hitchens, *No One Left to Lie To* (London: Verso, 1999), p. 26
1074. Ibid., p. 80
1075. Ibid., p. 84
1076. Ibid., p. 88
1077. Ibid., p. 89
1078. R. Morris, p. 441
1079. Brock, p. 220
1080. Isikoff, p. 242
1081. Ibid., p. 136
1082. J. Klein, p. 163
1083. Ibid., p. 208
1084. Jackson, p. 121
1085. Ibid., p. 107
1086. Ibid., p. 169
1087. Ibid., pp. 46-7
1088. Paul Fick, *The Dysfunctional President* (New York: Citadel Press, 1995), p. 126
1089. American Conservative Union, *Hillary Rodham Clinton* (Ottawa: Green Hill Publishers, 2005), p. 18

The Adulterer's Enabler

1090. D. Morris, pp. 212-3
1091. Tyrrell, p. 215
1092. Andersen, *Bill and Hillary*, p. 131
1093. Ibid.
1094. Brock, p. 59
1095. Oppenheimer, p. 133
1096. Brock, p. 59
1097. Milton, p. 5
1098. Andersen, *American Evita*, 79
1099. Olson, *Hell to Pay*, p. 87
1100. Hagood, p. 256
1101. Ibid.
1102. E. Klein, p. 32
1103. Ibid.
1104. Ibid., p. 93
1105. Carpozi, p. 186
1106. R. Morris, p. 440
1107. Brock, p. 253
1108. Olson, *The Final Days*, p. 108
1109. George Stephanopoulos, *All Too Human* (Boston: Little Brown & Company, 1999), p. 54
1110. E. Klein, p. 4
1111. Ibid.
1112. Ibid., p. 5
1113. Oakley, p. 511
1114. E. Klein, p. 32
1115. Ibid., pp. 32-3
1116. Jackson, p. 79
1117. E. Klein, p. 112
1118. Ibid., p. 110
1119. D. Morris, pp. 215-6
1120. Ibid., p. 216
1121. Oppenheimer, p. 262
1122. Ibid., p. 242
1123. Andersen, *American Evita*, 167
1124. Tyrrell, p. 34
1125. E. Klein, p. 32
1126. Carpozi, p. 185
1127. Ibid.
1128. Ibid., p. 224
1129. Flowers, p. 90
1130. Andersen, *American Evita*, p. 96
1131. E. Klein, p. 112
1132. Oppenheimer, p. 254
1133. Stewart, pp. 69-70
1134. Hagood, p. 202
1135. Andersen, *American Evita*, p. 160
1136. Tyrrell, p. 275
1137. Toobin, p. 242
1138. Emmett Tyrrell & Mark Davis, *Madame Hillary* (Washington: Regnery Publishing, 2004), p. 94
1139. Laura Ingraham, *The Hillary Trap* (New York: Hyperion, 2000), p. 136
1140. Ibid., p. 137
1141. Sheehy, p. 299
1142. Ingraham, p. 141
1143. Kuiper, p. 40
1144. Ingraham, p. 135
1145. E. Klein, p. 111
1146. Ibid.

Lesbianism + Hillary's Affair with Vince Foster

1147. Oppenheimer, p. 218
1148. Ibid.

1149. Ibid., p. 217
1150. Ibid., pp. 218-9
1151. Olson, *Hell to Pay*, p. 153
1152. Milton, p. 105
1153. E. Klein, p. 94
1154. Oppenheimer, p. 218
1155. Ruddy, Limbacher, p. 113
1156. Ibid., pp. 39-40
1157. Flowers, p. 80
1158. Texe Marrs, *Big Sister is Watching You* (Austin: Living Truth Publishers, 1993), 52
1159. Ibid.
1160. Ibid.
1161. Tyrrell, p. 276
1162. Ibid.
1163. Ibid.
1164. Austin, p. 119
1165. E. Klein, pp. 21-2
1166. Oppenheimer, p. 216
1167. E. Klein, p. 21
1168. Milton, p. 148
1169. Tyrrell, Davis, p. 78
1170. E. Klein, p. 21
1171. R. Morris, p. 444
1172. Olson, *Hell to Pay*, p. 153
1173. Brock, p. 227
1174. R. Morris, p. 444
1175. E. Klein, p. 21
1176. Brock, p. 228
1177. Olson, *Hell to Pay*, p. 154
1178. Limbacher, p. 162
1179. Milton, p. 147
1180. Andersen, *American Evita*, p. 97
1181. Milton, p. 147
1182. Carpozi, p. 187
1183. Toobin, p. 21
1184. Ibid.
1185. Andersen, *American Evita*, p. 98
1186. Ibid.
1187. Tyrrell, Davis, p. 111
1188. Brock, p. 389
1189. Olson, *Hell to Pay*, p. 154
1190. Limbacher, p. 140
1191. Ibid., p. 141
1192. Ibid., p. 142
1193. Austin, pp. 119-20
1194. Olson, *Hell to Pay*, p. 211
1195. R. Morris, p. 444
1196. Tyrrell, Davis, p. 78
1197. Aldrich, p. 80

Chapter Six:

The Kind of People They Really Are

The Phony Plastic Couple

1198. Christopher Andersen, *American Evita* (New York: William Morrow, 2004), p. 70
1199. Christopher Andersen, *Bill and Hillary* (New York: William Morrow, 1999), p. 11

Elitist Snobs

1200. Andersen, *American Evita*, p. 120
1201. Gary Aldrich, *Unlimited Access*, (Washington: Regnery Publishing, 1998), p. 253
1202. Ibid., p. 90
1203. L.D. Brown, *Crossfire* (San Diego: Black Forest Press, 1999), p. 84
1204. Ibid., p. 89
1205. Andersen, *American Evita*, p. 199
1206. Ibid., p. 90
1207. Brown, p. 84
1208. Roger Morris, *Partners in Power* (Washington: Regnery Publishing, 1996), p. 249
1209. Thomas D. Kuiper, *I've Always Been a Yankees Fan* (Los Angeles: World Ahead Publishing, 2006), p. 9
1210. Morris, p. 226
1211. David Bresnahan, *Damage Control* (Salt Lake City: Camden Court Publishers, 1997), pp. 44-5
1212. Barbara Olson, *The Final Days* (Washington: Regnery Publishing, 2001), p. 208
1213. Brown, p. 73
1214. Kuiper, p. 145
1215. Ibid., p. 141
1216. Joyce Milton, *The First Partner* (New York: Perennial, 1999), p. 331
1217. Ibid., p. 192
1218. Ibid., p. 97

Violence, Rage, and Intimidation

1219. Morris, p. 461
1220. Carl Limbacher, *Hillary's Scheme* (New York: Crown Forum, 2003), p. 88
1221. R. Emmett Tyrrell, *Boy Clinton* (Washington: Regnery Publishing, 1996), p. 217
1222. Lt. Colonel Robert Patterson, *Derelic-*

tion of Duty (Washington: Regnery Publishing, 2003), pp. 62-3

1223. Elizabeth Drew, *On the Edge* (New York: Simon & Schuster, 1994), p. 97

1224. Aldrich, p. 88

1225. David Maraniss, *First in His Class* (New York: Touchstone Books, 1995), p. 335

1226. Drew, p. 96

1227. Andersen, *Bill and Hillary*, p. 140

1228. David Brock, *The Seduction of Hillary Rodham* (New York: Free Press Paperbacks, 1996), p. 301

1229. Paul Fick, *The Dysfunctional President* (New York: Citadel Press, 1998), p. 185

1230. Joe Klein, *The Natural* (New York: Sentinel, 2005), p. 49

1231. George Carpozi, *Clinton Confidential* (Columbia: CLS Publishing, 1995), pp. 474-5

1232. Michael Kellett, *The Murder of Vince Foster* (Columbia: CLS Publishing, 1995), p. 5

1233. Bob Woodward, *The Agenda* (New York: Simon & Schuster, 1994), p. 259

1234. Ibid., p. 284

1235. Fick, p. 156

1236. Jeffrey Birnbaum, *Madhouse* (New York: Times Books, 1996), p. 160

1237. Ibid.

1238. Ibid.

1239. Morris, p. 466

1240. Patrick Matrisciana, *The Clinton Chronicles Book*, (Hemet: Jeremiah Books, 1994), p. 161

1241. Ibid.

1242. Ibid.

1243. Ibid.

1244. Dick Morris, *Rewriting History* (New York: Regan Books, 2004), p. 203

1245. Ibid.

1246. Gennifer Flowers, *Sleeping with the President* (New York: Anonymous Press, 1996), p. 12

1247. Ibid.

1248. Matrisciana, p. 157

1249. Ibid.

1250. Ibid.

1251. Ibid., p. 18

1252. Martin Gross, *The Great Whitewater Fiasco* (New York: Ballantine Books, 1994), pp. 69-70

1253. Candice Jackson, *Their Lives* (Los Angeles: World Ahead Publishing, 2005), p. 31

1254. Ibid.

1255. Ibid., pp. 31-2

1256. Ibid., p. 32

1257. Ibid.

1258. John Austin, *Rkansides* (Bloomington, 1st Books, 2000), p. 47

1259. Carl Limbacher, *Clinton Connected Bribes*, p. 2

1260. Rich Lowry, *Legacy* (Washington: Regnery Publishing, 2003), p. 154

1261. Ibid.

1262. Ibid.

1263. Ibid., p. 155

1264. Andersen, *American Evita*, pp. 102-3

1265. Barbara Olson, *Hell to Pay* (Washington: Regnery Publishing, 1999), p. 203

1266. D. Morris, p. 209

1267. Andersen, *American Evita*, p. 103

1268. Jack Cashill, *Ron Brown's Body* (Nashville: WND Books, 2004), p. 141

1269. Flowers, pp. 13-4

1270. Matrisciana, p. 19

1271. Richard Poe, *Hillary's Secret War* (Nashville: WND Books, 2004), p. 30

1272. Flowers, p. 108

1273. Austin, p. xvii

1274. Bresnahan, p. 90

1275. Austin, p. xvii

1276. Flowers, p. 108

1277. Carpozi, p. 642

Thieves Fleece the White House

1278. Edward Klein, *The Truth About Hillary* (New York: Sentinel, 2005), p. 203

1279. Ibid.

1280. D. Morris, p. 181

1281. Ibid., p. 182

1282. Ibid., p. 183

1283. Olson, *The Final Days*, p. 73

1284. D. Morris, p. 181

1285. Ibid., p. 183

1286. Ibid.

1287. Andersen, *American Evita*, p. 11

1288. Limbacher, *Hillary's Scheme*, p. 58

1289. Ibid.

1290. Patterson, p. 83

1291. Kuiper, p. 48

1292. Andersen, *American Evita*, p. 5

Booed Off the Stage

1293. Olson, *Hell to Pay*, p. 145

1294.   E. Klein, p. 95
1295.   Kuiper, p. 17
1296.   Ibid.
1297.   Andersen, *American Evita*, p. 191
1298.   Ibid., pp. 142-3
1299.   Olson, *The Final Days*, p. 29
1300.   Tyrrell, p. 258
1301.   Andersen, *American Evita*, p. 99
1302.   Carpozi, p. 267
1303.   Andersen, *American Evita*, p. 99
1304.   Carpozi, p. 267
1305.   R. Morris, p. 438
1306.   Charles Allen & Jonathan Portis, *The Comeback Kid* (New York: Birch Lane Press, 1992), p. 126
1307.   Olson, *Hell to Pay*, p. 200
1308.   Meredith Oakley, *On the Make* (Washington: Regnery Publishing, 1994), p. 363
1309.   Olson, *Hell to Pay*, p. 200
1310.   Oakley, pp. 362-3
1311.   Andersen, *American Evita*, pp. 229-30
1312.   Amanda Carpenter, *The Vast Right-Wing Conspiracy* (Washington: Regnery Publishing, 2006), p. 114
1313.   Poe, p. 10
1314.   Ibid., p. 3
1315.   Limbacher, *Hillary's Scheme*, p. xi
1316.   Poe, p. 2
1317.   Limbacher, *Hillary's Scheme*, p. 123
1318.   Poe, p. 12
1319.   Limbacher, *Hillary's Scheme*, pp. 130-1
1320.   Andersen, *American Evita*, p. 230
1321.   Poe, p. 5
1322.   Ibid., p. 6
1323.   Ibid., p. 5
1324.   Limbacher, *Hillary's Scheme*, p. 131
1325.   Andersen, *American Evita*, pp. 230-1
1326.   Poe, p. 3
1327.   Andersen, *American Evita*, p. 231

The Jewish Problem

1328.   Kuiper, p. 104
1329.   Limbacher, *Hillary's Scheme*, p. 95
1330.   Andersen, *American Evita*, p. 187
1331.   Limbacher, *Hillary's Scheme*, p. 93
1332.   Andersen, *American Evita*, p. 187
1333.   Oppenheimer, p. 155
1334.   Limbacher, *Hillary's Scheme*, p. 93
1335.   Ibid., p. 92

1336.   Andersen, *American Evita*, pp. 187-8
1337.   Kuiper, p. 95
1338.   Ibid., p. 104
1339.   D. Morris, p. 67
1340.   Ibid.
1341.   Christopher Ruddy & Carl Limbacher, *Bitter Legacy* (NewsMax: West Palm Beach, 2001), p. 107
1342.   Kuiper, p. 94
1343.   Ibid.
1344.   Cashill, p. 97
1345.   Carpozi, p. 357
1346.   Ruddy, Limbacher, *Bitter Legacy*, p. 117
1347.   Representative Paul Findley, *They Dare to Speak Out* (Westport: Lawrence Hill & Company, 1985), p. 95
1348.   Limbacher, *Hillary's Scheme*, p. 110
1349.   Andersen, *American Evita*, p. 193
1350.   Limbacher, *Hillary's Scheme*, pp. 110-11
1351.   Ibid., p. 111
1352.   Andersen, *American Evita*, p. 186
1353.   Limbacher, *Hillary's Scheme*, p. 108
1354.   Ruddy, Limbacher, *Bitter Legacy*, p. 109
1355.   E. Klein, p. 180
1356.   Ibid., p. 168
1357.   Ibid., p. 169
1358.   Ibid., p. 188
1359.   Oppenheimer, p. 275
1360.   Ibid., p. 160-1
1361.   Ibid., p. 161
1362.   Cahsill, p. 102
1363.   Robert E. Levin, *Bill Clinton: The Inside Story* (New York: S.P.I. Books, 1992), p. 146
1364.   Ibid., p. 147
1365.   Paul Roer, *The Rants, Raves & Thoughts of Bill Clinton* (Brooklyn: On Your Own Publications, 2002), p. 92
1366.   Levin, pp. 155-6
1367.   Ibid., p. 156
1368.   Christopher Hitchens, *No One Left to Lie To* (London: Verso, 1999), p. 58
1369.   Ruddy, Limbacher, *Bitter Legacy*, p. 37
1370.   Ibid., p. 38
1371.   Gordon Thomas, *Gideon's Spies* (New York: Thomas Dunne Books, 1999), p. 108
1372.   Ibid., p. 3
1373.   Ibid., p. 108
1374.   Ibid.
1375.   Ibid.

1376.   Ibid.
1377.   Ibid.
1378.   Ibid.

Culture of Death

1379.   Emmett Tyrrell & Mark Davis, *Madame Hillary* (Washington: Regnery Publishing, 2004), p. 145

1380.   Texe Marrs, *Big Sister is Watching You* (Austin: Living Truth Publishers, 1993), 188

1381.   Ibid., p. 189
1382.   Carpenter, p. 97
1383.   Tyrrell, Davis, p. 145
1384.   Marrs, pp. 50-1
1385.   Allen, Portis, p. 182
1386.   Ibid., p. 183
1387.   Ibid.
1388.   Ibid.
1389.   Ibid., p. 184
1390.   Ibid.

Bibliography

PRIMARY SOURCES

Aka, Dr. Charles K. *Bill Clinton: Man of the Public*. Bloomington, Indiana: 1st Books, 2002

Aldrich, Gary. *Unlimited Access: An FBI Agent Inside the Clinton White House*. Washington: Regnery Publishing, 1998

Allen, Charles F. and Portis, Jonathan. *The Comeback Kid: The Life and Career of Bill Clinton*. New York: Birch Lane Press, 1992

American Conservative Union. *Hillary Rodham Clinton: What Every American Should Know*. Ottawa, Illinois: Green Hill Publishers, 2005

Andersen, Christopher. *American Evita: Hillary Clinton's Path to Power*. New York: William Morrow, 2004

Andersen, Christopher. *Bill and Hillary: The Marriage*. New York: William Morrow, 1999

Austin, John. *Rkansides: The Legacy & Body Count of Bill Clinton*. Bloomington, Indiana: 1st Books, 2000

Birnbaum, Jeffrey H. *Madhouse: The Private Turmoil of Working for the President*. New York: Times Books, 1996

Blumenthal, Sidney. *The Clinton Wars*. New York: Plume, 2003

Bradford, R.W. *It Came From Arkansas: The Bill Clinton Story*. Port Townsend, WA: Liberty Publishing, 1993

Bresnahan, David M. *Damage Control: The Larry Nichols Story*. Salt Lake City: Camden Court Publishers, 1997

Brock, David. *The Seduction of Hillary Rodham*. New York: Free Press Paperbacks, 1996

Brown, Floyd G. *Slick Willie: Why America Cannot Trust Bill Clinton*. Annapolis: Annapolis-Washington Book Publishers, 1993

Brown, L.D. *Crossfire: Witness in the Clinton Investigation*. San Diego: Black Forest Press, 1999

Brummett, John. *High Wire: The Education of Bill Clinton*. New York: Hyperion, 1994

Carpenter, Amanda B. *The Vast Right-Wing Conspiracy's Dossier on Hillary Clinton*. Washington: Regnery Publishing, 2006

Carpozi, George. *Clinton Confidential: The Unauthorized Biography of Bill and Hillary Clinton*. Columbia, Maryland: CLS Publishing, 1995

Cashill, Jack. *Ron Brown's Body: How One Man's Death Saved the Clinton Presidency and Hillary's Future*. Nashville: WND Books, 2004

Clinton, Bill. *My Life*. New York: Alfred P. Knopf, 2004

Clinton, Hillary Rodham. *Living History*. New York: Scribner, 2003

Drew, Elizabeth. *On the Edge: The Clinton Presidency*. New York: Simon & Schuster, 1994

Evans-Pritchard, Ambrose. *The Secret Life of Bill Clinton: The Unreported Stories*. Washington: Regnery Publishing, 1997

Fick, Paul. *The Dysfunctional President: Inside the Mind of Bill Clinton*. New York: Citadel Press, 1995

Fick, Paul. *The Dysfunctional President: Understanding the Compulsions of Bill Clinton*. New York: Citadel Press, 1998

Flowers, Gennifer. *Sleeping with the President: My Intimate Years with Bill Clinton*. New York: Anonymous Press, 1996

Gross, Martin L. *The Great Whitewater Fiasco: An American Tale of Money, Power, and Politics*. New York: Ballantine Books, 1994

Harris, John F. *The Survivor: Bill Clinton in the White House*. New York: Random House, 2005

Hitchens, Christopher. *No One Left to Lie To: The Triangulations of William Jefferson Clinton*. London: Verso, 1999

Ingraham, Laura. *The Hillary Trap: Looking for Power in All the Wrong Places*. New York: Hyperion, 2000

Isikoff, Michael. *Uncovering Clinton: A Reporter's Story*. New York: Crown Publishers, 1999

Jackson, Candice E. *Their Lives: The Women Targeted by the Clinton Machine*. Los Angeles: World Ahead Publishing, 2005

Kellett, Michael. *The Murder of Vince Foster*. Columbia, Maryland: CLS Publishers, 1995

Kellett, Michael. *Phantoms of the World Stage*. Columbia, Maryland: Evidence First Publishing, 2006

Kelly, Virginia Clinton. *My Life: Leading with My Heart*. New York: Pocket Star Books, 1994

Klein, Edward. *The Truth About Hillary*. New

York: Sentinel, 2005

Klein, Joe. *The Natural: The Misunderstood Presidency of Bill Clinton.* New York: Broadway Books, 2002

Kuiper, Thomas D. *I've Always Been a Yankees Fan: Hillary Clinton in Her Own Words.* Los Angeles: World Ahead Publishing, 2006

Limbacher, Carl. *Hillary's Scheme: Inside the Next Clinton's Ruthless Agenda to Take the White House.* New York: Crown Forum, 2003

Limbaugh, David. *Absolute Power: The Legacy of Corruption in the Clinton-Reno Justice Department.* Washington: Regnery Publishing, 2001

Levin, Robert E. *Bill Clinton: The Inside Story.* New York: S.P.I. Books, 1992

Lowry, Rich. *Legacy: Paying the Price for the Clinton Years.* Washington: Regnery Publishing, 2003

Maraniss, David. *First in His Class: The Biography of Bill Clinton.* New York: Touchstone Books, 1995

Matrisciana, Patrick. *The Clinton Chronicles Book.* Hemet, California: Jeremiah Books, 1994

McDougal, Jim and Wilkie, Curtis. *Arkansas Mischief: The Birth of a National Scandal.* New York: Henry Holt and Company, 1998

Milton, Joyce. *The First Partner: Hillary Rodham Clinton.* New York: Perennial, 1999

Morris, Dick. *Rewriting History.* New York: Regan Books, 2004

Morris, Roger. *Partners in Power: The Clintons and Their America.* Washington: Regnery Publishing, 1996

Moser, Edward P. *Willy Nilly: Bill Clinton Speaks Out.* Nashville: Caliban Books, 1994

Noonan, Peggy. *The Case Against Hillary Clinton.* New York: Harper Collins, 2000

Oakley, Meredith L. *On the Make: The Rise of Bill Clinton.* Washington: Regnery Publishing, 1994

Odom, Richard. *Circle of Death: Clinton's Climb to the Presidency.* Lafayette, Louisiana: Huntington House Publishers, 1995

O'Leary, Bradley S. *Top 200 Reasons Not to Vote for Bill Clinton.* Austin: Boru Publishing, 1996

Olson, Barbara. *Hell to Pay: The Unfolding Story of Hillary Rodham Clinton.* Washington: Regnery Publishing, 1999

Olson, Barbara. *The Final Days: The Last Desperate Abuses of Power by the Clinton White House.* Washington: Regnery Publishing, 2001

Oppenheimer, Jerry. *State of a Union: Inside the Complex Marriage of Bill and Hillary Clinton.* New York: Harper Collins, 2000

Patterson, Lt. Colonel Robert "Buzz". *Dereliction of Duty: The Eyewitness Account of How Bill Clinton Compromised America's National Security.* Washington: Regnery Publishing, 2003

Poe, Richard. *Hillary's Secret War: The Clinton Conspiracy to Muzzle Internet Journalists.* Nashville: WND Books, 2004

Reed, Terry and Cummings, John. *Compromised: Clinton, Bush and the CIA.* New York: S.P.I. Books, 1994

Roer, Paul. *The Rants, Raves & Thoughts of Bill Clinton.* Brooklyn: On Your Own Publications, 2002

Ruddy, Christopher. *Vincent Foster: The Ruddy Investigation.* Tulsa: United Publishing, 1996

Ruddy, Christopher and Limbacher, Carl. *Bitter Legacy: The Untold Story of the Clinton-Gore Years.* West Palm Beach: Newsmax, 2001

Sheehy, Gail. *Hillary's Choice.* New York: Random House, 1999

Stephanopoulos, George. *All Too Human: A Political Education.* Boston: Little Brown & Company, 1999

Stewart, James B. *Blood Sport: The President and his Adversaries.* New York: Touchstone Books, 1996

Stone, Deborah J. and Manion, Christopher. *Slick Willie II: Why America Still Can't Trust Bill Clinton.* Annapolis: Annapolis-Washington Book Publishers, 1994

Timperlake, Edward and Triplett, William C. *Year of the Rat: How Bill Clinton and Al Gore Compromised U.S. Security for Chinese Cash.* Washington: Regnery Publishing, 1998

Toobin, Jeffrey. *A Vast Conspiracy: The Real Story of the Sex Scandal That Nearly Brought Down a President.* New York: Touchstone Books, 1999

Tyrrell, R. Emmett. *Boy Clinton: The Political Biography.* Washington: Regnery Publishing, 1996

Tyrrell, R. Emmett and Davis, Mark W. *Madame Hillary: The Dark Road to the White*

House. Washington: Regnery Publishing, 2004

Warner, Judith. *Hillary Clinton: The Inside Story.* New York: Signet, 1993

Watson, Kevin H. *The Clinton Record: Everything Bill & Hillary Want You to Forget.* Bellevue, Washington: Merril Press, 1996

Woodward, Bob. *The Agenda: Inside the Clinton White House.* New York: Simon & Schuster, 1994

SECONDARY SOURCES

Bainerman, Joel. *Inside the Covert Operations of the CIA & Israel's Mossad.* New York: S.P.I. Books, 1994

Beaty, Jonathan and Gwynne, S.C. *The Outlaw Bank: A Wild Ride into the Secret Heart of BCCI.* New York: Random House, 1993

Borjesson, Kristina. *Into the Buzzsaw: Leading Journalists Expose the Myth of a Free Press.* Amherst, New York: Prometheus Books, 2002

Cockburn, Alexander and Silverstein, Ken. *Washington Babylon.* London: Verso, 1996

Cockburn, Alexander and St. Clair, Jeffrey. *Whiteout: The CIA, Drugs, and the Press.* London: Verso, 1998

Coleman, Dr. John. *Socialism: The Road to Slavery.* Carson City, Nevada: Joseph Publishing Company, 1994

Cooley, John K. *Unholy Wars: Afghanistan, America and International Terrorism.* London: Pluto Press, 1999

Dowbenko, Uri. *Bushwhacked: Inside Stories of True Conspiracy.* Pray, Montana: Conspiracy Digest, 2003

Ehrenfeld, Dr. Rachel. *Evil Money: The Inside Story of Money Laundering & Corruption in Government, Banks & Business.* New York: S.P.I. Books, 1992

Farren, Mick. *CIA: Secrets of "The Company".* New York: Chrysalis Books Group, 2003

Findley, Representative Paul. *They Dare to Speak Out: People and Institutions Confront Israel's Lobby.* Westport, Connecticut: Lawrence Hill & Company, 1985

Griffin, Des. *Descent Into Slavery.* Clackamas, Oregon: Emissary Publications, 1980

Griffin, Des. *Fourth Reich of the Rich.* Clackamas, Oregon: Emissary Publications, 1976

Hagood, Wesley O. *Presidential Sex: From the Founding Fathers to Bill Clinton.* New York: Citadel Press, 1995

Hidell, Al and D'Arc, Joan. *The New Conspiracy Reader.* New York: Citadel Press, 2004

Hopsicker, Daniel. *Barry & the Boys: The CIA, the Mob and America's Secret History.* Eugene, Oregon: Mad Cow Press, 2001

Hopsicker, Daniel. *Welcome to Terrorland: Mohamed Atta & the 9-11 Cover-up in Florida.* Eugene, Oregon: Mad Cow Press, 2004

Jackson, Devon. *Conspiranoia: The Mother of All Conspiracy Theories.* New York: Plume, 2000

Kick, Russ. *You Are Being Lied To: The Disinformation Guide to Media Distortion, Historical Whitewashes and Cultural Myths.* New York: The Disinformation Company, 2001

Kwitny, Jonathan. *The Crimes of Patriots: A True Tale of Dope, Dirty Money and the CIA.* New York: W.W. Norton & Company, 1987

Lee, Martin A. and Shlain, Bruce. *Acid Dreams: The Complete Social History of LSD – the CIA, the Sixties, and Beyond.* New York: Grove Weidenfeld, 1985

Leveritt, Mara. *The Boys on the Tracks: Death, Denial, and a Mother's Crusade to Bring Her Son's Killers to Justice.* New York: St. Martin's Press, 1999

Marrs, Jim. *Rule By Secrecy.* New York: Perennial, 2000

Marrs, Texe. *Big Sister Is Watching You.* Austin: Living Truth Publishers, 1993

Marrs, Texe. *Circle of Intrigue.* Austin: Living Truth Publishers, 1995

Marshall, Jonathan. *Drug Wars: Corruption, Counterinsurgency and Covert Operations in the Third World.* Forestville, California: Cohan & Cohen Publishers, 1991

Marshall, Jonathan and Scott, Peter Dale and Hunter, Jane. *The Iran-Contra Connection: Secret Teams and Covert Operations in the Reagan Era.* Boston: South End Press, 1987

Martin, Al. *The Conspirators: Secrets of an Iran-Contra Insider.* Pray, Montana: National Liberty Press, 2001

Mayer, Martin. *The Bankers: The Next Generation.* New York: Plume, 1997

McNally, Patrick. *From Chappaquiddick to New York and Washington through Oklahoma City.* Bloomington, Indiana: Author House, 2004

Millegan, Kris. *Fleshing Out Skull & Bones: Investigations Into America's Most Powerful Secret Society.* Walterville, Oregon: Trine Day, 2003

OKBIC. *Final Report: The Bombing of the Alfred P. Murrah Federal Building.* Oklahoma City: OKBIC, 2001

Palast, Greg. *The Best Democracy Money Can Buy.* New York, Penguin, 2002

Perloff, James. *The Shadows of Power: The Council on Foreign Relations and the American Decline.* Appleton, Wisconsin: Western Islands, 1988

Phillips, Kevin. *American Dynasty: Aristocracy, Fortune, and the Politics of Deceit in the House of Bush.* New York: Viking, 2004

Piper, Michael Collins. *The Judas Goats: The Enemy Within.* Washington: American Free Press, 2006

Reavis, Dick J. *The Ashes of Waco: An Investigation.* Syracuse: Syracuse University Press, 1995

Rappoport, Jon. *Oklahoma City Bombing: The Suppressed Truth.* Los Angeles: Blue Press, 1995

Roberts, Craig. *The Medusa File: Secret Crimes and Coverups of the U.S. Government.* Tulsa: Consolidated Press International, 1997

Scott, Peter Dale and Marshall, Jonathan. *Cocaine Politics: Drugs, Armies, and the CIA in Central America.* Berkeley: University of California Press, 1991

Scott, Peter Dale. *Drugs, Oil, and War.* Lanham, Maryland: Rowman & Littlefield Publishers, 2003

Shattuck, David. *Forbidden Knowledge: From Prometheus to Pornography.* New York: St. Martin's Press, 1996

Simon, David R. *Elite Deviance.* Boston: Allyn & Bacon, 1982

Southwell, David and Twist, Sean. *Conspiracy Files.* New York: Gramercy Books, 2004

Stich, Rodney. *Defrauding America.* Alamo, California: Diablo Western Press, 1994

Tabor, James D. and Gallagher, Eugene V. *Why Waco: Cults and the Battle for Religious Freedom in America.* Berkeley: University of California Press, 1995

Tarpley, Webster and Chaitkin, Anton. *George Bush: The Unauthorized Biography.* Washington: Executive Intelligence Review, 1992

Thomas, Gordon. *Gideon's Spies: The Secret History of the Mossad.* New York: Thomas Dunne Books, 1999

Thomas, Gordon. *Seeds of Fire: China and the Story Behind the Attack on America.* Tempe, Arizona: Dandelion Books, 2001

Thomas, Kenn and Keith, Jim. *The Octopus: Secret Government and the Death of Danny Casolaro.* Portland: Feral House, 1996

Thomas, Kenn. *Parapolitics: Conspiracy in Contemporary America.* Kempton, Illinois: Adventures Unlimited Press, 2006

Thorn, Victor. *The New World Order Exposed.* State College, Pa: Sisyphus Press, 2003

Thorn, Victor. *The OKC Bombing-Elohim City Connection: A Study in State-sponsored Terrorism.* State College, Pa: Sisyphus Press, 2005

Trento, Joseph J. *The Secret History of the CIA.* Roseville, California: Prima Publishing, 2001

Truell, Peter and Gurwin, Larry. *False Profits: The Inside Story of BCCI, the World's Most Corrupt Financial Empire.* New York: Houghton Mifflin Company, 1992

Tucker, Jim. *Bilderberg Diary.* Washington: American Free Press, 2005

Vankin, Jonathan and Whalen, John. *50 Greatest Conspiracies of All Time: History's Biggest Mysteries, Coverups & Cabals.* New York: Citadel Press, 1995

Webb, Gary. *Dark Alliance: The CIA, the Contras, and the Crack Cocaine Explosion.* New York: Seven Stories Press, 1998

Wilson, Robert Anton. *Cosmic Trigger: Final Secret of the Illuminati.* Tempe: New Falcon Publications, 1977

Zepezauer, Mark. *The CIA's Greatest Hits.* Tucson: Odonian Press, 1994

ARTICLES AND WEBSITES

Adams, James Ring. *What's Up in Jakarta?* The American Spectator, September 1995

APFN, *Hillary Directed Waco,* February 10, 2001

Arkancide Clinton Body Count website

Baehr, Richard. *Can TWA 800 Shoot Down Hillary?*

Barsamian, David. *The CIA & the Politics of Narcotics.* University of Wisconsin with Professor Alfred McCoy, February 17, 1990

Blair, Mike. *Oklahoma City Bombing Witnesses Are Dying Fast*. Washington: Spotlight, May 19, 1997

Brandt, Daniel. *Clinton's Long CIA Connection*. NameBase News Line, October-December, 1996

Brandt, Daniel. *Clinton, Quigley, and Conspiracy: What's Going on Here?* NameBase News Line, April-June 1993

Brewda, Joseph. *George Bush's Opium War*. Executive Intelligence Review, November 26, 1999

Chossudovsky, Michel. *Who is Osama Bin Laden?* Centre for Research on Globalization, September 12, 2001

CBC News. *Afghanistan Leads World in Opium Production: UN Report*, June 26, 2007

Clinton Circle of Death website

CNN. *U.S.: Afghan Poppy Production Doubles*. November 28, 2003

Cockburn, Alexander. *Chapters in the Recent History of Arkansas*. The Nation, February 24, 1992

Connolly, John. *Dead Right*. Spy Magazine, January 1993

Dead People Connected with Bill Clinton

Dee, John. *Snow Job: The CIA, Cocaine, and Bill Clinton*

Denton, Sally and Morris, Roger. *The Crimes of Mena*. Penthouse, July 1995

Donahue, Tom. *Terry Reed-John Cummings Interview*. America's Town Forum, April 27, 1994

Dowbenko, Uri. *Up Against the Beast: High-Level Drug Running*. Nexus Magazine, April-May 2000

Dowbenko, Uri. *Defrauding America* (book review). Conspiracy Digest, 2001

Downside Legacy Research website, February 6, 2001

Duffey, Jean. *The Mena Connection Is Made*. May 29, 1997

Emerson Review. *Clinton Body Count*. Frederic, MI., February 8, 2007

Evans-Pritchard, Ambrose. *Smugglers Linked to Contra Arms Deals*. London: Sunday Telegraph, October 9, 1994

Evans-Pritchard, Ambrose. *Foster Hired Detective to Spy on Clinton*. London: Sunday Telegraph, July 15, 1996

Evans-Pritchard, Ambrose. *Phone Call Rings Clinton Alarm Bells*. London: Sunday Telegraph, October 6, 1996

Evans-Pritchard, Ambrose. *Student Bill Clinton 'Spied' on Americans Abroad for CIA*. London: Sunday Telegraph, June 10, 1996

Farah, Joseph. *The Clinton Body Count*. World Net Daily, September 24, 1998

Franklin, Richard L. *101 Peculiarities Surrounding the Death of Vince Foster*. The Progressive Review

Gritz, Bo. *Letter to George Bush, Sr.* February 1, 1988

Gumbel, Andrew. *The Unsolved Mystery of the Oklahoma City Bombing*, Truthdig, February 21, 2006

Guyatt, David G. *Deep Black: The CIA's Secret Drug Wars*. West Sussex, United Kingdom: Nexus Magazine, February-March, 1998

Hansson, Lars. *A Nation Betrayed (transcript of Bo Gritz interview)*, June 1, 1990

Hicks, Sander. *From Vince Foster to Venezuela*, interview with Greg Palast

Hoffman, David. *National Security Council Link in Oklahoma Bombing?* The Washington Weekly, February 3, 1997

Hoffman, David. *The Death of an Oklahoma Bombing Witness*

Hopsicker, Daniel. *CIA Linked to Seal's Assassination*. The Washington Weekly, August 18, 1997

In Aaron's Own Opinion website, December 3, 2005

Insight on the News. *True Crime or Pulp Fiction: Clandestine Operations in Mena, Arkansas*. January 30, 1995

Ireland, Doug. *Partners in Crime*. July 17, 1996

Khun Sa, Vice Chairman Thailand Revolutionary Council (TRC). *Letter to U.S. Justice Department*. June 28, 1987

Kimery, Anthony. *The BCCI Affair*. July 10, 1997

Lee, Martin. *Ex-CIA Agent Calls Drug War a Fraud*. Insight Features, October 1, 1990

Lee, Marvin. *Mena: The Investigation of Barry Seal* (interview with former Arkansas State Police Investigator Russell Welch), March 1996

Lee, Walter. *Vicky Weaver: Fire and Rain*

Leveritt, Mara. *The Mena Airport: Why*

Arkansas's Biggest Mystery Won't Die. Arkansas Times, August 1995

Limbacher, Carl. *Clinton-Connected Bribes, Break-ins, Beatings, Death Threats.* October 12, 1998

MacMichael, David. *The Mysterious Death of Danny Casolaro.* Covert Action Information Bulletin, Winter 1991

Mizrach, Steve. *Untangling the Octopus: October Surprise, Iran-Contra, Noriega, Iraqgate, and BCCI.* December 13, 2001

Momenteller, Bob. *Deep Inside the Clintonian Reich: Chinese Intelligence, Travelgate, and the Arkansas Connection.* Ether Zone, November 1, 1998

Morrison, Micah. *A Place Called Mena: Just Some Facts.* New York: Wall Street Journal, March 3, 1999

Myers, Lawrence, *Why Did Bill Clinton's National Security Council Fund ATF "Experiments" in Building Home Made ANFO Truck Bombs in 1994?* Media Bypass Magazine, November 1996

Nadler, Eric. *George Bush's Heroin Connection.* San Francisco: Rolling Stone Magazine, October 6, 1994

News Commentary. *Did Hillary Clinton Order Waco Assault?* Winter, 2001

Norman, Jim. *Fostergate.* Media Bypass, August 1995

O'Camb, Michael A. *Unresolved Deaths in Oklahoma.* December 10, 2000

Officer.com website, *Don't You Ever Forget Terrence Yeakey*

The Oklahoma Bombing: Witnesses Allege Government's Prior Knowledge and Complicity

Poe, Richard. *Hillary's Secret War: How Clintons Took Control of Federal Law Enforcement.* World Net Daily, July 7, 2005

Political Friendster, *Connection between Jackson Stephens and Bank of Credit and Commerce International.* November 18, 2005

Progressive Review. *Clinton Legacy: Most Convictions, Crookedest Cabinet, 31 Deaths.* August 12, 2000

Quinn, Jim. *Quinn Interview with Jim Norman.* Pittsburgh: WRRK, December 7, 1995

Revolutionary Worker. *Drug Lords, War Lords and the U.S. Military*

Ridgeway, James. *Software to Die For: Inslaw Lawyer Elliot Richardson Talks About Murder and the CIA.* (New York: *the Village Voice*, September 24, 1991)

Ridgeway, James & Vaughan, Doug. New York: *The Village Voice*, October 15, 1991

Ruddy, Christopher. *Arkansas' Murderous Ways.* Newsmax, October 22, 1998

Shannan, Pat. *OKC Bombshell Implicates Feds in Murrah Blast.* Washington: American Free Press, January 7, 2004

Shannan, Pat. *Who Killed Terrence Yeakey?* APFN

Smith, Sam. *Arkansas Connections: A Timeline of the Clinton Years*

Sprunt, Hugh. *The Third Man.* March 1998

Stelzer, C.D. *Danny's Dead: The Casolaro Files.* 1996

Stratton, Richard. *Altered States of America.* New York: Spin Magazine, Volume 9, Number 12, 1994

Swirsky, Joan. *Hillary Clinton's Culture of Corruption: The Scandal Queen.* The New Media Journal, March 13, 2006

Tumulty, Karen. *Hollywood Scuffle.* New York: Time, March 5, 2007

Valentine, Tom. *Bush-Clinton Have Two Things in Common: BCCI, Iran-Contra.* Washington: The Spotlight, August 31, 1992

Webb, Gary and Kramer, Pamela. *Series on CIA-Run Drug Ring Sparks Call for Probe.* San Jose Mercury News, August 29, 1996

What Really Happened website. *The Activities at Mena*

White, Mack. *Waco, Vince Foster, and the Secret War.* October 24, 2000

William Clinton Memorial Library

York, Byron. *Hillary's Webb – Webster L. Hubbell; Hillary Rodham Clinton.* (New York: National Review, July 26, 1999)

Index

SUBSCRIBE TO *AMERICAN FREE PRESS* NEWSPAPER AND GET FREE BOOKS!

AMERICAN FREE PRESS ORDERING COUPON

Item#	Description/Title	Qty	Cost Ea.	Total
	SUBTOTAL			
	S&H: No S&H inside U.S. Outside U.S. add $6 per book			
	Send a 1-year subscription to AFP for $59 plus 1 free book*			
	Send a 2-year subscription to AFP for $99 plus 2 free books**			
	TOTAL			

*NOTE ABOUT FREE BOOKS: For a one-year subscription to *American Free Press* newspaper ($59), we'll send you one free copy of Michael Collins Piper's *The High Priests of War*. **For a two-year subscription we'll send you *The High Priests of War* PLUS *The New Jerusalem: Zionist Power in America*—almost $40 in free books! (Domestic USA only.)

PAYMENT OPTIONS: ❏ CHECK/MO ❏ VISA ❏ MASTERCARD

Card # _____

Expiration Date _____ Signature _____

CUSTOMER INFORMATION: HS1/18

NAME _____

ADDRESS _____

CIty/STATE/ZIP _____

RETURN WITH PAYMENT TO: AMERICAN FREE PRESS, 645 Pennsylvania Avenue SE, Suite 100, Washington, D.C. 20003. Call 1-888-699-NEWS (6397) toll free to charge a subscription or books to Visa or MasterCard.